Both My HOUSES

Both My HOUSES

FROM POLITICS TO PRIESTHOOD

Sean O'Sullivan

WITH ROD McQUEEN

KEY PORTER·BOOKS

Canadian Cataloguing in Publication Data

O'Sullivan, Sean, 1952-
  Both my houses: from politics to priesthood

Includes index.
ISBN 1-55013-002-1

1. O'Sullivan, Sean, 1952- . 2. Catholic Church – Canada – Clergy – Biography. 3. Canada – Politics and government – 1968-1979.* 4. Legislators – Canada – Biography. 5. Canada. Parliament. House of Commons – Biography. 6. Cancer – Patients – Canada – Biography. I. McQueen, Rod, 1944- . II. Title.

BX4705.078A32 1986	282'.092'4	C86-094488-3

Key Porter Books Limited
70 The Esplanade
Toronto, Ontario
Canada M5E 1R2

Design: Don Fernley
Typesetting: Computer Composition of Canada Inc.
Printing and Binding: John Deyell Company
Printed and bound in Canada

86 87 88 89 6 5 4 3 2 1

For all who are helping
win the war on cancer . . .
NEVER SURRENDER!

CONTENTS

FOREWORD

I first approached this project both afraid and reluctant, twin concerns that eventually gave way to determination and a simple hope. I don't like to hurt or disappoint people, but I'm afraid that this book may well do a little of both. First, because I've tried to tell my story as honestly as I recall its mix of people, places and events. Sometimes, the truth hurts. Second, others might be disappointed because they find no mention of themselves in these pages even though they know that I care deeply for them as friends. Indeed, as my father told me after the outpouring of concern when my leukemia was diagnosed in 1983: "Sean, I don't know anybody who has so many people claiming to be his best friend."

Well, Dad, neither do I. And I would dearly love to acknowledge publicly all the people who have so enriched my life with their love and their friendship. Alas, a book of recollections such as this must condense much and omit many of the memories so special to the individuals involved.

So I begin by asking for understanding and forgiveness, particularly from the countless people who have made a personal difference in my life by sharing parts of the journey with me. True friends will understand that a passing mention in these pages is not nearly so important as being forever cherished in my heart.

This book was first urged upon me by Jack MacDonald when I was in hospital. He lobbied me to "tell a unique story that people need to hear." I wasn't sure that it was unique; I was less sure that anyone wanted to listen. Moreover, I wasn't really ready to tell it then.

Two years later, I found myself speaking to a group of Canada's future leaders – a collection of cabinet ministers' assistants in Ottawa.

In their youth, zeal and fervent right-wing approach I saw so much of my younger self and realized that I did have a relevant message for them, although it may not have been the one they expected. Rather than a barn-burning diatribe, they heard a message that day promoting peace and reconciliation.

Among those in the audience was Peter White, then a senior advisor to Prime Minister Brian Mulroney. He became enthused with the idea of a book containing my political anecdotes and personal reflections and mentioned it to Anna Porter, of Key Porter Books Ltd. When Anna approached me, I contacted Rod McQueen, one of Canada's most respected journalists and authors, as well as a good and trusted friend from our Ottawa days. Rod also thought that the book was worth doing and freed himself to make the idea become a reality. Without him, there would be no book. Without countless others, there would be no story.

So, foremost, I thank Rod for his tireless efforts and professional acumen in turning my rambling recollections into a form that would otherwise defy all logic, chronology and grammar. I thank him especially for his enduring friendship, together with that of his family – Sandy, Mark and Alison – as they lived this project with me, forever patient and frequently shoring up my flagging spirits in the face of self-doubts and discouragement.

I thank those whose memories I tapped to refresh my own: Merle Martin, Dr. Lewis Brand and Jack MacDonald for the political content; Don McCutchan for the 1983 leadership convention; and Father Gregory Cormican regarding the Irish College in Rome.

Much of my time in hospital had been blurred by the protective mechanism of a fuzzy memory. To Doctors Peter Powers, Greg De Marchi and Mo Ali go my sincere appreciation for helping me recall those days and weeks with clarity. Similarly, I am grateful to Sister Joan O'Sullivan and her staff at St. Joseph's Hospital for patiently responding to our many requests for all kinds of details.

Significant portions of the material about my political days were gleaned from my parliamentary papers kept at the National Archives and efficiently made available by the most courteous Kathy Hall and her colleagues. As always, the faithful and loyal Marjorie "Bunny" Pound gave freely of her time to help me locate the relevant papers.

Anna Porter not only invited Rod McQueen and me to collaborate on this book, she and her staff gave us constant encouragement and sage advice along the way. I am especially grateful to Anna, to editor-in-chief Phyllis Bruce and to editor Margaret Woollard; indeed, to all the friendly and helpful people at Key Porter.

I owe particular thanks to Gerald Emmett Cardinal Carter who gave me permission to produce these memoirs and who never once suggested or imposed any strictures on them. The freedom he gave me is just another example of his caring for me as one of his priests and his openness in letting me explore a variety of ways to feel useful again.

The process of arriving at a point where I could even feel like recalling and reliving certain events has been long and painful. So, while this book is of recent writing, it would not have been possible without those who saw me through my own sinner's version of "the dark night of the soul." I thank Fathers Sam Restivo, Ronald Kelly and Peter Watters for praying for me and prodding me through months of anguish toward wholeness and those first refreshing glimpses of hope.

As they helped me take the first steps toward recovery, so am I grateful for the leap made possible by my Alma Mater, Brock University. In particular to President Alan Earp and Vice-president William Matheson who, in June of 1985, invited all the family for our first get-together since my hospital room two years earlier. The occasion was the university's spring convocation where they truly honoured us all by presenting me with a doctorate of laws, the first Brock graduate to receive an honorary degree from Brock.

There are many special friends who have always been there to lend advice and ideas. They include Marc and Sarah Giacomelli and Michael McTeigue. I am grateful, too, for the wise counsel of Rory Cornale. And, of course, Sharon Curley, one of life's greatest treasures as a true friend, avid supporter and so often my toughest and most honest critic. Bless them!

I also want to acknowledge and thank all those other galoots who make my parents proud and have helped me write a life's story from day one: my sister, Kathleen Petch, and my brothers Joe, Paul, Terry, Tim and Jacques O'Sullivan. Most of all, I want to thank my parents.

Any good I may have done in life I owe to them. While I have accumulated a few titles and received many introductions, it remains my proudest boast to be known as the son of Paul and Helen O'Sullivan.

Much of this book has been written while my official assignment was to guide *The Catholic Register* through a period of transition. If there has been any success with either project, it is because I have leaned upon the goodwill and co-operation of the *Register* staff, in particular Paul Podesta, Brian O'Hearn, Norma Lumsden and Stan Koma. Similarly, during this period, I have been made welcome at the Church of the Transfiguration, Weston, Ontario. Fathers Patrick Doran and Gianni Carparelli have generously ensured me sufficient time for such extra projects as this.

The hours of intensive interviews took place over a period of weeks, largely at Malafield, near Campbellville, Ontario, where we enjoyed peace and tranquility in addition to the unmatched hospitality of Lillian Maloney and her daughter, Martha. Thanks to similar thoughtfulness and generosity on the part of Susan and the late John F. Bassett, we were also able to retreat for the final sessions to the warmth and friendly welcome of Longboat Key, Florida.

Above all, I thank those who have so faithfully continued to pray for me, providing the strength and determination so essential to such a painstaking task as this. I assure all my spiritual benefactors and all others involved that your contributions to this book have only been positive. Any shortcomings remain with me.

Finally, in an era of confused and troubled lives for so many, I am thankful for the gift of hope, which gives this book its purpose. For that is the simple goal of all this effort. To offer people hope. Young people making life decisions; those who need idealism rekindled for their own political quests; others anxious about their faith; and all of us who have that particular bond of being part of the war against cancer.

Through all the ups and downs and uncertainties of life, we need hope. That has been my experience of life. That's what I'd most like to share through these pages.

S.O'S.
June 1986

"There is no leisure about politics, for they are
ever seeking an end outside political practice,
for instance power or fame. Political life neither
provides our final end nor contains the happiness
we seek for ourselves or others . . . The purpose
of temporal tranquility, which well-ordered policies
establish and maintain, is to give opportunities
for contemplating truth."

St. Thomas Aquinas, *Commentary on the Ethics*

CHAPTER ONE

THE OLD CHIEFTAIN

As an Irish Catholic, I fit all the stereotypes: stubborn, even bull-headed; loyal and often sentimental; good-humoured but subject to mood swings from madcap to melancholy. I have fed from this life's offerings and now await its true fulfilment in life eternal. Meanwhile, events conspire to teach me humility.

My very name is a levelling device. When I give it on the telephone or offer it in person while not wearing my cleric's collar, I'll frequently be asked, "Are you *the* Shawn O'Sullivan, the boxer?" "No," I reply, "*he's* Shawn O'Sullivan, the boxer. I'm Sean O'Sullivan, the fighter."

Contrary to popular belief I did not combust on a street corner full grown, wearing a nine-piece suit and spouting Tory propaganda. I was born on New Year's Day, 1952, in St. Joseph's Hospital, Hamilton, Ontario. I arrived two weeks early. As my friends will attest, I've never been early since; in fact I'm rarely even on time.

My father, Paul O'Sullivan, was a hotelier. After service in the Second World War where he rose to the rank of captain, he returned to his first hotel job, so far from the front desk and the manager's suite that it was beyond reach of even the switchboard. He was a stock-room clerk in the bowels of the Royal Connaught Hotel in Hamilton, a job that would one day be my introduction to the hospitality industry as well.

Our lives did not correspond to the Hollywood version of the hotelier's family; home was not a luxurious suite with room service and hot and cold running maids. Being in the hotel business in those days was much like being manager of a bank branch; lots of prestige but little pay. A man on his way up had to be prepared to pack his clean shirts, go where he was posted without question and send for

1

his family later. A few months after my birth, my father was transferred to Montreal to become personnel manager for the Sheraton Mount Royal and the Laurentien. We lived in a typical Notre Dame de Grace fourplex. The resident families were a microcosm of the races and religions in Notre Dame de Grace: they included the St. Maurice family (French); the Morris family (WASP); the Dick family (Jewish); and the Irish O'Sullivans.

There were only two types of Irish families, shanty Irish and lace-curtain Irish. Both were poor; the latter were poor but proud. We were the lace-curtain variety. That meant that no matter how badly off you were, you bought lace curtains, hung them in the front window and said everything was all right. There were seven children born to my parents, Paul and Helen – six boys and a girl, spread over thirteen years. My two younger brothers (I was the fifth child) were born in Montreal. By then, the family had run out of Irish names; one of them had to be called Jacques.

In later life, after I had achieved some political success, I always found it ironic that many people assumed I must have been a spoiled child, even the scion of a wealthy family. If only they could have seen the O'Sullivans crammed into that apartment. We lived like raisins stuffed into a muffin. Four boys shared two sets of bunk beds in one room, the two eldest boys had a second bedroom, my sister had the third bedroom and my parents slept every night on a pull-out couch in the living room. There were so many of us that we even attended Sunday Mass in shifts.

My parents are the two most gentle people I have ever met. They gave us the rich gift of a stable and loving family. They taught me ambition, self-confidence and duty. O'Sullivans, we were told, weren't just ordinary folk, we were gifted, even though there were few famous O'Sullivans on the family tree. My great-grandfather was born in Hamilton, Ontario, making me fourth-generation Canadian. We had no known kin in Ireland; indeed, we had no knowledge at all of our Irish background. The assumption was simply made that the blessings of our birth meant service to community and country according to those gifts. My parents set high standards for achievement, and when report cards came home from school it was my father's view that mattered, not the teacher's. My mother, like most women of her generation, did not work outside the home. She devoted her life to raising us with a mixture of patience, contentment and simplicity.

While family was first, church came a close second. Faith was not paraded in public; it was practised in private. It was a personal pact with God. Although I went through the usual period of boredom with the church that every teenager endures, for the most part the Catholic church was a major force in my life and formed my very fibre. It was part and parcel of our Irish heritage and our family expectations. We were also blessed with good priests. Among them was Monsignor Gordon Ryan, one of those mellow, Irish priests of the old school. He would come into the schoolyard at recess or into the classroom unannounced, an impressive sight in his black cape and biretta with purple pompom and piping. He knew everyone by name and spoke to us in his wonderful, melodious voice, answering any and all questions, even one I remember about the cost of his vestments. He regularly visited families in their homes and was a presence of tremendous influence in the parish. There are now eight serving priests of a similar age who grew up in that area, a large number from one small part of a city, given the shortage everywhere today.

In addition to good parish priests, we O'Sullivans had some excellent role models within our own family. A great-aunt, Sister Celestine, was superior general of the Sisters of St. Joseph, Hamilton Diocese. My Aunt Joan, a nurse, entered the convent of the Sisters of St. Joseph in Hamilton and later became director of St. Joseph's Hospital there. When I was young, she would visit us in Montreal wearing the formidable black nun's habit with its veil, starched bib and rosary at the side even when on holiday.

A great-uncle, Joseph Anthony O'Sullivan, was archbishop of Kingston, Ontario. Two or three times a year his long, black Cadillac, driven by his priest-secretary, would pull up in front of our Montreal house and Uncle Joe would sweep in. He stood well over six feet tall and, with the cross hanging from his neck and a huge ring on his finger, looked like Central Casting's idea of an archbishop. As we children lined up to listen to his flowery oratory, he seemed to fill the entire room. His hands constantly made grand gestures as he ques-

3

tioned each of us and bestowed episcopal blessings. At the close of the visit, he would reach into his pocket and pull out a five- or ten-dollar bill – in later years, a twenty – and give one to each of us children, saying: "Here, have a holy picture." Then, he'd fix each of us boys in turn with a cold stare and add: "Get a haircut."

The family was the centre of our world. And a competitive world it was. As the shortest and slightest of the O'Sullivans, I was neither athletic nor physically well co-ordinated. Instead, I set out to become the most stubborn and outspoken, the offspring who didn't always want to go along. I succeeded. My first rebellion came early, when I was only nine. It was 1961 and my father announced that we were moving back to Hamilton because he had been named general manager of the Connaught. For him it was a promotion at last; for me it was purgatory at best. I was shattered to leave good friends and grade school in mid-year. I wrote a letter of protest to the president of the hotel chain demanding that he change his mind. Fortunately, I didn't mail it.

While Hamilton brought the trauma of new surroundings, it also meant we moved several steps up the social ladder. When we arrived at our new home in the east end, I was immediately impressed by its size compared to our modest portion of the Montreal fourplex. As it turned out, the building I was admiring was merely our garage, a four-car affair. The house was even bigger and had four large bedrooms. After sleeping four boys to a room in Montreal, it was a luxury to share digs with only one of my brothers, Terry.

Still, even a larger house did not make the world less hostile. Moving from the warm bosom of Montreal to the cold shoulder of Hamilton made me feel like a deep-sea diver who suffers the bends by coming up too quickly from the bottom of the ocean. Although I was moved ahead a grade, Hamilton still seemed in the Dark Ages. In Montreal, we had been using newfangled ballpoint pens for two years; in Hamilton, it was back to lead pencils, straight pens and inkwells. It took me two years to overcome the traumatic uprooting. During that time I developed severe eczema on the palms of my hands and the soles of my feet. I was trooped from general practitioner to dermatologist and back again in the search for a cure to these painful blisters and running sores. They tried everything: antibiotics,

4

purple dye, creams and salves, even herbal teas. No one could find a cure. Finally, in desperation, someone suggested an experimental treatment that involved bombarding my palms and feet with x-rays. The aberrant procedure was followed two or three times a week for months. According to one of my doctors today, those x-rays may well have been the time bomb that later became leukemia. Eventually, the eczema cleared up, probably just because it ran its course, not because any particular treatment worked.

I encountered other health problems as well. In Grade Five, I cracked my left ankle and acquired a limp that remains with me today. That was followed by severe pains in the leg and lower back. After two weeks in hospital, a tumour was discovered on my left hip. An operation was required to remove it surgically; fortunately, it was benign. Then, at fourteen, a disc had to be removed from my lower spine. At an age when most boys are developing physical skills by learning and playing team sports, the eczema, the leg, the tumour and the back problems kept me sidelined for about four years. There were simply too many visits to doctors and too much pain for anything like a normal childhood.

Fortunately, throughout, my marks in school didn't suffer. In Grade One my average was 98 per cent; in succeeding years, it remained near 85 per cent. In Grade Two, I won first-place prizes in my class for every subject except one – religion. Years later, when *The Selling of the President* was published, it described Richard Nixon as a pain-in-the-ass kid who received a briefcase for Christmas – and loved it – when everyone else got a football. He was, the writer added, the type of kid who always had his homework done and never let anyone copy it. I photocopied that passage and sent it around to several of my friends; I saw a fair amount of myself in the description. After all, with few outside outlets for my energies, my only game was schoolwork, my only scorecard was high grades.

I had an uncanny ability to memorize long passages, and that soon led to public speaking. By 1964, I was enjoying some success on a stage of sorts. I gave speeches on salmon and the loyalty of dogs and endlessly practised a version of "Casey at the Bat" for weeks in the empty four-car garage. My rendition, including the appropriate bat-swinging gestures, won third place in the boys' section of the lyric and dramatic recitation portion of the Catholic Youth Organization Crusader Drama Festival. There were a number of other budding politicians in the event. The winner of the girls' section for her version of something called "Gertrude McFuzz" was Sheila Copps, daughter of Hamilton mayor Vic Copps. Her presentation included acting out the different animals in the barnyard. She stole the show. Her routine may also have helped her understand her surroundings when she went on to win a seat in the Ontario Legislature in 1981, then in the House of Commons, after she switched to federal politics in 1984.

Not content with such solo performances, toward the end of elementary school I began to stage variety shows, with myself as host. My school chums and I mimicked the format of *The Garry Moore Show* and did comedy skits we wrote ourselves or stole from *MAD* magazine, musical routines and parodies of other television shows, such as *What's My Line?* We booked the church hall, issued tickets and, knowing the value of a star attraction as gate builder, invited Mayor Copps. He agreed to participate as the mystery guest. All was going well until the school principal discovered our plan. She was furious that we had invited the mayor (I assume because she wasn't consulted) and ordered me to withdraw the invitation. Looking back, I guess the youthful rebellions I later led had their roots there.

Just as I was learning to resent some authority figures, I learned to respect others. That was the period when I met the man who would dominate my life for the next dozen years. Because of my father's position as manager of Hamilton's best hotel, I got to see some of the famous personages staying there and was on hand for any celebrations staged in the hotel. In 1962, when I attended a dinner there to celebrate the success of the local Junior A hockey team, I was not only impressed by the hockey champions, I quickly identified an unlikely hero – Ellen Fairclough, a local MP and a cabinet minister in the government of John Diefenbaker.

Even as a ten-year-old, I could see that the cheerful, energetic Mrs. Fairclough had a sparkle and charisma that no one else in the room could match. In the days and weeks after, I began to follow her exploits in the local paper and to identify with her and the Progressive Conservative Party.

A year later, toward the end of the 1963 election campaign, my father took several of us in the family to dinner at the hotel. There was excitement in the air because the Right Honourable John George Diefenbaker, then prime minister, was campaigning in the area and was scheduled to come through the hotel lobby. After dinner, my father lined us all up where we'd have a good view, then prepared to meet the dignitaries as they arrived. Outside, a cavalcade of cars pulled up with much horn blowing, and the entourage burst through the front doors led by television cameras and a Scottish piper. Dief arrived to much applause and was greeted by my father; then suddenly Ellen Fairclough steered him over to meet the children of the general manager. John Diefenbaker was a grand and imposing figure in overcoat and homburg. He stopped and said "Hello," or "How are you?" to each of us, shook our hands and then was carried away in the crush of the cheering crowd. It was only a brief encounter, but the gaze of those piercing blue eyes above which his big eyebrows bounced with obvious delight made a deep impression on me. I became an instant fan. I was just like any other kid meeting Gordie Howe. The election was a few days later, and I stayed up as late as I was allowed to hear the results – a Liberal minority government. I was bewildered at the loss, but I felt a boyish admiration for this great man. Politics fascinated me. If rough-and-tumble sports were out, this was an indoor contest I could enter. I was hooked. Politics became my blood sport.

Dief's minority government had given way to Lester Pearson's minority government, and early in 1964 I finally gathered the courage to write a three-page letter to my hero, commiserating with him and extending my best wishes. I said I knew he was coming to Hamilton the next month for a speech and that I would watch for him in the hotel lobby again. As it turned out, however, my father was away and I couldn't be in the lobby. I wasn't worried because I thought either that the letter wouldn't reach him or that he would forget about it even if he did see it. I was wrong on both counts. As Diefenbaker entered the lobby, he looked around, didn't see me, and asked the assistant manager, "Where is he?" After a flurry of phone calls and some surprise at home (my mother didn't know I had written the letter) I was hustled over to the hotel.

His speech ran late, so it wasn't until about 9:45 p.m. that the Diefenbakers arrived and I met him and his wife, Olive, in the lobby. We rode the elevator with some local dignitaries to the couple's seventh-floor VIP suite. A number of people, mostly strangers to me, were assembled in the court of this travelling king. When we were all seated, he pulled my letter out of his briefcase. I couldn't believe my eyes. Not only had he read it, he'd brought it with him! Stapled to my letter was a note that said: "Mr. Diefenbaker, one of the most touching I've ever read." It was signed M.P., the initials, I later learned, of his secretary Marjorie ("Bunny") Pound. He made to show the letter around until Olive quietly said: "Now, John, you know we don't read our personal mail to other people." "She's right," he said, returning it to his briefcase. "We don't." He produced some photos of himself and asked who wanted one autographed. There was a hallelujah chorus of "Yes, please" in the room.

Dief had brought supplies of two different shots with him. One showed him patting his dog; in the other he was gazing out of his parliamentary office window with a small bust of Sir John A. Macdonald in the foreground. I hesitated, not knowing which photo to choose; I liked them both. Finally, Olive, realizing my predicament, motioned me to come closer to her and whispered: "Tell him you would like one of each." I repeated to him what she had said and Dief snapped: "Did she tell you to say that?" "Yes," I replied. "Well, she's the boss," he laughed and proceeded to sign both.

Among the people I met that night was Jack MacDonald, who would later become mayor of Hamilton and a great supporter of mine. As well, there were members of the Hamilton Young Progressive Conservative Association. At the time, YPC members had to be at least sixteen. I was not a member. Dief allowed as how he wasn't a member, either. "I'm too old to be a member, so I'm an honorary member," he said. Then he turned to the YPC members present and asked, "So couldn't we do the same for Sean? Make him an honorary member?" They quickly agreed.

After an hour had passed, I made ready to go, clutching my photos like talismans for the future. As he bade me goodbye, Diefenbaker said: "You write an excellent letter. I want you to keep on writing to me." With a conspiratorial air he gave me his home address and added, "We won't have any of these nosy secretaries interfering." I had been the centre of attention throughout; I was on cloud nine. Before our meeting that night I was just his fan; now I felt like his best friend.

During the next few months, I put my honorary membership to work attending the YPC meetings. For the first few sessions, my mother accompanied me on the bus. After the second night out, she commented on the way home that this was all very nice but was I planning to go to every meeting? "Oh yes," I assured her. Fortunately, members with cars began to give me rides and my mother didn't need to worry about my travelling alone at night. In June, Dief was back in Hamilton and I joined him for breakfast in his suite. We talked about everything from Judy LaMarsh to fishing. It was clear he preferred the latter. Other visitors included a reporter from the Hamilton *Spectator* and potential candidates in the next election. I was allowed to stay through all the meetings like some trusted confidant. Afterwards, I tagged along for his news conference, a wreath-laying ceremony at the statue of Sir John A. Macdonald in Gore Park and a picnic at Stoney Creek.

In the 1965 election campaign, I worked for local Tories, Lincoln Alexander (now lieutenant-governor of Ontario) in particular. One of my main tasks was to travel with Linc when he toured the riding in an open car. He would sit on top of the back seat, waving to passers-by. I hunched on the armrest of the back seat, with my arms hooked around his legs so he wouldn't fall out when the car lurched around corners.

During that year, Dief and I – the young whippersnapper and the old warrior – continued to exchange letters. I would write regularly and reverentially, telling him all the local political news and, of course, swearing eternal allegiance to him as only a young man of that age can to a hero of such mythic proportions. Dief would respond with equally kind words. Typical was this line: "Your loyalty is surpassed only by your enthusiasm." Nothing phased me as I learned more about the old man, not even the time Olive showed me the wringing wet undershirt Dief had just removed, after a speech. I regarded that rolled-up relic with an awe bordering on reverence. Soon, I was signing my Christmas cards, Sean O'Sullivan FPM –

Future Prime Minister. I'm still embarrassed by such youthful exuberance, ambition and arrogance.

In March 1966, my parents allowed me to travel alone to attend the YPC national convention in Ottawa. I arrived by train, checked my bag in a locker at the station downtown and walked down Wellington Street to Parliament Hill. I was carrying a photograph in a brown envelope under my arm. Although some protesting students were being thrown into a paddywagon in front of the Centre Block, no one stopped me as I walked in the front door, climbed the stairs and found a seat in the public galleries of the House of Commons. I must have looked more like a messenger boy than a student at a sit-in.

At first, I was taken aback at the haphazard and relaxed atmosphere below me. When an MP rose to speak, few listened; some read newspapers and others dozed. Many seats were vacant, including the prime minister's; none of the Hamilton-area MPs was in sight. Dief, however, was in his front-row seat, and I cheered inwardly when he rose to speak. He attacked Justice Minister Lucien Cardin and they seemed to spend a great deal of time glaring at each other. Earlier that week, the Liberals had dropped a bombshell in the House: the name of Gerda Munsinger. Indiscreet links between Munsinger and former Diefenbaker cabinet ministers Pierre Sévigny and George Hees soon became public, as did concerns over breaches in security. At this point, the public inquiry had not yet been set up and little was known, so debate about the issue was mostly mudslinging. Still, as I watched the proceedings, I thought that nothing could be more rewarding than one day to join Diefenbaker on the floor of the Commons.

Suddenly, Dief left the House, and I scrambled to find his suite of offices. After a few minutes' wait, I was ushered in to see him. I had brought along a photograph taken of the two of us in Hamilton for him to sign. We chatted briefly and then listened to the first few minutes of the news as he made ready to leave for a speech he was delivering that evening. "We'll have to have you out to the house," he said. "Keep your ears open at the convention and call me tomorrow with some ideas for my speech." He gave me his home telephone number, then added: "Don't let any of those birds over there [at the convention] get it."

On Sunday, the Diefenbakers did invite me out to Stornoway, the official residence of the leader of the opposition. Dief gave me what he called "the fifty-cent tour" that included everything from his collection of letters written by Sir John A. Macdonald to the basement where he kept rows of filing cabinets popping with documents from his days in power. Among the many interesting items I spotted was a record on a table in the hall entitled "Learn French." I had heard him speak some French the day before in his address to the YPC convention. His pronunciation wasn't good; but I was impressed that he was still struggling to improve after all his years in public life. After the tour, we sat in the den at the front of the house and he predicted: "We'll have you in Parliament at eighteen." Later, he leaned forward in his chair, stared solemnly at me and said: "I will be going soon. Remember – this is our secret." With that, the conversation was ended, the audience over.

My next Ottawa visit was for the November 1966 general meeting. I was not a delegate. There were few YPC delegates from Ontario, and the executive had quickly snapped up those positions. I could only register as a guest. The place was abuzz with revolt. National President Dalton Camp wanted a leadership-review mechanism written into the party constitution. The device was merely a front for his dump-Dief views. The loyalists who wanted Diefenbaker to stay were represented by their candidate for president, Arthur Maloney. The clash between the two was widely seen as a pro- or anti-Dief battle.

I wasn't without delegate status long. Dr. Lewis Brand, one of the seventy-one MPs who were loyal to Dief and supported Maloney against Camp, gave me his delegate's ribbon so I could get into more meetings. When I asked if this transfer was legal, he replied: "I certainly don't see why not after the way Camp treated the MPs at the National Executive meeting yesterday. Why, he treated us as if we were dirt."

I arrived at the Château Laurier ballroom at 6:00 p.m. to secure a good seat for Dief's speech, which was scheduled for 8:15. Already the Campites had occupied the front rows. I could hear the whispered instructions passed among them: "Don't stand up when Dief comes in." They sat on their hands when he entered, they jeered his

11

views and they hurled insults as he spoke. In an attempt to find out what had changed Camp's mind about his leadership, Dief read back some of Camp's previous supportive statements. Camp stared at the floor. After the speech, I sought out Hamilton-area delegates for their reaction and was shocked to learn that Lincoln Alexander, a candidate Dief had supported heartily in 1965, was backing Camp. Alexander was chief returning officer; he would cast the deciding ballot in the event of a tie. I confronted Linc. He said he only hoped to God he didn't have to vote; I could only agree.

On Tuesday, Camp and Maloney both spoke. As he stood outside the ballroom waiting his turn, Camp shook several hands, including mine, then stared at my Arthur Maloney badges and moved away. As I stood there watching him, I couldn't help but think how alone he looked, even unhappy. I was seized with the sudden urge to race over, grab his speech notes and flee down the hall, leaving him without his text minutes before he was due on stage. I lacked the courage, however, and didn't follow through. I thought Maloney's speech was the better of the two efforts. He called for loyalty and respect for Diefenbaker, with his now-famous line, "When John Diefenbaker enters a room, Arthur Maloney stands up!"

The speeches over, I walked over to Dief's parliamentary office. He asked me who I thought would win. I said Maloney's speech should give him the edge. "Well, if it's Camp, you won't see me crying," said Dief. "I won't let it disturb me. Besides, he's not the brains behind it all anyway. No, it's [former cabinet ministers, E. Davie] Fulton and [Douglas] Harkness and [Wallace] McCutcheon." I asked him if he would be returning to the convention. "What! And put up with those young scuttlebutts? I shouldn't have to put up with them and I won't!" He continued: "I would have gone six months ago – if only they had left me alone. But they began complaining and I will not go as long as they are fighting to destroy me."

Before the ballots for president were counted, I asked Lincoln Alexander if he would tell me the outcome on his way to the stage to make the official announcement. It was my intention to phone Dief with the results. Linc refused, saying that all delegates should be told at the same time. It made sense to me, so I took my seat in the hall beside New Brunswick MP Gordon Fairweather. Imagine my surprise a few minutes later when someone whispered to Fairweather that Camp had won by fifty-eight votes! Fifteen minutes passed before Linc made the announcement that confirmed what I had heard on the floor. I was upset, but decided to accept the election results and began removing my Maloney badges to put it all behind me. Said Fairweather: "No, keep wearing those. He put up a good fight and you should wear those proudly." I did.

The next day, word spread that more than half of the seventy-one loyal MPs might form a new party called the Canadian Conservative Party and serve as the Official Opposition in Parliament. The loyalists were also told that Dief was coming to the Château Laurier at 11:00 a.m., and we packed the lobby for his brief visit and speech. Among other rousing comments, he quoted Sir Andrew Barton, an Elizabethan soldier:

> Fight on, my men . . .
> I am wounded but I am not slaine
> I'll lay me down and bleed awhile
> And then I'll rise and fight againe.

I was distraught, not just with the emotion of the moment, but with the realization that while my leader was pleading for understanding and support in the lobby, a few feet away his fellow party members were voting on various policy matters, uninterested in his views or vision. The convention ended in turmoil. Dief's final speech and the closing banquet were both cancelled. The final indecency was done: there was an affirmative vote calling for a leadership convention before January 1968. Through it all, it was Olive who seemed to feel the deepest hurt. After the meeting she said to me: "Sean, we both know that he would be going soon. I am only sorry that he has to go like this. But, you know," she continued, "those men are the kind that will soon go and will be forgotten. It is John who will be remembered." The awful 1966 convention was over, but its effects were just beginning in the party.

I concluded that Dief was perhaps the most misunderstood prime minister Canada had ever had. Canadians had voted for a hero in 1957 and 1958; he could not live up to their expectations. He had been surrounded by a treacherous cabinet and a disloyal party. I thought

Camp and his followers were evil incarnate. I continued to admire Dief and hope that I could be half the man he was. At the same time, the disappointment he felt and poor treatment he was given soured me. There was a tremendous bond between Dief and me. I saw what his own party did to him and learned quickly that even among supposed friends and colleagues it was impossible to know who could be trusted. For me, attending the November 1966 convention was like being at the slaying of my own political father. Overnight, at fourteen, I became anti-establishment, suspicious, warped and Machiavellian. That would be the Tory way – and my way – for the next dozen years.

CHAPTER TWO

THE YOUNG REBEL

M y naive belief that the best man always won was further battered by my immersion in high-school politics. I became involved in politics as soon as I started in Grade Nine at Bishop Ryan High School because I thought that was one way to emulate Dief and become adept enough to join him in the House of Commons. We newcomers went by the derogatory tag of "minor niners." I was determined to win equal rights for freshman students, so I ran for class representative and won on a platform to make my fellow Grade Nine students an equal part of the school. It was a good start, and I did want to do positive things through the democratic process. But after seeing the national defeats and personal setbacks handed to Dief, I also learned fast that politics was often unfair and cruel. To succeed, I thought that I had to be the same.

In Grade Nine, Sheila Copps and I ran against each other for president of the Social Action Club. A formidable opponent with a high-profile name, she plastered her father's old election signs everywhere. When the day came to make our final speeches to the school, she listed her plans in a serious tone. I took an entirely different tack – I cracked jokes. My closing line was typical of the frothy tone I took: "I just want to restate that, with me as president, the Social Action Club will once again take as its hero our great friend Superman and defend truth, justice and the Canadian way." As he listened, I could see that the principal, Father Ronald J. Cote, was incredulous. I didn't care; especially when I won.

Winning was just the beginning. In keeping with my new hardball ways, I was not a gracious president. After a few weeks, I concluded that Sheila was not really interested in the role of vice-president that automatically went to the candidate who finished second, and I decided to do her in. At a club meeting she did not attend, I painted her as a sore loser, convinced the others that she would not be an effective member of the executive, and moved to have her impeached! She was. As a young politician, I learned early to stomp on any opposition before it had a chance to rally and take back power.

My uncle the archbishop, or "Big Joe" as he was known to his priests, later gave me some sage political advice that was along those same lines. When I was running for office in the Young Progressive Conservative organization, he met someone who told him about one of my opponents and the dire plans that were apparently in store for me. Uncle Joe was not a turn-the-other-cheek churchman or politician. His advice on how to deal with this upstart was: "You've got to spike them first before they spike you." I guess I was practising that political philosophy even before he preached it.

Just as there were some political leanings in my family, there was also not a little rebellion. My aunt Mary Merryman was a rebel from her youth. She looks and sounds like Bette Davis; she smokes and drinks like a gangster's moll. She is very opinionated and is the great character of the family. During the Second World War, she worked for British Intelligence in Washington and from there was posted to Bolivia. Clearly, she must have upset the local authorities because she was suddenly given twenty-four hours to leave the country. She shipped her belongings home in a trunk to her father. This very proper man barely knew where she was, and because of the secrecy of her work, certainly didn't know what she was doing. One day, her trunk mysteriously arrived without explanation and without Mary. When he opened it, he found a shotgun inside.

The rebelliousness of Mary Merryman, the tough advice of Uncle Joe, the sight of Dief being crucified by the party, all came together to turn me into a negative force in high school. After an idealistic start in Grade Nine, by Grade Eleven I had become the angry young man who was going to battle the administration or anyone else who got in the way. Impeachment had worked so well against Sheila Copps that I had the mischievous idea of using it against the school authorities. My friend Marc Giacomelli and I wheedled our way onto a committee that was drawing up a new constitution for the student council.

16

He did the writing, I did the sales job, and council passed it. The rewritten version duly named such council members as the principal, vice-principal, advisor to students, and class representatives; a few pages further on came the clause that a two-thirds vote of council could impeach any member. It didn't take Father Cote more than one reading to realize that we had voted ourselves the power to impeach him. He summoned a special meeting of council and announced that the rewrite was unacceptable. The teacher advisor resigned in embarrassment and, needless to say, Marc and I were unceremoniously turfed off the constitution committee.

There were additional run-ins. Among other activities, I ran chocolate-bar campaigns and a raffle to raise money for the school. In the raffle, the prize was a new car. The campaign was going swimmingly and it looked as if we would make $8,000, until the police arrived. It seems we had forgotten to obtain the necessary provincial permission and licence for the raffle. Father Cote made us set up a hotline to tell buyers there was no car and to offer refunds. Fortunately, few purchasers wanted their fifty cents back; we were able to keep nearly all of the proceeds. Because there was no prize to buy, our profits were even higher than anticipated. We made $11,000 and erected new bleachers on the school grounds with the proceeds.

Other activities included helping to edit the school newspaper and managing the football team, excellent training for politics. After all, anyone who can handle a group of rowdy football players can control the wide assortment of types who are attracted to politics. I also coached a class basketball squad. I was not an expert. I knew little about the game, not even how many players were allowed on the floor at once. If anyone asked for a playing turn, I would agree. The player he replaced didn't always return to the bench right away. I just kept sending men onto the floor and when I could slip in an extra one, well, I didn't mind. After all, they just wanted to play and it did seem to help our side.

My reputation with the administration kept deteriorating and I found that to keep involved I had to hide behind a front man. This soon turned into what passed for machine politics in high school. We put up a candidate for president, a mild-mannered, extremely likeable student, as our stand-in. Even though we blitzed the school with campaign literature, he lost, finishing well down the list. The top two students were so close that Father Cote announced there would be another vote. Knowing full well that our man didn't stand a chance in the rerun either, I seized the moment to make a statement that would allow us to withdraw with gusto if not with grace. I drafted a letter to Father Cote over the signature of our candidate. It read: "Due to the gross, unwarranted intervention of the administration in a student attempt at a democratic election, irreparable damage has been done to my candidacy. Accordingly, I am withdrawing and shall not stand in the election."

Father Cote knew very well who had written the letter and called me into his office the following day. As a teacher first and administrator second, he began by noting that I had spelled *irreparable* "irrepairable." Then he continued: "There's an old rule in the German army that you might well heed and that is not to make a complaint in the heat of the moment. You should wait at least a day." I replied in my most pompous-twit tone that a day had passed and if I had to do it all over again I would write the same letter.

Father Cote looked out the window of his office for the longest time and finally said: "It could well be, Mr. O'Sullivan, that it would be better for you and for us all if you found yourself another school that might cater to your particular demands. I am, however, unaware of the existence of any such institution." I stayed on to graduate from Bishop Ryan. The line beneath one photo in the yearbook reads: "Sean O'Sullivan: with his iron will and determination, has a reputation for getting things done."

My interest in national politics and my unwavering loyalty to Diefenbaker continued unabated throughout this period. In the summer of 1967, I read that a Youth for Diefenbaker committee had been organized in Toronto. I wrote to William Hatton, one of its co-founders, saying that I was a delegate and would like to help. He jumped at the offer. I met Hatton and his associate, Keith Martin, in Toronto. Keith, later Dief's executive assistant, would become one of my closest friends until his death in 1984. He counselled me often and kept the legend of Dief intact; I still think of him as one of the canniest politicos I've ever met.

In that summer of 1967, Martin and Hatton were operating a

storefront political office that was no more than smoke and mirrors. The whole thing was run from the firm where they worked, Eastern Personnel Agency, on Yonge Street. Behind the public-relations façade there was little substance to the Youth for Diefenbaker "movement." The office was a tiny place with an air conditioner that gave the occupants two choices. If the machine was off, they were roasted alive; if it was on, everyone was freeze-dried. There were a few desks and a telex machine that spewed messages on tape. There were standing orders that, on the rare occasions when the phone rang, the telex machine was to be fired up to make the office sound busy. Whoever else was in the room would shout during the telephone conversation. The standard background lines went something like, "It's another riding; we've just picked up three more delegates in Algoma," to give callers the impression that the place was abuzz and that Youth for Dief had momentum. It was the classic political boiler room, pumping out nothing more than hot air.

Youth for Dief saw me as a real catch and milked the publicity. I signed on as its youngest (and first and only) conscript in July. There was a brave news release announcing that I would be western-Ontario organizer and even braver talk about national tours to rally all YPC delegates to Dief – or, if he didn't choose to run, behind the candidate he designated. On July 4, 1967, I issued a news release (or rather the Hatton-Martin machine issued one in my name) appointing me to the Youth for Dief committee. In the press release, I made much of my three-year friendship with Dief, our correspondence and the several meetings we'd had in Hamilton and Ottawa. Among other gushy sentences in the news release was this gem: "That he would befriend a boy, who cannot even vote, in this way, is another of the many proofs that John Diefenbaker is a great man."

The press release also took the opportunity (few were missed) to castigate those who dumped Dief at the November 1966 meeting. Proclaimed I: "I was at that meeting and saw a carefully planned plot executed by a small but loud group of parasites who represent not the feelings of Young Conservatives but rather the height of poor manners and that cheap form of politics which has no place in the Conservative Party." I predicted Dief would run for leader and said, "That is why our slogan is 'Keep the Chief.'" I was prepared for the inevitable question: "Who will you support if Mr. Diefenbaker does not run?" My well-rehearsed reply was: "I will support the candidate whom Mr. Diefenbaker, in his wisdom, indicates is worthy to succeed him." We weren't just supporters, we were true believers and zealots in the cause. Dief, of course, was delighted with the whole operation and my participation in it. Both he and Olive wrote to congratulate me.

In addition to beating the press bushes, I had some practical duties. I was in charge of lining up high-school friends from Hamilton to attend the convention with signs and other pro-Dief paraphernalia. One of my Hamilton recruits was paid a retainer and inserted as a volunteer in the Robert Stanfield organization as a mole, with instructions to report any helpful news he heard about their campaign. From him we gleaned such valuable information as the fact that there would be Stanfield girls at the convention dressed in tartan outfits and handing out roses. We immediately ordered roses, too, and announced that a crew of Diefenbaker girls (recruited by my sister) would be handing out roses. We thought this theft of their tactics would cause all sorts of turmoil in the Stanfield campaign, until word came back from our mole that Stanfield's organizers saw our plans as just a coincidence, the kind of thing that happens at a convention with several candidates. They would be going ahead anyway. The mole was not a great success.

There were other scams. I lined up a Hamilton radio reporter to perpetrate one of them. We got him to phone a youth organizer for Stanfield and pretend he was conducting an interview. His line of questioning went something like this: "Are you aware that certain delegates committed to your candidate were elected at meetings where proper notice wasn't given? Are you aware that Mr. Keith Martin and Mr. William Hatton of Youth for Diefenbaker are even now flying to Ottawa to hold a press conference that will expose all?" The startled voice at the other end was that of Larry Grossman, now opposition leader in Ontario. This was meant to throw the other side into disarray, but if it did, it wasn't for long. We had no case; there was no news conference.

At fifteen, I was the youngest delegate among the approximately 2,250 who gathered for the convention, from September 5 to September 9, in Toronto. I spent the time in Toronto, when I should have been attending classes at Bishop Ryan, doing everything from pouring drinks in the hospitality suite at the Royal York Hotel, through handing out "Keep the Chief" buttons, to organizing the pitiful band that only knew one song: "Hail to the Chief." Convention week is a most unreal time. People try to decipher every clue and seize upon even the most insignificant event as if it were a fingerprint at a murder scene. Much of the guessing game revolved around the will-he-won't-he question of whether Dief would run. In our view, Dief's indecision was our strongest card. If he announced at the last minute, we argued, everyone else would be sent reeling and one great speech would sweep the delegates. We thought other candidates like George Hees, Michael Starr and Alvin Hamilton would drop out and return, delegates in tow, to the Diefenbaker fold.

The plain fact was that each of the candidates was anathema to Dief, and none was very likely to support him or send delegates in his direction. Hees had resigned in 1963 and, Dief argued, helped cause his electoral defeat in the general election that year. Diefenbaker loved to tell the story about Hees and Fulton arriving one day at 24 Sussex Drive. Fulton heaped praise on Hees as a successor to Diefenbaker then phoned later to withdraw everything he had said. As for Hees, Dief thought he was an able salesman and very friendly but not too bright. He had never forgiven him for demanding Dief's resignation at a caucus meeting, breaking down in tears, declaring party unity to the media then resigning a few days later. After the Munsinger affair became public, Dief said he was convinced that the Liberals had known about it in 1963 and blackmailed Hees into resigning. Dief was particularly irate that Hees fled to ski in Switzerland. "Where was he when this party needed him?" Dief would ask; then answer his own question with all the disgust he could muster: "Skiing in Switzerland!"

Dief could also put on quite a show repeating what he claimed were actual quotes from RCMP tapes of Gerda Munsinger's dalliances with Hees and Pierre Sévigny. As he listened to the Sévigny portion, Dief claimed, he had to ask the RCMP what all the thumping was. He'd playact his own question and repeat the RCMP answer in his own words. "What's all this damned banging and thumping? It was his leg, his wooden leg." As for Hees, in Dief's account there was little lovemaking, just endless narcissism as Hees kept asking her: "Have you ever seen a body like mine? Have you ever seen such a physique? How old do you think I am?" I always doubted that the stories were true, but it certainly meant that any Hees-Diefenbaker alliance was unlikely. Even in 1965, when Hees ran again and Dief agreed to appear in his riding, it was a perfunctory performance. The photographer got one shot of the two together and asked if he could take a second. Dief refused.

Nor was Dief much of an Alvin Hamilton fan, even though they were fellow Westerners. Dief would rise to the bait quickly whenever Hamilton's name was mentioned. He did not see him as a credible leadership candidate. Instead, Dief believed he was an amateur with no support who tried unsuccessfully to portray himself as a thinker, a doer and an innovator. What irked Dief most was Alvin Hamilton's claim to have sold Canadian wheat to China. "He had nothing to do with it," Dief would fume. "It was all done. I authorized and I sent it. He just happened to be minister and I allowed him to announce it. He never sold one bit of wheat and that's all."

As for Robert Stanfield, Diefenbaker had fewer negative things to say about him. Dief knew that, as leader of the party in Nova Scotia, Stanfield had campaigned hard for him in federal elections; even so, there was one line that just ended all discussion. Stanfield was Camp, that was it, full stop. Camp, Dief assumed, wanted to be party leader himself but knew he couldn't win and had found a willing puppet in Stanfield. Camp, Dief surmised, took himself out of the running after he realized how unpopular he was across the country. After all, Dief would point out, wasn't the loyal Jimmy Johnston (who looked like Camp) attacked by two women with umbrellas in a hotel lobby because they thought *he* was Camp? Now, I don't think Camp had any intention of running, but it served our purposes to spread that story and rally the loyalists to Diefenbaker's banner.

In all, even though our organization was weak, we did not think it was impossible for Dief to win the convention. A few of Dief's loyalists, men like Senator David Walker, Dr. Lewis Brand, broadcaster Joel Aldred and former party national director Jimmy Johnston arrived to help, but for the most part, the only bodies were the miserable few produced by Youth for Dief. There certainly were no spotters in stands tracking delegates, no walkie-talkie technology, no deals cooking with candidates. There was barely any literature beyond the one copy of the 101-page book I had written, entitled *My Friend the Chief*, that I presented to Dief that week.

After an arrival with police escort at the Royal York Hotel, Dief took up residence in a suite and dispatched people in all directions to gather information. Lists of delegates and nomination papers began to circulate. Dief hadn't made up his mind yet, but everyone else was ready. Without him, they had no access to even the modest power held by a leader of the opposition. Everyone was on hand for his speech Thursday evening, expecting he would declare himself in or out. He opened with the delightful line: "It's a hot, hot night, and were we of another generation the attractions of Yorkville would be beyond all telling." Then he picked up on his favourite theme, "One Canada," and scolded the party for adopting its "two nations" policy at the Montmorency conference a few weeks earlier. "I cannot be interested," he said, "in the leadership of this party under a policy that is borrowed from Liberalism." He held out the bogeyman that Quebec would become a separate nation and Canada would be divided like Germany. "I am not going to agree, whether it's popular or not, to build a Berlin Wall around Quebec. We don't want any Checkpoint Charlies in this nation."

The forty-five minute speech was a great rhetorical success, but everyone was still guessing what he would do. All the other candidates had spread the word that, after the debacle of 1966, delegates should be generous with their applause. They were; that just massaged him. Behind the scenes, matters simply got out of hand. Every aged retainer and semi-agile member of his retinue overestimated his support and reinforced everyone else's false views. When he returned to the hotel, the consensus was that he had to run to defend his view of Canada. He probably had intended to run all along. The deadline for nominations was 10:00 a.m. the following day. On Friday, I was one of the twenty-five delegates to sign the nomination papers.

To the convention delegates, however, he was just another candidate. On Saturday, his speech was desultory, the floor demonstration was ragtag and Dief was a humiliating fifth with 271 votes, just about half of the tally received by the front-running Stanfield. There was a lot of blame-placing among all of Dief's supporters because this was really the first televised convention in Canada and we finally realized how far behind the times we were even in the gimmick department. Hees had a slick campaign; Mike Starr had a chimpanzee; Wally McCutcheon had his blonde bombshells. Stanfield had the organization. By comparison, Dief had neither gimmicks nor votes. Almost one hundred of his delegates fled on the second ballot, dropping his total to 172. We weren't even well enough organized to get him off the third ballot in time and he suffered that humiliation as well, receiving only 114 votes.

On the final ballot, Dief didn't urge any particular direction. He didn't need to. After all, Stanfield was Camp. We knew we had to go to Duff Roblin (then premier of Manitoba) in order to try and stop Stanfield. I voted with a great lack of enthusiasm. To me, Roblin was the Thomas Dewey of Canadian politics; he looked like he belonged on the top of a wedding cake. By contrast, I found his wife, Mary, most gracious. After Dief was off the ballot, many of the key Diefenbaker people were taken into a Roblin holding room, but even then I refused to remove my Diefenbaker buttons when Mary Roblin pinned her husband's button on me. I must have appeared overcome emotionally, because she finally turned to me, put both her hands on my shoulders and said: "It's been difficult for us all."

The attempt to stop Stanfield was useless; he won by 1,150 votes to 969. After the appropriate announcements had been made, Diefenbaker took the podium. There was a hush, because no one knew what his position would be. Then he began: "My fellow Conservatives." Everyone roared with delight; it was a healing beginning. Then, the unrepentant fighter spoke: "I have nothing to withdraw in my desire and dream to see this one Canada, one country." He welcomed Stanfield and appeared to be urging support for him when he said, "Always remember those who have the mantle of leadership of the party are subject to persistent attacks." Then came the zinger: "But, my friends, as the fires of controversy burn around the leader, don't add gasoline to the flames."

For Dief the fight was far from over. Back in his hotel suite, he removed his suit coat and his shirt and sat, surrounded by his cronies, gloating over the humiliation that some of the other candidates had suffered. Dief was particularly pleased at Fulton's poor showing and just sat there shaking his head and repeating: "Poor Davie, he's devastated. There's *nothing.*" But what he relished most was his own statement about the gasoline. "You heard what I said about the fires of controversy?" he'd cackle, repeating it several times. As he asked everyone in the room for their reaction, he made sure they understood that the fires of controversy were already licking around Stanfield's right to the throne. He would be consumed by that fire soon enough; there was no need for anyone to add more fuel. Everyone, of course, snickered along with him and urged him to fight on. "Those babies," he'd say with a sneer, dismissing Camp and Stanfield and anyone else who hadn't been loyal.

That speech was the quintessential John Diefenbaker. He was capable of greatness in his ability to say the right thing, to offer the healing line as he did in his opening. He could also be the great warrior and statesman, defiant, unbowed and uncaring about what had been done to him and able to press on with his own strong views: "I have nothing to withdraw." But, in the end, he just couldn't resist the cheap shot at those who did him in. He was each of those things and came with an ego big enough to embrace them all. After I had returned to Hamilton, in a letter dated September 16, 1967, he wrote saying: "Today I walked down to the Mall for lunch and it took [venerable retainer] Mr. [Gilbert] Champagne and me three quarters of an hour to get away from the crowd who wanted to shake hands and extend good wishes. He estimated the crowd at 500 and he did not overdo it. Yesterday I was in Montreal and the reception at Expo from French Canadians was what I have always had – kindness, warmth and courtesy. Some of our followers are trying to find an excuse for their conduct and contend that I should have withdrawn." He obviously disagreed and ended the letter with thanks for my efforts and effusive praise. "You are the most unusual youth I have ever met and I only wish I could see you twenty-five years from now and through life as you make your contribution to Canada."

The Hatton-Martin coalition was not so fortunate. The Youth for Diefenbaker campaign, which was really the only organization Dief had, had run up close to $20,000 in bills. Some western oil men who were friends of Dief's had said they would pay, then reneged. Only through Dr. Brand's persistence did they ante up enough to silence the creditors.

If I had been bitter after the 1966 meeting, the 1967 convention made me twisted. An election held by the Hamilton YPCs shows just how Machiavellian I had become. I was already a member of the executive, and was well known as a Diefenbaker loyalist. The party, including the Hamilton YPCs, was filled with people who disliked one another. In this, I was both a cause and a target. I wanted to be president, yet I knew there were enough in the association who disliked me to make it unlikely that I would achieve my goal. A few of us got together and devised an ingenious plan. First, I would continue to claim an interest in the office but also be so obstreperous that the rest would want me stopped and assume that I stood no chance because of my cantankerous views. Second, we would introduce Marc Giacomelli as the political godfather of Bishop Ryan High School, the kind of young man needed in politics because he could quickly command and organize dozens of eager student workers. He would also be described as my mortal enemy. For Bill Knowles, the retiring president, there would be a certain appeal in seeing Giacomelli, my mortal enemy, win. Third, we set up the go-between, John Timmis, another member of the executive who was also part of the plot, to tell Knowles that he would act as a double agent and carry information from me to Knowles so Knowles could keep an eye on me. Further, Timmis would constantly remind Knowles that Marc was my enemy.

Over the next few weeks, Marc kept turning in names of Bishop Ryan students whom he purportedly was recruiting as members to support him. Unknown to Knowles, each $1 membership fee handed in with every name was paid by me, secretly funded in turn by Keith Martin. All the while, Knowles was chuckling, thinking to himself: "Isn't Sean going to be surprised when he shows up for the election and there are sixty new votes against him and for Marc?" At one point, I even wrote Knowles a letter indicating that I wouldn't be running. Of course, it was all just disinformation to keep them from guessing the real strategy. We convinced Knowles that the meeting required an impartial chairman in case O'Sullivan kicked up a fuss, a chairman who knew the party and was familiar with the rules. Knowles asked Marc and John Timmis for names. They suggested Keith Martin. Knowles unwittingly agreed.

On the night of the vote, Marc's students all showed up, as did the rest of us, and Keith took the chair. Bill Knowles, who was thirty-three, made a speech about how the group needed a leader from a new generation and then nominated Marc. He was duly seconded. Then Marc rose on a point of order, said he did not wish to stand and nominated me. That was seconded and Chairman Keith quickly asked if there were any further nominations. Everyone was too stunned to say anything, so he quickly added: "No further nominations. I declare Sean O'Sullivan duly elected president." With the support of the students Marc brought, we also managed to put people we wanted into just about every position on the executive. Knowles was stunned by the turn of events. His only comment came at the end of the evening when he said to Marc, "O'Sullivan must really have something on you." Spike 'em first.

That same month, I was also elected to the executive of the Ontario Young Progressive Conservative Association. That election was above board, at least on my part. I had decided to run for eighth vice-president but there was another candidate, a law student who put up various of his friends to muscle me out. I was taken aside a number of times and told to run for auditor where I would have been on the executive by acclamation. I stuck to my guns even when a heavy hitter spoke to me and said how it would be an awful shame if both these fine people running didn't get on the executive and why didn't I take a dive and run for auditor instead. The plea was made by Paul Godfrey, later chairman of Metro Toronto Council and now publisher of the *Toronto Sun*. I refused and went on to win. That put me onto the Ontario executive, which meant I could attend every meeting and Tory dogfight in the province.

I didn't wait for a dogfight to erupt, I started one. There was growing disunity at the grass roots, beginning with the 1966 meeting and hastened by the 1967 leadership convention. After a few months as leader, Stanfield decided to clean out some of the old Diefenbaker appointees in party headquarters. One of those to be sacked was the youth director, David Currie. Currie was a friend of Keith Martin's, and Currie's father, Colonel David Currie, had been appointed sergeant-at-arms in the Commons by Diefenbaker.

Currie became our righteous cause. We fired off a telegram to Stanfield protesting the dismissal and gathered our forces outside a Toronto fund-raising dinner where Stanfield was speaking. About ten of us picketed the hotel where the dinner was being held. Our signs read: "Keep Currie, Dump Camp." The shouting and parading was in neat juxtaposition to the formal affair inside. Ontario party organizer Eddie Goodman went nuts. He collared YPC President Ed Kowal at the reception and ordered him to fire me from my position as eighth vice-president and have me off the street or I'd be arrested. Kowal demurred with a wonderful line. In response to Eddie's verbal pyrotechnics, Kowal said: "I'd rather be the best man at a wedding than a pallbearer at a funeral." Our protest made the national news but no real change. Currie's dismissal was sealed. I was to be the only future member of Stanfield's caucus who began his political career by picketing his leader.

In June 1968, I was out of school early in the month and went to Prince Albert to help Dief in the general election with the youth vote in the riding. In the riding he was a different man from the one Ottawa saw. As he walked the streets, he was relaxed; he knew he was among friends. My first assignment was to scour the photo library of the local newspaper and collect all the photographs of him meeting world leaders so he could run an ad with the slogan: "He walked with kings, but he never lost the common touch." Next, I delivered the cards telling constituents where to vote. With my limited knowledge of Prince Albert streets, there were more than a few people who were sent to the wrong polling station. More memorable for me were the times I spent with him. Bobby Kennedy had been assassinated and we watched the funeral, complete with colour commentary from Dief. When Ted gave the very moving eulogy, for example, Dief's comment was dismissive: "He's the one who cheated at Harvard and got thrown out."

Among the helpers on the campaign was Dief's younger brother, Elmer. At various times he had been a salesman and a teacher, but by then he was retired. He was a gentle, quiet person who spoke laboriously and often took ages to say something so obvious that he was forever trying his brother's patience. Elmer made a cottage industry out of getting on Dief's nerves and driving Olive crazy. Once, while Dief was prime minister, Elmer accompanied the Diefenbakers on a round-the-world trip and at a reception in India was mistakenly introduced as John's son. I'm sure that was the low point of the trip for Olive. Dief gave Elmer money and Elmer's task during the campaign was to buy King Edward cigars and pass them out on the Indian reserves on behalf of his brother. Dief also requested James Gladstone to campaign on his behalf in order to remind the native people that Dief had given them the vote and had appointed Gladstone as the first native Canadian to the Senate.

Diefenbaker was paranoid about party headquarters. He never thought he was held in sufficient respect. At one point, a memo arrived announcing a mailing of policy papers produced by the party for distribution locally. Through some oversight, his own policy papers were not included in the shipment. He wrote on the memo: "I am not one of the candidates who count." Even when efforts were made to involve him, he frustrated the attempts. Much energy, for example, was expended to get Dief and Stanfield together for a rally. Saskatoon was the chosen location, and the negotiations were endless. Stanfield would be flying in on his campaign plane, a DC-7C, dubbed the "Flying Banana." Dief was angry that the plane chartered by the party for him on that occasion was smaller than Stanfield's. Dief finally accepted the size difference, but wanted the two planes to land at the same time in Saskatoon. He also wanted Stanfield to come to his plane to greet him. He didn't want it to look as if he had less standing than his leader. "He can come to me," Dief would say. "I know what those babies want."

Everyone soon realized that the plan wouldn't work because the two planes couldn't land at the same airport simultaneously. After more negotiations, it was agreed that Stanfield would land first, deplane and be on the tarmac to greet Dief after he landed. At the appointed hour, Stanfield's campaign plane was running late and Dief arrived first. He was convinced that the whole thing was a plot and that this had been the plan all along. He sat in the plane, as it perched on the tarmac getting hotter and hotter, and refused to leave.

Finally, Stanfield's plane landed and his son, Max, was dispatched to greet Dief and Olive and bring the two men together.

On election night, the polls closed hours earlier in the East than in Prince Albert, so results from Atlantic Canada were available. Dief, however, couldn't be seen to receive advance information directly, so while he and Olive and some of their friends sat in Room 1 of the Pink Flamingo Motel, I took calls in Room 5 and ferried information along to him. He was gleeful; all the devastation that he had predicted would happen without him had happened. Trudeau won 155 seats, the Conservatives 72. When he was interviewed on local television, his comment was succinct and, for him, succulent: "The Conservative Party," he announced, "has suffered a calamitous disaster."

In 1969, my father was transferred to manage the three Sheraton properties in Niagara Falls, Ontario. I would be leaving Bishop Ryan after Grade Twelve, so rather than take one year at a new high school, I enrolled at Brock University a year sooner than usual in a program for exceptional students. In addition to good marks, students needed a letter of recommendation from their principal. Father Cote's feelings toward me made him more than delighted to sign such a letter and I began an intensive six-week summer course to qualify for classes beginning in September.

I was not among my kind. On the first day I walked into a lecture hall filled with what looked like refugees from Berkeley. Flower children were in their heyday and every hippie in Ontario seemed to have been accepted into the program. Paisley shirts and bell-bottoms, beads, beards and long hair seemed to be the uniform. I, on the other hand, was a Young Progressive Conservative, just about the squarest kid you can imagine, wearing out-of-fashion clothes and short hair. They were quoting the poetry of Dylan Thomas and discussing the meaning of life. I had always been an achiever, but these people were intellectuals. When the subject of Latin came up during course selection, someone near me said: "Latin isn't a language, it's a disease." I was aghast; everything they said was an epigram. I was scared stiff I wouldn't make it against such brainpower. In the end, I did. Of the original 105 students, only seventy-eight registered in first year in the fall of 1969. At seventeen years old, I was among the top eight picked to begin university.

Most of the students were two years older than I was. For some, their ideas of a social life included alcohol and drugs and didn't jibe with mine. As a result, I went into political hyperactivity. I was forever cutting classes; or I would go missing for days because my idea of a great time was to climb on the bus in St. Catharines to attend a political meeting in London or Toronto or Ottawa. Wherever two Tories gathered, I wanted to be the third. Although I was not a devoted student, the professors put up with my absences because at Brock the course was called "Politics" (not the usual "Political Science") with an emphasis on the practical not the theoretical aspects. During the summer, for example, I worked in Ottawa for Dief as his special assistant. It was a wonderful apprenticeship and taught me more about how Ottawa worked than any course, no matter how practical, could have. Fortunately, my professors agreed.

By then some people began to worry less about my association with Dief and my past rebellions. As the 1970 Ontario YPC convention approached, I was called by the president, Ed Kowal. Ed was thirty, a typical age for a YPC at the time. His message surprised me: "I think you should run as president. I can pretty well guarantee you'll be elected." Until that point, I had only been eighth vice-president and, I thought, merely tolerated as a young upstart. He even said that a particular member of the executive who I thought detested me was behind the idea and would raise money for my campaign. I checked with Keith Martin, my political advisor (who had joined Dief as his executive assistant in 1968), and he urged me to accept – as long as I wasn't being set up.

There was no set-up, but as I later learned I did fit the party's needs. Apparently there had been some rudimentary polling done and the Ontario party had discovered it was weak among young people. Consideration was being given to lowering the voting age and Premier John Robarts wanted the party to have a new image. It wasn't that they were enamoured with Sean O'Sullivan; they just wanted a teenager. I was the right age. They also wanted a Francophone female for the executive but could find no one. They finally came up with a bilingual female from eastern Ontario who was made fifth vice-president, again all in the name of fresh-faced youth. Her name was Maureen McTeer. And so another career was launched.

Even though my candidacy was said to be secure, I knew nothing could be left to chance. Joining me at Elgin House near Port Carling, Ontario, that September was the 1967 "SWAT team" of Keith Martin and Bill Hatton. They immediately were concerned that, as things were shaping up, there would be too many independents on the executive. Hatton was nominated to run for auditor, the bottom rung, so I would be assured of at least one supporter at future executive meetings. Hatton made a classy candidate. He was known as "the Colonel" because he held a rank in the reserves, wore striped three-piece suits, and affected a British accent. His campaign slogan reflected his style: "If you liked Mountbatten, you'll love Bill Hatton."

Because the Hatton candidacy was a last-minute thing, his campaign material was patchy: signs were done with magic markers, buttons made from stickers. We needed a cover story to explain the hasty look. We told everyone that he was a well-to-do and adept politician who simply wanted to serve. We claimed that the truck carrying his material to Elgin House had broken down on the way and burst into flames, destroying his literature, buttons and signs. Not satisfied with that, we added more personal details to gain everyone's sympathy. There had been some unspecified family difficulties and, the *coup de grâce*, just last week his dog had been run over by a car and killed.

Robarts spoke at lunch and Stanfield addressed the dinner session. At the reception before the meal, Keith introduced Bill Hatton to Stanfield and proceeded to launch into the sorry tale about the truck fire, the family tragedy and the death of the dog. Stanfield listened stoically to the woeful story, then turned to Bill and asked: "What was your dog's name?" It absolutely convinced us that the man had no feelings. Of course, my position as a Diefenbaker partisan ensured that I also saw him as an ineffectual, boring man who didn't deserve to be leader, a puppet of the Camp people, and a man who was lost without his speechwriters.

The other big-name attendee from Ottawa was Alberta MP Jack Horner. He spent the weekend being a loose cannon rolling about the decks, arguing in the hospitality suites with anyone who would listen – and shouting at those who wouldn't – about the sad state of the Tory Party. The saddest part was the diversity that the weekend showed the party encompassed. Robarts was the chairman of the board, flying in and out of the meeting by float plane and lending the aura of a winner to the proceedings. By contrast, Stanfield slipped in almost unnoticed and seemed to wander aimlessly about, welcomed by some Conservatives and shunned by others. And Horner was taking potshots all the while.

In the end, however, we achieved our youthful goals. Most of the members of the new executive were under twenty. My message to the group was robust, if predictably naive. "Our enemy is apathy in young people, not the other parties. It's not a matter of most young people being committed to another party but the disillusionment of youth. We believe that youth can do something and we believe it can be done within the framework of our party."

On Sunday, as Stanfield ended his speech about continuing to fight the government, he said: "Sean and your colleagues, I look forward to your support." Pleasurable chills ran up and down my spine. Even if my mentor, Dief, thought Stanfield was a "horse's foot," I was now in the big leagues. I had arrived. Equally important, the weekend marked another beginning. It was there I met a fellow delegate, Paula Marsden, a respiratory technologist, with whom I would share a two-year romance. It became serious enough that some on the executive started referring to her as Olive. She was not amused.

My new position in the party did not mean, however, that I joined the establishment. In fact, I was more willing than ever to battle it. My first fisticuffs came within months, at the convention to replace John Robarts. The issue was whether delegates from the Ontario YPCs would be included among the delegates sent from every riding. In some ridings, YPC groups had not been included. In all, there were 11 ridings out of 117 where YPCs felt shut out. In eight, there may have been legitimate misunderstandings, but we chose three ridings in particular as test cases. They were Ottawa East, Carleton and York-Forest Hill.

The constitution of the Progressive Conservative Association of Ontario said that each delegation should include members of the local YPC club if it were recognized or, failing that, two people under thirty. The riding associations we complained about took the wording to mean recognized by *them*. Thus, if they didn't recognize the local youth group, they didn't have to send any youth delegates. Ottawa East was a particularly glaring example. In addition to the two youth representatives, each riding was to send four male and four female delegates. All of the Ottawa East delegates were male.

As a member of the convention planning committee I was supposed to be neutral, but I piled into this fight. One night, for example, my hotel bill showed that I had placed fifty-two outgoing calls from my room as I lined up support and sought information. The establishment didn't want to give in to randy youth so they produced a multipage legal opinion from Toronto lawyer Charles Dubin that was supposed to settle the issue (against the YPCs, of course) but we fought back with our own counsel, David McFadden, now an Ontario MLA who tore apart Dubin's opinion. Finally, after a four-hour meeting of the credentials committee, we won the right to have delegates in the three ridings.

The ridings, however, refused to comply. The battle with higherups that would dog me for years was joined. After all, one of the delegates was none other than Eddie Goodman, already a power in the party, and a man who was to become one of Premier Bill Davis's closest advisors. At the time, I assumed that there was backroom dealing to put specific people in place in various ridings who would favour a particular candidate. In addition to fighting for members of the YPC group I represented, I was also arguing for an open convention. After all, of the 1,700-odd delegates, about 500 were delegates-at-large anointed by party brass. There were no YPCs among that coterie. To shut us out from a few riding delegations was just too much.

The whole issue just fed my paranoia about the Tory Party and those who ran it. However, fearing nothing and no one, we threatened all manner of indignities including floor demonstrations at the convention when it opened in Maple Leaf Gardens. The whole messy affair was then handed over to Alan Eagleson, president of the Ontario Progressive Conservative Association. On Thursday, the debate went before the whole convention at Maple Leaf Gardens.

There was a series of speeches denouncing the YPCs. The most abusive was given by Jean-Paul Guertin, speaking on behalf of

34

Ottawa East: "This party will be ruined by young people just the way they've ruined some universities," he charged. Fortunately, most of the 3,000 or so people in the audience booed when he said it. The establishment side put up three speakers, so we were allowed three as well. When our turn came, however, we waived the three speakers and put up only one: me. I took the podium and made a seven-minute speech that I still believe was the best speech of my political life.

"This is not the time for argument," I began. "This is a time for decision. And the decision that you are called upon to make today is of crucial importance to the future of youth in this party." After a burst of applause, I continued: "The YPC position is clear and the principle of the entire question must not be forgotten. Young people want to participate in politics, in the Conservative Party.

"But the time has surely come to recognize that young persons have their own aspirations, their own style, and wish to make their contribution in a distinctly youthful fashion. No branch of this party can be made subservient to another; neither the women, nor the students nor the YPCs should be told by any other group that they cannot carry out their distinctive programs for the Progressive Conservative Party. Such a situation is an insult to democracy, a mockery of this party's heritage and would make a sham of the offer made so often to young people of meaningful involvement in the affairs of the province.

"The Ontario YPC Association wants to carry to all young people of Ontario the message that this is an open party, a democratic party, a party where they can be truly involved. You can make this message ring true today." I closed by reading an excerpt from a letter: "I know from personal experience that membership in the Ontario Young Progressive Conservative Association is stimulating and rewarding. My own political career started as a member of this organization." The letter, I told the convention, was dated just a month earlier. Then I told them the name of the author: the outgoing premier of Ontario, John Parmenter Robarts. The applause was immediate and lengthy.

There was some debate from the floor, but the applause for my position showed that if a vote were held the establishment would lose. They didn't want that, so a secret ballot was avoided when the main combatants disappeared to where all truly interesting party debates are eventually resolved – in the back room. In this case, the back room was an area behind a black curtain stretched across one end of Maple Leaf Gardens, with the delegates getting increasingly restless on the other side. Delegates could only sit staring at a vacant podium wondering what was happening.

Eagleson, known for negotiating tough deals for NHL hockey players, must have wondered why he even had to bother with this freckle-faced troublemaker. "I'm really on your side," he said. "I'm doing what I can. Trust me, trust me, trust me." When he said it the third time, he left the room. Another member of the executive turned to me and rolled his eyes.

Before the speeches, he had offered to let the six YPCs sit in a special observers' section – but they couldn't vote. I rejected this proposal as suitably thoughtless. Then he wanted the two delegates from each of the three disputed ridings to be split: one to be named by the YPCs, the other to be named by the riding. I refused. Eagleson was simply pandering to the establishment view, which feared that the party was about to be taken over and ravaged by radical youth. I refused to accept the compromise and words became heated. At one point, Eagleson grabbed my lapels as he made his points. My position was simple: we'd won before the credentials committee; why give in now? "No," I said, "let's have the vote, we're going to win this." A snooty man from York-Forest Hill replied: "I think you're being unreasonable." I blew up: "I don't have to listen to any more of your bullshit. We won. Let's vote."

Mr. York-Forest Hill was apoplectic. He turned to Eagleson and shouted, "Are you going to let him talk to me like that?" Eagleson led him away, then returned on his own and said, "Let's settle." Eagleson had found a new route. The six YPCs affected would become delegates and the six other delegates they displaced would be able to vote because they would suddenly be named delegates-at-large from the apparently bottomless bag held by Eagleson.

The battle took about twenty minutes behind the curtain. Goodman, who was not involved in the solution, was furious. He felt there should have been no compromises and told anyone who would listen that if delegates had been allowed to vote on the question, the YPCs would have lost. When I saw him the following day, he said: "That was a great speech you gave yesterday. Too bad none of it was true."

"Thanks, Eddie," I shot back. "I learned it all from you."

For my part, I was delighted with the outcome. The six delegates elected by their ridings could still vote; so could the six youth delegates, who also had the same rights. After handshakes all around, the nomination speeches for the various candidates began. I didn't stay. I had been up all night, and it was now 3:00 p.m. I went back to the hotel to sleep. After all, that's what all political warriors do after victory, isn't it? Even the young ones.

Politics is an arena where the emotions of the losers, and those on their way out, are on public display. There is no way to hide those emotions. Two vignettes demonstrate what I mean. As the voting went on, John Robarts and Ernie Jackson, a long-time London confidant, disappeared for dinner, to return reeking of booze and garlic in time to anoint the successor to Robarts, Bill Davis. With all the attention on the podium for the announcement, I happened to be backstage and saw a lonely figure standing at an open door, with his back to me, sucking in some cold February air and obviously trying to steady his nerves before turning over power. I tried to make small talk with Robarts, but backed off when I realized it was all he could do to keep his emotions in check. It was a bittersweet moment. When the time came for him to perform, the actor in him took over. You could see him turn on as he left the backstage area and strode to the podium. It was as if the band and the ballyhoo filled him up again, at least long enough to say his piece, congratulate Davis, then disappear into the night.

I saw John Robarts again a few days later at the Ottawa airport. He was waiting for a private plane that would take him north for some fishing. The plane was late, delayed by fog, and he was sitting alone. Gone were the retinue of aides and the other people who feed off the powerful like spigots tapping into a maple tree in the spring. His natty attire had been replaced by outdoor gear; he looked shrunken. His main concern seemed to be a lost newspaper. A similar sad scene was played out the morning after the vote as I breakfasted with Keith Martin in a Union Station restaurant, across from the Royal York Hotel. There at the curb was Allan Lawrence, two-dozen delegates short of being premier, loading his own luggage into the trunk of his car. The night before, hundreds had held his banners and wanted to be near him. Within hours, he and his wife were abandoned. Both scenes, Robarts and Lawrence, brought home to me the cruelty of politics and how it can make humans into hermits.

I didn't even vote for the eventual winner. My first ballot went to Robert Welch, because he was from the Niagara Peninsula and the closest thing to a native son I could find. The voting machines were fouled up and the results took hours. When it was finally announced that the ballot would have to be redone, I heard that Bert Lawrence had been low man. I cast my "second" first ballot for Bert, then switched to Allan Lawrence, who eventually finished second to Bill Davis. Eddie Goodman was a close Davis advisor; I knew that I was now a marked man. If Eddie decided that I had to go, that I was some sort of unguided missile ready to land on the premier's office any day, I was gone.

I worked that summer as a reporter at the Hamilton *Spectator* and tried to salvage my political career. My YPC executive meetings became rancorous; the youth organizer hired by the party, Darwin Kealey, began criticizing me behind my back, and Davis's henchman, Hugh Macaulay, sent a memo questioning YPC expenses. Eventually, I wrote to Davis saying that I intended to resign but didn't want to do so in a way that might cause him embarrassment. Davis asked to see me and said that the best route would be for me to receive an appointment to his campaign executive. His chief aide, Clare Westcott, would be in touch, said Davis.

The weeks passed and there was no call from Clare. My executive was getting anxious, awaiting my announced departure, but as yet I had no place to go with dignity. My mistake was in telling my executive I was resigning, then staying on. Clare Westcott did not return my calls, so I cornered Davis on a visit to Hamilton and put my case again. In the days following, there was still no response. Finally, I drafted a press release announcing my resignation as president and my appointment by the premier as a special advisor on youth matters. I phoned his office, read the release to one of the secretaries and told her to tell Davis that I was going to issue the announcement unless he told me not to. There was no call, so on July 13, 1971, I announced that I was to act as a liaison between the premier and the party's youth. My relations with Davis did not improve. Rather than give me a face-saving way out with an appointment that meant nothing to him, I felt he'd misled me and hung me out to dry.

In the fall, I attended a party meeting in Ottawa just to show everyone I was still alive. I worked the corridors in a long overcoat, feeling for all the world like Napoleon on the retreat from Moscow. I was a pariah. Youth activist Harry Burkman warned delegates to stay away from me. "During everyone's political career there is a time when there's a black X hanging over their head," said Burkman. "Sean O'Sullivan is carrying that black X these days." I had risen like a comet and crashed just as quickly. I had become an outcast. At nineteen, when most YPC members are just becoming active, my career seemed over. I felt burned out.

In December, when my world was most bleak, Keith Martin left his post as Dief's executive assistant to become executive director of the Manitoba PCs. Dief invited me to replace Keith. Classes at Brock, not as good as the real thing, were abandoned. I was off to Ottawa to be executive assistant to the Right Honourable Member from Prince Albert. At nineteen, it had been a mere eight years since I had first met him. To hell with Billy Davis, I would serve My Chief.

CHAPTER THREE

GREEN AS A BEET

My love affair with politics began with John Diefenbaker. He played many roles in my life – hero of my boyhood, mentor of my teenage ambitions, harsh taskmaster, parliamentary colleague and friend. I was happy to be in his shadow and to bear his shield. He helped me grow, and as I matured at his side over a full decade I came to know him as few did. He revealed himself to me and I revelled in what I saw. I saw him at his best and I saw him at his most bitter. In the early years, I was blind to his faults and bedazzled by his feats. With maturity, I can now see the flaws, but my devotion remains. As only Diefenbaker could say of himself, "I was sometimes wrong. But I was never on the side of wrong." Dief's presence in my life was a precious force. In befriending me, he sparked my passion for politics, opened the doors of opportunity and guided me toward a career in his beloved Parliament.

After John Diefenbaker lost the leadership in 1967, the Speaker of the House of Commons was at pains to provide him with a larger staff and more office space than an MP would normally have because of Dief's status as a former prime minister. During his time as prime minister he had occupied a corner office on the fourth floor of the Centre Block on Parliament Hill; and he had remained in that office after he became opposition leader. When he lost that post, he could have moved to a much larger suite than he did, but chose instead a fairly small office directly across the hall. It was as if he wanted to remind the new tenant that his own stay could be brief. The new office, which had belonged to Dief's former executive assistant, Thomas Van Dusen, was divided to accommodate devoted secretaries Iris Axford and Betty Eligh, and create a small sitting room and

41

an inner office for Dief himself. Down the hall were two offices housing two more secretaries, an assistant, and countless disorganized files. It was to this flame I was drawn to work in the summer of 1970. In 1971 the job became full time, and in 1972 I joined him in Parliament as an MP.

All the action was in his lair in the corner. The office windows faced north and west, overlooking the Ottawa River and Hull, Quebec. On one wall hung a huge portrait of Sir John A. Macdonald, and on another there was a stuffed swordfish Dief had caught and landed. Draped across a couch was an RCMP horse blanket. Every surface and all the available wall space were littered with photographs and other mementoes of past glory. The place was a scurry of people, a jumble of books and newspaper clippings and a flurry of speech notes. Out of sight the ever-present crackers and dried bits of cheese were squirrelled away in his desk drawers. When he was not in residence, the office was an unimpressive and empty place. But when he was ensconced, he presided over events like a nobleman in exile, eternally hopeful that the call of his people would come and restore him to the royal throne and his rightful heritage.

In the end, John Diefenbaker, prime minister of Canada from June 21, 1957, to April 22, 1963, thirteen times elected to the House of Commons, would come to fulfil the description first given him by my friend Marc Giacomelli when he saw Dief at the 1967 leadership convention. He said: "John Diefenbaker is a madman who thinks he's John Diefenbaker." A yeasty mixture made up this colourful, complex and controversial Canadian who so dominated my political life and this country's political landscape. He was steadfast in battle, no matter what the odds. He would not surrender no matter what the wounds. He taught me many things, including how to fight and keep on fighting. He did not, however, teach me how to be a graceful loser. Nor did I learn the power of reconciliation from him; that would have to wait for later in my life.

Throughout, the man I went to Ottawa to serve was demanding. I was never an early riser, but I tried to be there for 9:00 a.m., knowing full well he'd been lashed in the harness for hours. If his mood were expansive, he would look up and greet me with one of his favourite salutations: "News, views, interviews?" That signalled he wanted to hear all the gossip that hadn't made the newspapers or the morning broadcasts. You could also tell where your information fell on his Richter scale of interest by his response. When he was pleasantly surprised by something, he'd utter, "I gollies"; if the news was bad, it was "What the hell."

My most important function, I quickly discovered, as it had been with my predecessors, was to provide political intelligence. The more it served to feed his ego at the expense of the party and those who followed his nemesis, Dalton Camp, the better. Typical was this memo I once delivered: "Upon conversation with Edward Kowal, President, Ontario YPCs, I've learned that the rift between the federal and provincial parties has grown to crisis proportions. The latest development is a letter from Alan Eagleson complaining about statements by National Headquarters' people to members of the press blaming Toronto [office] for failure of party conferences. As a further development, [Eddie] Goodman has been completely cut off from any provincial influence including any rapport with the Premier." Dief *loved* stuff like that.

His reaction to such information was, by any measure, bizarre. If you told him about some minor feuding in the party, he would clench his left hand into a fist at his waist, slap it lightly with his right hand and say, very quickly: "Me-me-me-me-me-me-me." If the report were particularly salacious, the singsong would be the same but with a faster tempo and a slightly higher pitch. It was an incredible sight-and-sound show, and the only explanation I could ever come up with was that it was an absolutely unquotable response. If anyone ever said, "How did Dief react when you told him?" you couldn't possibly say. There *was* no response, only this indescribable sound. As a politician he was safe and couldn't possibly have his views come back to haunt him.

He would take such juicy news and spread it like the seeds of a thistle in the hopes that they would spring up and choke those who had once done him in. He would wave a memo he'd been handed or collar the information he'd just heard and shout: "Where's the list?" meaning the list of friends and supporters who received his regular calls and mailings. Often he'd phone Olive first, and his opening line was always the same: "It's everywhere." With the memo in front of him he'd begin: "What I'm hearing, you see, is this." And then he'd quote the best bits, sprinkling them with his own additions, such as "They're fighting and feuding."

After Dief had spoken to Olive, he'd start phoning the names on the list at random. Recipients of the call would include MPs such as Bob Muir, Bob Coates, Jack Horner and Dr. P.B. Rynard. Across the country, intimates included former party director and then newspaper publisher Jimmy Johnston, fund raiser George Cloakey, former cabinet minister Gordon Churchill and Brigadier Michael Wardell, as well as such ex-staffers as Gregor Guthrie, Thomas Van Dusen and Keith Martin.

If the information I brought was potentially embarrassing to the government rather than the party, he'd seize upon it as a possible topic for Question Period later that day or as an item to pass on to one of the few journalists he could abide in the Parliamentary Press Gallery. Among the ones he liked and would regularly favour with an interview or a pungent comment were broadcasters Mike Duffy of the CBC and Max Keeping of CJOH-TV and print journalists Arthur Blakeley of the Montreal *Gazette*, Victor Mackie of the *Winnipeg Free Press*, Stewart MacLeod of Thomson Newspapers, and Richard Jackson of the *Ottawa Journal*.

Jackson and Dief had an unusual arrangement. Dief didn't always like what Jackson wrote, but Jackson had known him for so long that he could get away with being a bit of a smart alec. Jackson would come around to Dief's office for an interview that would sometimes turn into more of a squabble than an interview; then he'd go away and write the story. When it was published, Dief might judge it to be 90 per cent accurate, but there might be one line that Dief didn't like and he'd call Jackson in and shout at him. But far more bothersome to the Old Man than Jackson's inaccuracies was his statement that, in return for all the favourable stories he'd written about Dief over the years and all the trial balloons he'd floated on his behalf, he wanted just one thing. Dick Jackson wanted to be remembered in Dief's will. He didn't want any money, mind you, just the mention of his name and some small trinket, a remembrance, to show Dief's eternal esteem. He hounded Dief about it so much that Dief was offended. (Jackson, needless to say, wasn't mentioned in the will.)

After the news, views and interviews had been heard and spread, Dief would turn to the mail. He had a fetish about following up every letter he received, making sure there was a reply – as well as searching the incoming mail for laudatory comments. If he found something he liked, he'd read it aloud to everyone within earshot. Then he'd disperse the day's mail around the office, with requests for information to be sought from cabinet ministers or civil servants and replies drafted for his signature. Many of the letters he received were from Canadians who felt they'd suffered some injustice at the hands of government or a stuffy bureaucracy. The turmoil of the Pearson years and the ignominy of 1966 were forgotten, at least by some ordinary Canadians, and Dief had returned to his populist role as a voice for them. People saw Dief as the defender of the little guy; and he saw his staff as his helpers to right all wrongs.

If he were scheduled to deliver a speech, the directives flew twice as fast. He wanted fresh research material from the Library of Parliament dug up, newspaper clippings he thought he'd seen somewhere assembled, famous quotations he vaguely remembered rooted out and copious notes drafted for his possible use. Typical was some rhetoric I gave him for a speech on Canadian youth. "Youth needs education; they're offered pornography. Youth wants constructive reform; they're offered violence."

Draft speech notes were the most frustrating request he made. Although I would labour long and hard to research and write what I thought was more than just passable prose, his only response was a muttered "Thank you," or maybe a muted compliment. No matter how much work I did or how many rewrites he ordered, John Diefenbaker delivered only two speeches anyway. One was what I called the "Dream your dreams" speech, which he gave at school openings, non-partisan dinners and to visiting school children. I could stand at the back of the auditorium or outside his office and predict precisely what he was going to say next. My favourite pair of sentences went like this: "Not every one of you can become prime minister or a cabinet minister, or even a member of parliament or a mayor. But each of you has in your heart of hearts that something of that something that makes you you." I've analyzed that second sentence countless times; it says nothing. It's gibberish. Yet Diefenbaker's delivery made grown men shiver and women weep, and mesmerized small children.

His other speech was called "Where are we going?" When the occasion required old-time political rhetoric, no one could serve it up like John Diefenbaker. He'd list the litany of Liberal failures, updated to include that week's atrocity, all linked with the repeated phrase: "Where are we going?" Or if he were stuck for another phrase, he might add: "I love Parliament." Either would serve as a transition to the next topic, when he wasn't quite sure where he was headed next. After he'd repeated "Where are we going?" half a dozen times, he'd go highbrow and just for variety would shout "*Quo vadis* – where are we going?" My Latin was even less fluent than my French at that point, but I was aware that "*quo vadis*" was the famous phrase spoken to St. Peter as he was fleeing Rome. It properly translates as "Whither goest thou?" I never told him he was using it inaccurately.

For the most part, the greatest orator on the Canadian political stage quite rightly ignored a lot of my speech drafts. He did not, however, stop demanding them. Nor did he cease demanding material for Question Period in the House, the daily showcase that proves, if there were ever any doubt, that in Ottawa there really are too many egos to feed. This was the highlight of his day, the time when he saw himself as the gladiator up against the Liberals, his chance to show the world that it had been wrong to reject him in 1963. If he had a good day, and he often did, he would return to the office glowing with triumph and dissect his victory in minute detail, chortling all the while: "Did you see the look on their faces?" Staff and friends were urged to quote good phrases back to him that he'd used in the House, because what he most enjoyed hearing was how well he had done. He'd sit back, preen a bit and say: "You have to laugh yourself." If he was relating how an audience had enjoyed one of his lines, he'd say, "They laughed like sixty." And if he was very pleased with his performance, he'd admit, "Sometimes I even amaze myself."

Next, we would wait for the "blues" (so called because coloured paper was used) – the typed first draft of the transcripts that would become *Hansard*, the permanent record of Commons debates. Within an hour or so of speaking in the House, each cabinet minister and senior MPs such as Dief would receive a copy of his remarks as transcribed by the *Hansard* reporters. The early copy was really just a courtesy to let an MP correct spelling or a particularly distorted rendering, so that *Hansard* was kept accurate. Usually, Dief only tinkered in a minor way with Question Period, but after he'd made one of his lengthy speeches in the Commons, he'd make revisions in the blues as if he had yet to deliver the speech and this was just some foolish first draft submitted for his approval by a gawky aide. Whole sections were changed, omitted or rewritten; great chunks were added; syntax and sentences were altered. If he had gone home early, he expected me to do it all for him. Knowing that the first thing he'd do in the morning would be to read the version of *Hansard* printed overnight, I worked assiduously to please him. Changes were still possible the next day, but only the egregious errors. The legend needed to be burnished immediately.

The rewriting task was difficult on two counts. First, trying to make logic and grammatical sense out of his rhetoric was sometimes simply beyond my ingenuity. What sounded like effective oratory filled with eloquent pauses and grand gestures could read like senseless ramblings when put into print. Second, the editors of *Hansard,* who all looked like devoted clerks from a Dickens novel, were supposed to accept and allow only minor changes in the text. After several hours of rewriting, I would sheepishly return the blues to them, having performed an editorial lobotomy. They always were gracious enough to accept the revisions just as if they accurately reflected what had really been said. In fact, as lovers of the language themselves, they often became co-conspirators in the effort to ensure that Dief's parliamentary interventions read with clarity and continuity.

If phrases from a speech he had given were quoted in a newspaper, he'd carefully read them aloud, pause, and then say, "It says something," indicating that although most parliamentary rhetoric was pretty empty, his was not. On the other hand, if a minister got the better of him during an exchange in the House, the matter was quietly dropped. Past incidents that some might see as failures could always be rationalized by Dief. His cancellation of the Avro Arrow in 1959, for example, was easily explained. "Exquisite in appearance, magnificent in design," Dief would say, then pause and add flatly, "but it wouldn't fly." Only rarely would he admit any shortcomings and only after sufficient time had passed. For example, even in his 1958 electoral sweep, few Italian-Canadians voted Conservative. This bothered him so much that regularly, and without warning, he'd sigh: "I could never get the Italians."

He enjoyed sparring with Pierre Trudeau in the House. Dief respected Trudeau's intelligence and admired his battling ways. But on the occasions when Trudeau got the better of him, Dief wouldn't admit it. He'd return to the office and just fall silent. If Dief scored, he'd be quite pleased with himself. He had a grudging respect for Trudeau and a residual respect for the office of prime minister. And it didn't hurt at all that people in Trudeau's office paid attention to such niceties as the anniversaries of Dief's election and his birthday. In 1970, Trudeau even invited him over for a private luncheon at 24 Sussex Drive. It was supposed to be hush-hush, just the two of them talking privately as parliamentarians. Diefenbaker couldn't stop telling everybody about the meeting even before it had happened. He went so far as to phone Dick Jackson in the Press Gallery. "Don't tell anyone, now, this is just for you," he said, "but, you see he wants me over for lunch, just the two of us to discuss things." Telling Jackson was like sending telexes door-to-door across the country.

Dief did not, however, like what Trudeau was doing to the country. He thought Trudeau was a leftist and had a questionable background. In private, Dief would ask why Trudeau had been denied entry into the United States. What was he doing in the canoe on the way to see Fidel? While Dief would never come right out and say it, his views would lead any jury of listeners to believe that Trudeau was a communist, if not now, then certainly in his youth. "They call him PET," Dief would splutter at visitors to his office as he drew attention to Trudeau's initials. "Did you ever look up *'pet'* in the Larousse dictionary?" His eyes would dance with delight as the visitor leafed through the book he handed them. Before they'd even found the reference, he'd say: " *'pet'* in French means 'fart.' It's the pejorative for *fart*."

Whenever Dief wanted to tell an off-colour joke, he blamed it on George Hees. Dief would hear a good story, but in keeping with his own particular self-righteous image of himself, he'd be reluctant to retell it. So, he'd put it in the mouth of Hees, a man to whom Dief regularly ascribed all kinds of improprieties. One of his favourites went like this: "Have you heard the one that Hees is telling? It's the most awful thing. He's going around asking people: 'What's the difference between a cactus and the Conservative caucus? On a cactus, the pricks are all on the outside.' " As he finished, Dief would laugh along with the rest and feel he was home free because he'd blamed the whole thing on Hees.

Without Hees as a foil, Dief's language was rarely foul. When he wanted to put someone down, as he frequently did, his usual expletives were: "He is a complete (pause) louse." If angered, he'd say "He's a complete horse's (pause). . . ." You'd wait for the appropriate part of the body to be mentioned, and he'd finally add "foot." If he learned that someone had been critical of him, he'd snap: "He can go to hell, with or without my compliments." Then he might call the person "Old Sizzerbell," a Diefenbaker expletive of unknown origin. Or he'd say, "He hasn't got a brain in his head," or, sometimes, "He's as crazy as a March hare." The pronunciation varied so that it sometimes sounded like "marsh hare." One day Keith asked him: "Sir, are you saying 'March hare' or 'marsh hare'?" "March," he said, as if there could be no doubt, "because you see in March rabbits are sexually crazy." Enemies were described with the adjective "offensive," as in: "He is the most offensive member." If he had sympathy for someone, he'd be "that pore little fella."

Liberals, for the most part of course, fitted into the offensive category. I watched the 1968 Liberal leadership convention with the Diefenbakers at their home. He was lying on a couch, propped up with pillows and covered with a mohair blanket. Because he'd removed his hearing aid, the television was turned up so loud that the console rattled and danced toward us all night. Olive was sitting in a chair darning his socks. He showed the deepest concern for Paul Martin because it was clear that Martin's delegate support was going nowhere. Diefenbaker kept muttering, "Poor Paul, poor Paul." Then he'd add, "He's lying, you know. He has that look, I can tell. Whenever Paul's lying he has that look. Olive, you see that look? Sean? He's lying, no, no, no, he's lying." Dief had a similar view of Lester Pearson, the man the Liberals were all seeking to replace. Pearson and Dief had fought four very bitter elections against each other.

49

Whenever Pearson's name was mentioned, Dief would say, "Oh yes, Pearson. Very friendly, very engaging individual." There would be a moment's pause, then the kicker: "And the biggest liar I ever met."

Both he and Olive liked Robert Winters, saw him as a gentleman and worried when his speaking voice went hoarse at the convention. "This will do him great damage," Diefenbaker offered. "This is very bad indeed." As for Paul Hellyer, Dief was not yet over Hellyer's 1966 unification of the armed forces, so whenever Hellyer appeared, Dief would mutter, "This damned unification business." He was unimpressed by Allan MacEachen, too, and was particularly scornful of his line that only a Nova Scotian could defeat Stanfield, another Nova Scotian. Snorted Dief: "What the hell!" His comments were not limited to the candidates. Jean Marchand, whose political career would flourish under Trudeau, was dismissed as "a funny little Frenchman."

He and John Turner were a mutual admiration society. The two seemed to have a relationship that forgot party boundaries. The painting of Sir John in Dief's office had been given to him by Turner. It was a monstrosity done in garish colours and measuring at least six feet by six feet. Turner had bought it and an equally ugly portrait of Sir Wilfrid Laurier at an auction. He was stuck with Laurier, but he found a home for Macdonald. Every so often, Turner would bring someone by on the pretext of showing off the painting, then take the opportunity to talk to Dief. Dief liked him because Turner was the consummate gentleman and always deferred to the Right Honourable Member from Prince Albert. They'd run into each other on holidays in Barbados. Turner was a bencher there and he arranged for Dief to be admitted to the bar also.

The story told in Turner's biography that he saved Dief from drowning is very likely true, although Dief never told the story himself. When he was in Barbados working on his memoirs with John Munro and Keith Martin, I know they had to make sure that someone was with him whenever he went into the water because he would wander. He could swim, but he'd lose his bearings and stray out where the water was too deep. So I have no reason to doubt the story.

While he had some friends, such as Turner, among the Liberals, he could get quite exercised by what the Liberals were doing with some of the country's traditional symbols, particularly anything to do with the monarchy. The Queen repaid his loyalty at one point by naming him a Companion of Honour, an award given by the monarch for "conspicuous services of national importance." Dief was vacationing in Barbados when the call came from Trudeau. After he got off the phone, he didn't say what the call was about, he just spent the day whistling and singing until the official announcement was made. Once he had collected the award in London and was flying home, he bragged to the Air Canada flight attendant about it. When he asked her if she'd like to see the honour and she said yes, he went rummaging around in his briefcase looking for it. What he mistakenly pulled out and waved at her was not his medal on the ribbon, but his truss. Keith Martin had to grab the truss, descend on the briefcase quickly before some other unmentionable was produced, and find the medal.

As keen an observer of Canadian affairs as Dief was, he most liked it when all eyes were on him. He regarded himself as something akin to a national shrine. And if you cared anything about him at all, he expected your homage always, but particularly on two days: his birthday, September 18, and the anniversary of his election to Parliament, March 26. In Ottawa, where national days, independence celebrations, and feast times were part of everyday life, for Dief and all who loved him these two occasions were especially to be honoured. Each year, both days would begin with him pretending they were nothing special. When the prime minister rose in his place in Parliament to pay tribute, Dief would feign surprise at achieving yet another milestone of age or gaining more lustre as the dean of the House of Commons. The ritual would continue later in his crowded office as he received personal greetings from MPs, staff and all sorts of people connected with the Hill. He paid close attention to who showed up and who stayed away. For days after, he'd pester staff and friends, saying: "Where was Mr. X? Why didn't Y show up?"

Knowing the command-performance level that each of these days had reached, I was fully aware I would be counted among the missing and presumed dead in March of 1977 when I was travelling with a parliamentary delegation in the Middle East. In order to stay in Dief's good graces, Claude Wagner, his wife, Gisèle, and I sent a joint telegram from Tel Aviv saying: "CONGRATULATIONS UPON ANNIVERSARY OF YOUR FIRST ELECTION." Feeling I had covered myself appropriately, I thought nothing more about it until I returned to Ottawa. Whenever one of his loyalists had been away, Dief expected to be first on the agenda upon your return, so I showed up at his office feeling jaunty and ready to flatter him with reports of how highly the Israelis thought of him. Before I opened my mouth he lit into me.

"Were you drunk?" he snarled.

"Sir?"

"Were you drunk? That is the only possible explanation."

I had no idea what he was going on about and could only repeat another dumbfounded, "Sir?"

"Don't play cutesy with me. This is the most damnable thing I've ever seen. And from you, of all people, I never . . ."

Finally, I was able to say: "I don't know what you're talking about."

"This is what I'm talking about." And he flung my telegram across his desk toward me. I picked it up and read the message: "CONGRATULATIONS UPON ANNIVERSARY OF YOUR FIRST ERECTION." I never was able to convince him that the mistake was unintentional.

As for Robert Stanfield, no amount of homage, short of resigning, would ever get him back in Dief's good graces. Stanfield was the butt of his endless scorn. Dief referred to him as "my leader" but the way Dief said it, the epithet dripped from his mouth like liquid sarcasm. Whenever Stanfield said something that Dief judged to be foolish, he'd predict that the statement would lose Stanfield "tens of thousands of votes across the country." It was always "tens of thousands." Or he'd shout: "I cannot understand this man. I have tried to help him but he will not listen." Stanfield's personal staff and headquarters employees were little better. "What," he would sneer," are the *little* men saying?"

Dief was equally scathing in his comments about how the party had treated him. Never mind the assassination, he didn't even think he'd received suitable recognition when he led them to victory. He'd regularly launch this line without provocation: "I've never asked for anything, prime minister, leader, member for all these years. I've never asked for anything, never received anything. Nothing." Then just in case you still didn't understand, he'd spell out their ingratitude with even greater emphasis: "Not one thing." His opinion of Joe Clark was not much better. He called him "Joe boy." Of course, Dief saw him as another one of the Red Tories who was in Camp's pocket; he loved to hang nicknames on them all. Prince Edward Island MP David MacDonald was a United Church minister and a Red Tory. Dief called him "Judas MacDonald."

He watched every move the party made with undisguised disgust. A few weeks before the 1969 party policy conference in Niagara Falls, Dief wrote to me to say that "in August 1967 the Party went over Montmorency Falls. Apparently, not satisfied, it is going to show it can successfully go over Niagara Falls." Montmorency was always a particularly galling meeting for Dief. That was the one where the Tories adopted the party's ill-fated "two nations" policy, a view of Canada Dief could not abide. In the same letter he also got after the man who would be leader after Stanfield. "In the hall adjacent to my office Mr. Joe Clark and his associates [in Stanfield's office] flit hither and thither whispering or speaking in low monotones apparently frightened that there [sic] strategy become known in advance of the gathering. They must have been in touch with some of the football coaches and learned first hand the value of secrecy."

He took particular offence at a newspaper article published early in 1972 that glowingly described the organization of the December 1971 party meeting in Ottawa. " Billed as a policy session," said The Canadian Press story, "the convention wound up as a pep rally with all the cheers for Mr. Stanfield personally. 'For the first time Stanfield himself felt he had the party behind him.' " said the article, quoting a party headquarters staffer. The staffer continued: " 'It was the last moment for Diefenbaker. That's when he died.' "

Dief was alive and livid in Ottawa. He dispatched me to see the party national director, Liam O'Brian, and make him aware of Dief's displeasure. O'Brian said that Stanfield had already seen the piece and told O'Brian, "This won't do. Get to the bottom of it." O'Brian said he "almost croaked" when he read it himself and assured me that neither he nor several other headquarters staff members with whom he had checked had made the statements. Dief, of course, did not believe the explanations and saw the whole thing as smear tactics aimed against him.

The respect Dief thought the party begrudged him, however, was more than made up for by the response he got from ordinary Canadians whenever he travelled. It was great fun to watch people recognize and interact with Dief. He strode the country gathering compliments and praise as easily as the leggings of a young boy collect burrs as he romps through a field. Dief would often seem to remember names of people as he met them, even the occasion of their last meeting, no matter how brief the contact had been. But what appeared to be an astounding memory on his part, on close observation was no such thing. Most people, on meeting him, would quickly volunteer their name and the last time they had seen him. He simply assented to this information with a knowing shake of the head. His own forceful presence did the rest. Invariably people went away repeating snippets of his conversation and convinced that they were on the most intimate of terms with the former prime minister.

When his memory didn't work, such lapses didn't worry him. At one Toronto reception, an eager guest shook Dief's hand and said: "My name is X and I believe you knew my father in Saskatchewan." "Ah yes," replied Dief, "I knew your father well. He was a butcher, wasn't he?" "No," said the nonplussed guest in surprise, "he was a surgeon." Dief simply moved on to the next guest, saying: "Ah yes, nice to see you again."

He loved to campaign and would go to great lengths to help a candidate he liked. This gave rise to some humorous situations. Once, when he was visiting Heward Grafftey's riding in Quebec, Heward took Dief and the touring press corps to see where the famous Brome Lake ducks are raised for dinner tables across Canada. As they stood gazing over ducks as far as the stomach could imagine, Heward enthused: "Isn't this marvellous?" Dief glared at him and replied, "Yes, Heward, but do they vote?"

Dogs, however, were an animal Dief couldn't get enough of, voters or not. Unlike some politicians who use babies or animals as a way to talk to their respective parents or owners, Dief liked to talk to dogs and would often pay no attention to whoever was at the other end of the leash. Riding in the car, he'd constantly point out dogs on the street, calling them all "doggie." Once, on Kent Street in Ottawa, when we were on our way by car to the airport, we stopped at a red light and a car pulled up beside us containing a family and the family dog with its head stuck out the window. The family saw the special licence plate, 2000, realized it was Dief and saw that he was rolling down his window. Assuming he wanted to speak to them, they rolled down their windows to say hello, but all they got was John Diefenbaker twittering at their pet, "Hello, doggie, nice doggie," before the light changed and his car pulled away.

Half of the difficulty of being a Dief aide was caused by the "Mrs. Diefenbaker factor." If she took a dislike to a staff member, that was the end of his or her employment. More important, Dief's bitterness and anger at both his party and his life in general was fuelled by us every day at the office and by Olive every night at home. No one ever stood up to him and said, enough, the battle's been fought and it's time for all Conservatives to pull together. Olive's bitterness had its beginnings in 1963 when resigning cabinet ministers left "her John" in the lurch; the feelings were compounded by the assassination at the 1966 general meeting.

After that meeting, Olive wrote to me in her distinctive turquoise ink and backhand script to say that the 1966 meeting "was a deeply hurtful experience." She continued: "I can meet the world with my head held high, but I will never get over the hurt, and I don't want anyone offering 'soporifics.' Therefore," she concluded, "I won't talk about it." She signed her name, then, immediately forgetting her vow, added a postscript: "Did you see Dalton Camp on television last night? If ever there was a guilty face!" In 1971, she wrote to me again: "Things look worse and worse for R.L.S. I almost feel sorry for the man. Almost."

There was quite a lengthy list of enemies she thought had brought harm to her John. In public, she ranks among the best political wives I've ever seen. She could be as smooth as a kitten's wrist. In private, however, her claws came out and she could be devastating. She carried enough bitterness and anger within her for both of them. All of us sycophants and hangers-on didn't much help to calm matters. In order to please her we supplied her with ample material to feed her enduring hurts. A typical conversation with Olive would begin with the mention of a name known to be on her enemy list. Predictably, she would begin the litany: "He's a dear, dear friend and we're very fond of him, but, oh-oh-oh . . ." Then the axe would fall and she'd continue with, "He just collapsed under the pressure of the Camp forces when John needed him," or "He has no common sense," or "He can't handle a drink." One day she was sitting in the visitor's gallery to see Dief deliver a scheduled speech. Beside her was another Tory wife, there to lend moral support to her own husband. The other man was recognized by the Speaker before Dief, and Olive was not amused. The Tory MP had just nicely begun his speech when Olive turned to his wife and asked: "Is your husband not well?"

Her attacks on people sometimes had their humorous side. Keith Martin's brother, Glenn-Gary, and I took Olive out to the Ottawa airport one day to meet Dief as he returned from an out-of-town speech. The flight was delayed, she was impatient and we were desperately trying to keep the conversation light and off the topic of the delay. She was not in a mood to hear good things about anyone. Glenn-Gary mentioned that the son of a former Diefenbaker executive assistant had just won a scholarship and that his parents were rightly very proud of him.

"They think that he is a genius," said Olive. "Well, I used to be assistant Head of Guidance in the Province of Ontario, and I know something about these things. He's a dear boy and a very bright boy, but he is no genius. He is no genius at all because he has no attention span, no attention span whatever."

Not quite hearing her last words, Glenn-Gary asked: "No what, Mrs. Diefenbaker?"

"No what what?" she replied, demonstrating an amazing lack of the same herself.

Much of Olive's bitterness stemmed from the fact that she had neither close friends nor family in Ottawa, so she couldn't enjoy the warmth any human being craves and requires. Further, she was regularly in great pain from arthritis and often walked with a cane. The condition was said to have originated during a flight with Dief, during his time as prime minister, when the aircraft in which they were travelling took a sudden drop and flung her roughly against the ceiling. In addition, she also had intermittent heart trouble. As a result, she couldn't travel with her husband as often as she wanted to and so became isolated in Ottawa, stewing in the bitter brew of her memories and ladling out servings for him.

Troublesome as her general condition was, however, Dief did tend to exaggerate Olive's health problems. One morning he announced: "Olive died six times last night." He then became quite angry when it was suggested that perhaps she should be hospitalized. Olive was equally fond of hyperbole when describing her condition. Once, when I picked her up at home to take her to an event in my riding, she greeted me with: "You know, Sean, I really shouldn't be going. I had a slight heart attack last night."

Still, the two were as close and as happy together as newlyweds leaving the church. He could get absolutely mushy when he spoke to Olive on the phone. His favourite name for her was "Sweets." She was his closest advisor and ablest confidante. Much has been made about the so-called cover-up of the first Mrs. Diefenbaker, who died in 1951. The allegations that he tried to keep secret both the marriage and Edna's contribution to his early career surprised me, because I never found the Chief reticent about her. He usually referred to her as "the first Mrs. Diefenbaker," although rarely within earshot of Olive. I think the simple truth was that, out of deference and love, he avoided talking about her around Olive. Perhaps more important, Dief had a difficult time dealing with death, anyone's death. The recollection of Edna's lingering death from leukemia was a source of terrible pain for him.

Early in his career, Edna gave him a belief in himself. Dief was seen as a confident man, but when he first came to Ottawa from the Prairies he was frightened and insecure. Edna built him up. She held happy parties where liquor was served (he was later a teetotaller) and carefully raised his social standing in Ottawa. But as he became consumed with his career, she was moved aside. At the end, when she was dying, Dief couldn't deal with her death. All he could bring himself to do when he visited her in hospital was come to the door of the room and yell, "Is there anything you want? Is there anything I can get you?" The charge, however, that he tried to wipe the first Mrs. Diefenbaker from his life is nonsense.

There were other aspects of his past, however, that he did studiously avoid discussing. The real story of his exploits in the First World War, for example, will probably never be known. He always maintained that he had been invalided home. If you drew the conclusion from that information that he had been injured in battle, well, that was just fine with him. On other occasions, he would say he had been hit by a truck and so been unable to serve in the trenches. Pearson used to tell his intimates that he once sent for defence department files wherein the problem was listed as hemorrhoids. Dief vehemently denied that story. In one of the last conversations I had with Keith Martin before Keith's death in 1984, he talked about Dief's war record. It was as if he'd finally pieced the puzzle together and could see it clearly for the first time. He had concluded that Diefenbaker, a cocky young man with an obviously German name, had been shipped over to Britain and beaten up pretty badly by his fellows. National Defence, argued Keith, had covered it up and, rather than risk another beating, shipped him home.

Although he was frightened by death, including the thought of his own, Dief was fascinated by anything to do with medicine. Any MP who was also a doctor could always get in to see Dief no matter how tight his schedule. The MD MP might want to talk politics; Dief would want to talk medicine. MP Dr. Lewis Brand, for example, was forever being asked by Dief for a diagnosis of this or that ailment, real or imagined. Finally, in the hopes of halting free advice to his friend, Brand told Dief he could only offer advice if he were allowed to do a physical examination. Dief immediately stripped, right there in his office, so Brand could give him a once-over. Nor was Dief reluctant to offer opinions on other people's health. He regarded me as too pale and was forever urging me to eat more beefsteak. As for Keith, who liked to take a drink as much as most politicos in Ottawa, Dief thought he was dehydrated and should take in more fluids.

One of the health fads Dief enthusiastically embraced was a treatment propounded by Dr. R. Glen Green, a naturopath from Prince Albert who also tried out his new remedies on inmates at the penitentiary there. One of Green's experiments involved megadoses of nicotinic acid that Green claimed offered relief from a wide variety of ailments. Dief became a great fan, claimed it worked wonders and told everyone he met to try it. "Don't be put off by the initial reaction," he told people. "It's wonderful, but it makes you feel prickly all over."

His interest in medicine gave rise to one of my favourite descriptions of myself as an aide. Whenever anyone asked exactly what the executive assistant to John Diefenbaker did, I replied: "When it gets late in the day and dusk is settling over Parliament Hill, I get to hold the oil lamp while Dr. P.B. Rynard is applying the leeches." My real role was more often than not covering up for him. Once, he had to go into hospital to have a hernia repaired. He wanted a press release issued to explain his disappearance from the House, but he did not want to use the word *hernia*. Because he had recently been taken ill in Europe with a bleeding stomach, we didn't want people to think this hernia was anything serious, but we couldn't mention it, so the press release was written and rewritten numerous times. He was never content. Finally, the release mentioned that he'd "suffered a strain while on a fishing trip." He entered hospital and had the operation, but there were complications. He was bleeding into the scrotum. If he didn't want to mention the hernia, he certainly didn't want to mention that. We just kept saying that "he was mending" until he was back in the House and everybody, including him, could forget about it.

I've always thought that Keith Martin should have received the Order of Canada for his heroic efforts in keeping the legend of John Diefenbaker alive and intact in the Old Man's last days. Keith had worked for Dief off and on since the Youth for Dief movement in 1967. He covered up for him, made excuses for him and cleaned up his messes – sometimes literally. After Olive's death, Dief had visions that she visited him in the night. As a result, the bedroom would be a wreck in the morning. Keith and the housekeeper would put it back together pretending all the while that nothing had happened. Toward the end, though he was still usually alert and lively, he was coming apart. Perhaps the most noticeable indication of this was his failing memory. Aboard one flight, he told Keith that when they returned to Ottawa, he was going to make an appointment to see Prime Minister Mackenzie King about some important matters.

In addition to health troubles over time, John Diefenbaker was a mercurial man. His moods could never be predicted. One day he'd be upbeat and co-operative, signing everything placed in front of him, agreeing to all speaking engagements and any impossible demand placed on his time by MPs who wanted to bring around groups to pay their respects. The next day, he would be in foul form. He'd slash through entire pages of correspondence he had dictated the day before, all the while demanding: "Who perpetrated this monstrosity?" He would arbitrarily decide that he was being used by persons unknown and would announce the cancellation of appearances at events where he had been scheduled weeks earlier as the guest of honour. After a while, as the executive assistant charged with bearing this bad news, you got used to the plaintive wails from people who saw their plans abruptly ruined after tickets had been sold and the hall booked to capacity for later that week. Such cancellations happened so often that I learned to steel myself to the pleas from organizers across the country. I felt like a bank manager calling a loan. You'd heard the cries for sympathy before, but you went ahead and called the loan anyway.

Next to invitations to speak, the most frequent requests were for his autographed photo or for a signed copy of the Bill of Rights he had passed in 1960. Usually, he was happy to sign, but he liked to do them in batches. Once in a while, however, he'd remember that he was paying for these "free" photos that were being mailed out, and he'd rant "What the hell!" and refuse to sign any of them when they were presented. Not wanting to arouse his ire, the secretaries kept such requests a low priority and, as a result, considerable backlogs accumulated. Frequently, we'd find ourselves without the job done on the eve of an event or publication date that required an autographed photo.

After trying several unsuccessful ploys with him, I took another route. Using a pen like his, I practised the inscription, "To (name) with best wishes," and his sweeping signature until I had it all down pat. I then signed the photos myself. We not only cleared the backlog, we avoided future problems. Whenever the secretaries complained to me that he was "in one of those moods," they would hand over the stack of photos and I would return them the next day, signed and ready for mailing, no questions asked. Across Canada, there are scores of treasured photos of the Right Honourable John Diefenbaker signed by my own hand, not his. In my defence, I can only plead this: At least they arrived on time.

Because of the generous receptions and ongoing requests for appearances that he received, Dief was convinced that there was a great following in the country waiting for word from him. He thought that on any given issue he could easily rally public opinion to his side and win over the country. The campaign was simple and consisted of eight speeches. No matter what the issue – bilingualism, capital punishment, the next election – just eight speeches. He'd begin, "I've been thinking about this most awful tax bill, eight speeches. Eight speeches across this country and that would be it." Then he'd begin to list the cities where he planned to speak, starting with Vancouver, on to Winnipeg, then Toronto and Moncton. By the time he'd named four or five cities, however, he'd get confused and have to backtrack; then he'd end the list by repeating, "eight speeches." In all the times he rolled that strategy I never heard him name the eight different cities he had in mind. Nor did we ever set out on such a tour. The only time we came close was in 1974 when Stanfield asked Dief to stump through a few ridings in a show of party solidarity. Dief travelled in fine style, with an entourage of four or five and unlimited expenses. The bill for ten days on the road probably ran to $50,000.

Some views he held were not for such broadband announcement. He loved to be in on secrets and to spread them. But you always knew when Dief was *not* sharing a secret with you alone. If you came into his office and he lowered his voice and said, "Now, no one else has this," you knew that everyone he had talked to that morning had heard the same opening gambit and the news that followed. Among the "secrets" he regularly laid claim to knowing was information that he kept locked in a cabinet in his office. At various times he said it contained proof that Dalton Camp had made exorbitant amounts of money from government advertising contracts, evidence as to why the young Trudeau could not enter the United States, or the goods on why Lester Pearson covered up for the suicide of Ambassador Herbert Norman in Cairo. "I'm going to tell the story," he'd say, looking you straight in the eye as if the nation would come to a standstill when he did. He never told those stories. At his death, no such papers were ever discovered.

As his years on Parliament Hill drew to a close, Dief became increasingly demanding and testy and eternally obsessed by trivia. Only with Keith's help and the collaboration of the rest of the office staff could the appearance of normalcy be maintained. They had to do it. He was, after all, a national treasure. But he was like an aging actor whose one famous role had been usurped; his former glory had dwindled to fewer fans, some faded clippings and the endless replaying in his mind of past scripts and praiseworthy scenarios.

In the stuff of our friendship there is also some sadness; for although John George Diefenbaker was a man touched by greatness, he was not all he could have been. If he wasn't the best prime minister Canada has ever seen, he was arguably the best opposition leader in our history. He was devoted to his country and gave us great oratory, something that is sadly lacking today. He could rouse crowds and rally public opinion. He could also evoke feelings of great frustration and anger in those of us who wanted him to be superb always. His pettiness and egocentricity were upsetting, and his vindictiveness sometimes frightened even me. Those characteristics of his dark side drove good people away from him.

When Lester Pearson died in 1972, I paid my respects in the Hall of Honour, and visited Dief in his office. We chatted about Pearson and Dief said: "You've seen my funeral plans and you know that it'll be different for me – my casket will be open."

"Well, you know, sir," I offered, "why Pearson's had to be closed?"

"No," exclaimed Dief, showing a sudden and dramatic interest as he leaned forward at his desk to await every word of the explanation.

"Well, in addition to the cancer which killed him, Mr. Pearson developed jaundice at the end and this causes a lot of discoloration."

"Well, this is it!" said Dief triumphantly. "You see, I knew there had to be something. Well, what in the world." And with that, Dief pounced upon his phone and dialled a number with which I was very familiar. "Olive," he shouted into the mouthpiece. "He was as green as a beet."

I could hear Olive's incredulous response even from where I was sitting. "Who?"

"Pearson. He's as green as a beet!" Now, I never knew jaundice to turn someone green, nor had I ever seen a green beet. Perhaps he meant to say green as a bean. In any event, he kept saying it as he redialled the phone to call all his cronies across the country with these most strange tidings. I slipped out of the office, now regretting that I had ever raised the topic.

A few days later, as all of official Ottawa gathered at Christ Church Cathedral for Pearson's funeral, I happened to be sitting where I could see Dief. His head shook and wobbled more than usual, but throughout the service he kept his eyes fixed on that coffin. And as I sat there, I knew Dief well enough to know that as he stared, he was trying to imagine the mortal remains of his former nemesis as he was being laid to rest. And green. Green as a beet, Olive.

CHAPTER FOUR

REAR WINDOW:
TAKING MY SEAT

After I attended the March 1966 Conservative Party meeting in
Ottawa, I wrote to John Diefenbaker and said that I was sure
he would be prime minister once more. And one day, I
optimistically predicted, "I will have the honour of serving with you
in the House!" Of course, the 1965 election had resulted in a Liberal
minority government, and he never led the party into another election. Although he didn't become PM again, I was determined to have
at least one of my two predictions come true. In 1972, at only twenty
years of age (but with eight of them in party politics), I decided to run.

For all his love of Parliament and his supposed view of me as his
protégé, however, Dief was not pleased when I told him. In principle,
he approved, but in practice he wanted me to continue as his executive assistant. I had planned to work for him until the fall of 1972,
helping him through the anticipated summer election, and then to
enter law school. (I had been accepted for law at both the University
of Windsor and Osgoode Hall.) Only when I was established as a
lawyer would I seek a seat in Parliament. At least that was the original
plan. Instead, after working for Diefenbaker on the Hill for only four
months, I was preparing to leave his service.

The change in plans was precipitated by a call that spring from a
Dundas, Ontario, realtor, George Pawley. According to him, some of
the locals had made a shopping list of possible Progressive Conservative candidates and my name was included. Would I be interested
in running in the riding of Hamilton-Wentworth? Frankly, I was
dumbfounded by the call. Their interest in me was unexpected. I had
grown up in the constituency of Hamilton East and had lived
in Hamilton West, but other than attending school in Hamilton-

Wentworth, I had little knowledge of that riding.

On the map, the constituency seemed almost like an afterthought. A horseshoe-shaped riding, it stretched for about forty-five miles from working-class east-end Hamilton around the city to suburban Ancaster and Stoney Creek and on to the rural farmland of Wentworth County in Glanford, Binbrook and Saltfleet townships. In 1968, the Liberals had won with about 14,000 votes, the NDP was second with 12,000 and the Tories finished third with 10,000. Even though the Trudeau government had become unpopular since, winning would not be easy.

The key Tory force in the riding was Jack MacDonald. A generation earlier he had been the boy wonder of Hamilton politics. MacDonald had been the youngest alderman, then the youngest controller, and had served on city council for years before running for mayor. He was defeated but would later return as a controller again and eventually be elected mayor twice. In 1972, his brief absence from public office meant he was the party's elder statesman, godfather and guru in the region. His opinion and support would be crucial.

MacDonald is a chronic and infectious optimist. However, he is also a realist, and the riding was a long-time Liberal bastion held at the time by Colin Gibson, a man in his late forties. In fact, the term "sacrificial lamb" seemed an apt description for any Tory candidate challenging Gibson. Well, I thought, even such an animal as that could press on with law school and resume his earlier plans. I decided to plunge ahead and seek the nomination. When I told Dief, he reached for his copy of the Parliamentary Guide, reviewed the riding's voting history, pronounced my plan "nonsensical" and would hear nothing more about it.

Dief, of course, was not without self-interest in all of this. He properly expected my help as his executive assistant in his own riding. Trudeau had lowered the voting age to eighteen for this election, and Dief was working himself into the usual lather that preceded his customary easy, personal victory. In an attempt to get a stay of execution, I convinced him that I should at least go to Hamilton-Wentworth and assess the strength of the promised support first-hand. It didn't take me long to discover that local Tories were simply looking for an unusual angle around which to rally support. A well-regarded high school teacher, twenty-eight-year-old John Miller, had already indicated he was interested in running, but my early boosters thought a twenty-year-old with a Diefenbaker connection offered a bit more excitement.

The prospect of running certainly excited *me*. Local party people put the best face on the situation and blithely assured me that they thought I could win. They promised that I would not be saddled with any campaign debts. That was a most important commitment. I had little money of my own and no family financial resources to fall back on. My recent job as Dief's executive assistant had brought me my first real salary. After four months' work at $12,000 a year, I had hardly saved enough for a modern-day campaign. With the riding association's financial commitment, I returned to Ottawa to tell Dief that this opportunity was too good to pass up. He reluctantly offered me his blessing, but claimed that he had talked to people he would not name who had told him I would lose so badly it would be most embarrassing.

The next step was to win the nomination, but before the election writ was issued and while Parliament remained in session, I felt committed to continue serving Dief. I also needed the income. My main campaign tool became long-distance telephone calls as I asked party members who could vote at the nominating meeting for their support. At first I worried that without the personal touch my case would suffer. In fact, the phone turned out to have advantages over a face-to-face approach. First, I had free access to the government tie lines and could massage each person regularly; second, my telephone voice made me sound older than I was and much older than I looked; third, it was no small help to have the dulcet tones of the Peace Tower carillon chiming in the background while I made my pitch as someone who knew Ottawa. The Tory candidate in the previous election, Jim Ridge, agreed to help, as did Colonel Bill Brigger (they would later be my co-campaign managers). They were two key supporters in the community. Mind you, Bill's vote wasn't so much for me as it was against the other candidate. With typical candour he told me his reason: "I'm not interested in having any goddamned school teacher as my MP." In politics you take the votes where you find them.

As I gathered other supporters to the cause I learned not to expect automatic backing from youth as "their" candidate. John Miller also had the support of young people because of his teaching position. On the night of the nomination meeting, for example, he arrived with the entire high school band in tow. For my part, I had an even more loyal bunch: the O'Sullivan clan. My brothers and sister, even my great-aunts, approached just about everyone they had ever met, sold them the Tory Party membership required for voting and brought them along on that May fifth evening to Marritt Hall in Ancaster. There were clowns, cheerleaders and placards by the score. One thousand people gathered, including 647 delegates, to choose between Miller and myself.

The usually amiable Colin Gibson was not much impressed with what this young pipsqueak O'Sullivan had already been saying about him. I had pointed out that Gibson was all but invisible in Ottawa; few there could even name the member from Hamilton-Wentworth. His constituents, I argued, were not being well represented by him. In four years, he had spoken in the House for a grand total of four hours. Stung, Gibson responded rather stuffily: "When some neophyte politician stands up and says that Hamilton hasn't had effective representation in the House of Commons, I want to take this opportunity to deny it flatly."

In response, I dismissed Gibson out of hand by telling the crowd at the nominating meeting that he had become both "offended and offensive." I continued in my most self-righteous tone: "I'm content to let the voters of this constituency tell Mr. Gibson how monumental is the task of representation in this riding." The incumbent had made the mistake of rising to the bait offered by someone who was not yet a candidate. I had drawn him onto my ground. That showed the incumbent took me seriously and made me appear as his Tory opponent. I won the nomination by a 120-vote margin. The real fight could begin.

As I would learn so often in life, however, everything did not go according to the tidy schedule that I had projected or planned. I expected to lose a summer election, then head off to law school in the fall. Trudeau fouled it up by announcing that there would be no summer election. I was stuck in Ottawa with the riding far away and the election even further off. I even lost my $75 deposit for law school because I had to withdraw my application. Trudeau's decision, however, was beneficial. The country began to suspect he was afraid to call a national election. It also gave us several more months to prepare.

We opened three headquarters including one at the Ancaster Garden Centre. As a local newspaper columnist pointed out, the choice was a wise one: it had always been known as a great place from which to spread fertilizer. Jack MacDonald, the old pro, taught me how to "take" a room filled with people by entering it with a flourish, shaking every hand while fixing the eye of each person for a few intense seconds, repeating the person's name and asking for his or her support. Under Jack's enthusiastic tutelage, I toured pubs and drank my first beer (it tasted awful). For my first "main-streeting," Ishbel Ridge, Jim's wife, took me to a rural part of the riding. I discovered that as a politician I was as green as that spring's freshly sprouting crops. At one point I listened carefully to a farmer talking about the problems he'd been having with Seneca. He was referring to a variety of corn he'd planted; I thought he was having trouble with a local Indian band.

Among the early meetings I had was a session with the chief Ontario organizer, Paul Weed. He called me to Toronto for a forty-five minute briefing and pep talk that was offered to all new candidates. He urged me to use my initials, SOS, in my campaign material and mentioned a campaign in California as a parallel. When Pierre Salinger, former press secretary to John F. Kennedy, ran for office there, his buttons read: "P.S. I love you." The idea began to lose its appeal for me when Weed went on to say that Salinger had lost. Weed's second suggestion was even less appetizing. He urged me to have someone from my campaign team pick up the garbage from my opponent's headquarters every day and sift through it for insights into the opposition's plans and problems. I did not follow his advice. Knowing that such mentality was abroad, however, I did arrange for the garbage from my own committee rooms to be split up and taken home daily by various members of the staff so it was spread around the city.

I was still juggling the two jobs, candidate and executive assistant, when I accompanied the Diefenbakers to Stratford, Ontario, for a testimonial evening to honour a former Diefenbaker cabinet minister, J. Waldo Monteith, and his wife, Mary. The evening was also an excuse and an opportunity to get Dief and Robert Stanfield together on the same stage in order to show some semblance of party unity. The event, held in the Festival Theatre, was marred by tragedy. One of the first speakers, Mr. Justice King, collapsed in mid-sentence and had to be carried from the stage. As doctors worked to resuscitate him in the wings out of sight of the audience, the responsive acoustics of the theatre carried his every gasp and cry out to the hushed crowd. After several terrifying minutes, King died and the rest of the evening's program was cancelled. The Diefenbakers and I drove back to our motel in an uncomfortable silence that was broken only by Olive's unfortunate attempt to pay tribute to the dead jurist. "Well," she sighed, "it was a great last act."

Back at the motel where we were to stay overnight, Dief and Olive had more to say. Because the walls were thin and Dief had removed his "earpiece" (as he referred to his hearing aid), their conversation in the room next door was plainly audible. "You know, Olive, Sean is not going to make a very good candidate," Dief rumbled. "He's just too young for it and that's all."

Olive concurred: "John, I've been telling you this from the beginning. It's a very bad mistake he's making."

"He'll be ruined," continued Dief. "He'll never be able to run again. It's awful; it's the most awful thing." I finally fled to the reception desk, demanding to change rooms so I didn't have to listen to my lack of qualifications as enumerated by my employer.

Still, the Diefenbakers agreed to come into the riding in June to campaign on my behalf, although we did make a $500 contribution to Dief's re-election coffers in Prince Albert to assure the Chief that the trip wouldn't be a totally lost cause. Dief and Olive met local Tories, he held a news conference and gave a speech at a beef barbecue – his first appearance in the area in more than three years. In his speech, Dief attempted a cheerful reference to my nocturnal work habits. "Some people are larks, and some are . . ." and he paused while he groped for the appropriate bird to describe me. "Er – hawks." "Owls," Olive added in a stage whisper. "That's right," Dief continued, as if he'd said it himself, "and I happen to be a lark." We taped his entire speech in the hope of finding a rousing endorsement of me that could be used in radio advertising, but it was a typically rambling Dief speech and when the sentences were parsed, there was little that was helpful. The best we could do was to salvage this line: "If you return Sean O'Sullivan as your member, the people of Canada will know where Hamilton-Wentworth is." Weak as it was, that quote was replayed countless times during the campaign, when the election was finally called for October 30.

My campaigning style and methods improved after my awkward beginnings with that farmer worried about Seneca. One of the more enjoyable events was a return to Bishop Ryan, the high school where I had stalked the halls as a student just three years before. During an all-candidates meeting with the current crop of students, I had some fun at the expense of teachers who were still on staff. There was one nun in particular, I recalled in my opening remarks, who would tell the girls not to cross their legs because they would get varicose veins. The howls of delight arising from the students told me they knew exactly who I meant and that she was still offering the same dour advice. I also carried a serious message: "Canada has become a country," I told them, "where it is more profitable to collect unemployment insurance than to work. The Liberals have made welfare a way of life. The Conservative Party believes that the government should interfere in the lives of the people as little as possible. The government should be the servant not the master of the people."

The rest of my campaign views were equally clear-cut: reduce taxes to stimulate the economy; halt government job programs and let the private sector create jobs; end reliance on welfare. I was against the legalization of marijuana and in favour of capital punishment. Above all I was against Pierre Trudeau. In the election of 1972, that was enough. Because Trudeau had lowered the voting age, it was the first time someone under twenty-one could run; that gave me some notoriety. Second, and more telling, the tide had gone out for the Liberals.

Not everyone admired my youth or lack of elective experience, so my campaign literature was designed to make me look older. We ran photos of me carrying my young nephew and niece. If voters wanted to deduce that I was older than I really was and that these two were my children, well, they were welcome to do so. At one point, the NDP actually hired a sound truck to tour the riding and blare the unremarkable message that I was only twenty, single and had no children. Obviously, the "aging" strategy worked; at least we upset the opposition.

There were other borderline gambits. We published a single edition of a newspaper with this blazing headline: "Polls indicate O'Sullivan in the lead." They were, of course, our polls. My dumbest attempt to gain publicity, however, was a contrived romance with Stanfield's youngest daughter, Mimi. Mimi, a bright and attractive young woman who captivated both the press and the public, was accompanying Stanfield on his cross-country tour, along with her mother. As a publicity stunt, some overzealous campaign workers promoted a romantic liaison between Mimi and myself. The Stanfield campaign plane was due to land in Hamilton one day early in October but was diverted to Toronto because of fog at Mount Hope airport. Undeterred by the change in venue, I raced over to Toronto to meet Mimi and have my picture taken with her.

Poor Mimi, little did she know that my headquarters had previously prepared a press release to accompany the anticipated photo of the two starry-eyed friends. As the statement brightly noted: "Mr. O'Sullivan isn't admitting to anything serious, but two weeks ago he acted as escort for Mimi Stanfield at the Conservative campaign kick-off in Oakville." The news release also pointed out that I "went to a lot of trouble for a brief reunion with Miss Stanfield." Also mentioned, without comment, was the fact that though the elder Stanfields had left the airport by car for a campaign stop, Mimi had stayed behind. The implication, of course, was that she wanted to be with me. Mimi, a wise campaigner, knew a set-up when she saw one and was justifiably furious at my attempt to hook up with the boss's daughter. In the end, I received my just desserts. While this fake romance was being "heated up," the real thing was cooling. My relationship with Paula Marsden, ongoing since I had met her at the YPC meeting in Port Carling in 1970, was all but over. My few-minute public "affair" with Mimi was the beginning of the end. That December, when I gave Paula her Christmas present, she gave me the door. Mimi later married Murray Coolican, a former Stanfield staffer and a longtime friend of mine. In 1986 I helped officiate at the wedding of Paula to Scott Spearn.

On election day, with the campaigning done – both the trumped-up and the truthful – you pass the anxious hours as best you can. I continued a tradition that Jack MacDonald had begun twenty years earlier and headed out election morning without a tie looking to buy the gaudiest one I could find – for luck. I visited a few polling stations, handed out flowers to workers, went to 5:30 p.m. Mass and bolted an uneasy supper. Although I had two speeches ready, one if I won, the other if I lost, I have to say that by that point I was ready to win. A great campaign team presented me with a victory by 3,856 votes and allowed me to become Canada's youngest Member of Parliament. I wouldn't turn twenty-one for another two months.

Among the victory messages was one from Dief: "Congratulations and hail to the conquering hero. My wife and I are jubilant. You leading your loyal workers have put Hamilton-Wentworth on the national map." In fact, the entire Hamilton-Niagara Peninsula area had been painted Tory Blue; we'd won ten of the thirteen ridings in the region. In Ontario, the PCs won forty seats to thirty-six for the Liberals. Nationally, it looked for a time as if we might even form a government. At one point the PCs were leading, and Stanfield appeared before the television cameras in Halifax to accept lusty cheers from his workers. As the results were finalized over the next few days, however, it became clear that the Liberals had elected 109 members to 107 for the Tories. The thirty-one New Democrats would hold the balance of power in the minority government. Even though we had beaten the Liberals, both in seats and the popular vote in every province except Quebec, the Tories were still in opposition.

My own election-night champagne celebration with campaign workers was held in the Crystal Ballroom of the Royal Connaught Hotel. Someone asked me if this was the first step on the way to becoming prime minister. I attempted humility in my response: "I just want to be the very best MP I can." Looking back, I probably thought I *had* taken the first step. But what was perhaps more on my mind that night was the fact that nine years earlier I had shaken the hand of a man in the lobby of that very hotel. I was about to realize the dream that he inspired and join the Chief as a fellow member of

Parliament on the floor of the House of Commons in a way no one could ever have predicted. A precious dream had come true.

John Diefenbaker liked to refer to his beloved Parliament in rather grandiose terms. He called the Commons the "cathedral of democracy." In fact, for those of us who revere the place as he did, his words are accurate. He saw its inhabitants as a special breed. As he once said in a speech in the House: "Mr. Speaker, this institution must not fail. Without it there is no freedom. We are here today not only as the custodians of the present and the inheritors of the past but, Mr. Speaker, we are as well the hope of this institution's future."

If a person must work at all in this world, then it is best to work in such a place as Parliament. When winter grips Ottawa, sometimes the only thing that seems to keep the city warm is its self-sustaining insulation from the rest of the country. The Commons, however, can heat hearts all on its own. In those early days as a new member I could feel the chamber drawing me as I strode across the marble-floored rotunda, past the ornate columns and the Manitoba limestone walls, through the swinging wood and glass doors into the lobby, up a few steps, then through the thick, green curtains into the chamber itself. The Commons can still move me to an unusual quiet with its beauty. It is an architectural wonder, alive with history and vaulted heights, with a ceiling of hand-painted linen and glowing stained glass windows saluting the provinces and the territories with a confection of colours amid a beautiful gathering of wood and reverence.

After a deferential bow to the Speaker, I'd slide into the seat polished by my peers from my country's past. What had once been a vague dream had become vibrant drama. For years I had pursued this goal with all the ardour of a suitor chasing an elusive woman. I had wooed her and won her, a conquest that brought me into an exclusive club that has frustrated and foiled many more wealthy and powerful Canadians than I. It was my seat. Uniformed pages could be summoned by a snap of the finger. Mail could be dispatched across the country merely by signing my initials in the corner of the envelope.

So I felt quite pleased with myself – even arrogant about my accomplishments. After all, as a boy just seven years earlier I had looked down into this crusader's battlefield from the visitors' gallery; I had matured and I had arrived. I had longed to be here and I knew I belonged. I was not only in the House, I was home.

Unlike most new MPs, I felt very familiar with Parliament. After all, Dief had provided me with an apprenticeship available to few. I already had friends on the Hill. That did not mean, however, that I was universally accepted. The day Parliament opened, the members of the House of Commons gathered at the bar of the Senate to hear the Speech from the Throne. For a while, everyone listened, but then MPs got on with what they do best: talk. One MP standing nearby looked at me, turned to a colleague, and said with more than a tinge of incredulity, "Who is that youngster?" "Don't you know," came the response, "that's Sean O'Sullivan. He's the youngest member. He's only twenty." Sniffed the first, "What does a twenty-year-old know about being a member of Parliament?" That stinging rebuke came from another new MP who years later held a special prayer breakfast for my recovery – Jeanne Sauvé.

Even this putdown could not puncture the emotion that I enjoyed as we were summoned to the chamber by the division bells. There was a real sense of excitement to the proceedings. This was a minority government and we were only two seats away from power. There was a widespread belief that the Trudeau government could collapse at any moment. Every debate was critical; no member could stray far from Ottawa if a key vote was expected. Even MPs who were hospitalized were hauled to the House for votes. The parties stayed in a state of constant readiness. Because we Tories expected to become the government any day, all MPs were conscious of keeping a close eye on the riding in case there was a quick election. As well, of course, we wanted to be diligent and successful so that when Stanfield went looking for talent, we would be his shining stars.

I was not, nor did I ever become, a key player in Stanfield's inner circle. I couldn't have been more a backbencher unless carpenters had installed another row of seats behind the curtains. I was in the very back row. The seat did, however, offer an excellent view of the debates. I sat immediately behind Stanfield, so I could see beyond him toward Trudeau and the rest of the Liberal cabinet. I didn't move from that backbench seat for the next five years. Some might have protested and demanded to sit closer to the front ranks. Not me. That seat put me at the centre-field stripe for the political football game. Nothing could escape my eye. I enjoyed myself so much that a comment attributed to me helped quell a later, minor rebellion in party ranks. After Brian Mulroney's Conservatives won 211 seats in 1984, MPs had to be dispersed some distance from the prime minister and far from the Speaker's eye. In trying to calm the rabble, then Deputy Prime Minister Erik Nielsen quoted my comment on that back row seat more than ten years earlier: "There's no such thing as a bad seat in the House of Commons." I don't remember being so eloquent. Or so brief. But the sentiment is real.

Trudeau clearly dominated the House in that minority Parliament, and many members were in awe of his brilliance. You took him on at your peril. He intimidated people and could be a verbal bully. He might be unpopular in the country, but most of us in the 1972 crop of new MPs owed our election to him. Still, Canadians forgave him just about everything. He was forever getting away with things that no other politician could.

Awe for Trudeau didn't mean unbridled respect. We were suspicious of his motives and his game plan. Ottawa was always awash with rumours that he had been trained by communists, and some of our caucus members were convinced that Trudeau was a Soviet plant. There was also the popular speculation that Trudeau would never let power slip from his hands. He would, the story went, pull an Indira Gandhi, declare martial law and suspend sittings of Parliament in order to maintain his grip on power. Some were convinced that the 1970 invocation of the War Measures Act was just a trial run to see how far he could go in suspending civil liberties in Canada.

After the first session of Canada's twenty-ninth Parliament opened on January 4, 1973, I quickly entered the fray. During the first week, I asked questions of Transport Minister Jean Marchand about Mount Hope Airport outside Hamilton. I was surprised and secretly delighted when he confused it with another Ontario airport. That all made for good local fodder about the hopeless Liberals. The main issues in those early weeks were the government's so-called secret police, the security planning and analysis group under the solicitor general (I had been named secretary of the caucus committee on that department), management of Hamilton Harbour, capital punishment, and the defects of the government's Opportunities for Youth (OFY) programs. I busied myself as an MP in Ottawa on weekdays and back in the riding each weekend.

My seatmate was Peter Reilly, the Conservative MP from Ottawa West. He was a former broadcaster, and the two of us made a scrappy Irish pair, offering a running commentary about the scene around us. He revelled in his own colourful past and told stories on himself, escapades that usually involved women – and always liquor. Once, at a campaign meeting, a bristling question came from an older woman: "Mr. Reilly, is it true that you have a drinking problem and have been married three times?" Reilly faced it head on. "Madam," he said coolly. "If you'd been married three times, you'd have a drinking problem, too." On another occasion when he'd been out on a bender, he returned home late and tried to sneak in quietly. He shed his shoes and his clothes on the way to bed and crawled under the covers, congratulating himself for not waking anyone. He was ready for sleep when he suddenly realized that he'd come to the wrong house and had climbed into bed with a previous wife.

Reilly was forever up to high jinks. When the Ontario Liberal leadership was up for grabs, he penned two notes on House of Commons notepaper. Each read: "Returning to the riding this weekend to meet with delegates to the leadership convention. Will line them up for you if you are ready to run. Please let me know today." Then he affixed an indecipherable signature to the bottom of each. Liberal cabinet ministers John Munro and Eugene Whelan were each sent one of the notes. We then sat back and watched as each of the recipients read his note, squinted at the signature, then turned on his radar screen and looked hopefully around at his colleagues in a vain attempt to identify which Liberal backbencher had sent it.

In the early days of the 1973 session, the new Conservative MPs were briefed by senior caucus members about how to set up an office, how to ask questions and other first-day-of-school information. The best speech came from George Hees, the party's perpetual cheerleader. If a letter with a question came from a constituent, said Hees, you sent it on to the appropriate cabinet minister and then proceeded to take credit for whatever happened. Even an acknowledgement should be passed along to the constituent to let him know you were hard at work on his behalf. "When the minister does reply," went the litany in the rah-rah voice that George could muster for any occasion, "the answer is going to be yes or no. If it's yes, you take credit. If it's no, you blame the government and say 'That's those damn Grits for you.' " What, Hees was asked, would happen if we became the government and our own minister said no. "Well," he replied, "you blame it on those sons of bitches at Treasury Board. Nobody knows who they are, but they're the bad guys."

Hees had another daily song-and-dance routine. As he left the House and passed my desk, he'd gently punch me in the shoulder and say: "That's my boy, Sean. Keep up the great work." One day, George was specific in his kudos. "Saaay, that was a great question you asked the solicitor general yesterday. You keep asking questions like that and we're gonna embarrass this government, we're gonna form a new government and you're the type of guy who's gonna help us do all this." Even my ego couldn't swallow this and I responded, "George, I didn't ask a question. I wasn't even here yesterday." George didn't miss a beat. "Thaaat's my boy, Sean, you know there's not one goddamned vote in that whole department, anyway. You know when to stay quiet, just keep doing that and we'll embarrass this government, we're gonna form a new government and you're the type of guy who's . . ." It was vintage George in overdrive.

My office was in the Confederation Building at the west end of Parliament Hill. There I had two secretaries and kept two more busy in the riding office trying to keep my constituents happy. I became involved in committees on the Hill, particularly Justice and Legal Affairs, because I still retained the hope I would eventually go to law school. I was also interested in the Department of the Solicitor General, so I approached the Tory critic in that area to see if I could assist him. The chief critic was Erik Nielsen, who soon became something of a mentor to me. In those days, Nielsen was a firewagon partisan who detested Liberals and loved to ask tough questions in the House. As a widower who needed money beyond his MP's salary to support his children, he spent a lot of time working as a lawyer in his Yukon riding. His interest in me meant that I could learn much;

his regular absences meant that I could try out my talents in his stead.

Dief and I walked over together to the West Block for the first caucus meeting of the new session. In the recent past, he had rarely attended the weekly Wednesday morning meetings. I convinced him to attend at least this one. I was very excited to be able to go with him. After that first time he didn't return, and my attendance soon fell away, too. I quickly concluded that caucus meetings were a waste of time among windbags making rambling speeches. For a meeting behind closed doors, where everything was supposed to be secret, there was a great deal of posturing. It seemed particularly useless, since as near as I could tell all the major decisions were taken away from caucus in the leader's office anyway. Rather than go and grow in my frustrations with the party, I became content to take the morning off and sleep in.

As the youngest member, I was regularly lumped together with Perrin Beatty, another Ontario member, who was an elderly twenty-two when he was elected for the first time in 1972. While he wanted to be friendly, I was wary of Perrin. He was bright and ambitious and I assumed that, like me, he aspired to reach the top. The age question was tougher on him because he'd often meet people who'd mistakenly say: "Oh, you're the member from Hamilton," or "You're the youngest MP," and he was forever having to establish that he wasn't Sean O'Sullivan. If being Perrin Beatty had its complications, being me wasn't always fun, either. I felt self-conscious about my age and from time to time my innate shyness would return like an unwanted memory to dampen my enthusiasm. I always found it a strain to meet new people and "work" a room of voters, and I am still a bundle of nerves before a major speech.

Although I was reluctant to take on the role, I was cast by some as a spokesman on youth issues. In one sense, it was ironic because my early involvement in politics was at the price of those attitudes and experiences we usually associate with our youth. As an MP, I tried to keep my interests broadly based and stay away from the concerns of youth, but it was a topic on which I had firm views. In one speech, I was particularly hard on my fellow young Canadians. "This country has gradually adopted a policy of overemphasizing the importance of youth, catering to its whims, smothering its difficulties and pampering it at every opportunity," I told a meeting of the Rotary Club of Hamilton on Junior Achievers' Day. "The approach seems to be that a young person need not worry about anything except doing what he pleases. Progress now seems to be measured along a route that starts with student loans – not necessarily to be used for education. And you know you've really made it if you manage the system well enough to collect welfare and unemployment insurance at the same time. Young Canadians have not been done any favours by schemes, however well intentioned, that render them lazy and too contented, lacking ideals; without initiative or self-pride, or concern for their neighbours. If this trend continues, then the meek shall indeed inherit the earth. Nobody else will want it."

I wanted to be the MP for all of Hamilton-Wentworth, however, not just the member for youth. And I wanted to be Sean O'Sullivan, the individual who had earned his seat through the electoral process, not just a protégé of Dief's. At the same time, I was reluctant to charge in; I decided to take my time and wait to earn my stripes. It soon became clear that there was plenty of time. Within a very few months, we were beginning to realize that, with NDP support, the Liberals under wily House Leader Allan MacEachen would be in power for a while. On several occasions, for example, we actually put forth non-confidence motions copied precisely from NDP motions in the previous Parliament. The NDP, worried about being slaughtered in a snap election, preferred to swallow their principles and vote with the government, thus maintaining the Liberals in power.

Questions in the House were a major source of publicity, and every member hoped for the single issue that would make his name a household word. Often such reputations, however, were made at the expense of another MP. My only chance to bring a minister into disrepute came in the form of allegations from two people in my riding that John Munro and some of his cronies had been involved in arranging contracts for Canada Mortgage and Housing Corporation. Rather than raise the matter in the House, I decided to turn the documents over to the RCMP for investigation. Two officers arrived in my office to hear what I knew. During their questioning, they seemed distracted and more interested in a plant that was sitting in the office than the CMHC matter. They wanted to know where the plant had come from. I told them it was a gift from a Hamilton florist. They informed me that it was a marijuana plant. Aghast, I was greatly relieved when, on closer inspection, the plant turned out to be plastic and clearly a joke played by my florist friend. The allegations against Munro were found to be equally lacking in substance.

In looking to learn my craft as an MP, there were many role models around me. I was much impressed with Tory frontbenchers Claude Wagner and Paul Hellyer. Wagner was certainly the best catch of the class of 1972 and inspired me to work hard at becoming bilingual. In the early going, you could tell which MPs were anxious to move up; they were the anglophones who studied French. I was among them. For his part, Hellyer took an active interest in helping young MPs. In that first week, he invited Perrin and me to dinner with his family. It was an evening that began my treasured friendship with Paul and his wife, Ellen.

As the weeks passed, it became clear that not everyone could live up to his advance billing. Claude Wagner was one disappointment. There were such high expectations for him that I don't suppose anybody could. But he was not the politician and tough guy his reputation indicated. Many favourably remembered that he had protected the Queen in Quebec with armoured cars and ordered an attack on protesters that is remembered as "the Saturday of the truncheons." But that hardhat act had been almost a decade earlier, and he was much changed. After his time in Liberal provincial politics, he had served on the bench before becoming a Tory and winning a seat for us in Quebec. But for all his reputation in English Canada as the "hanging judge," he actually could be quite indecisive and was easily rattled. When the going got tough in the 1976 leadership campaign, for example, he wanted to drop out and disappear from the race. For a potential leader, he was soft in the crunch.

In my view, the best parliamentarian from any party was John Turner. He was an impressive figure who even treated new members with respect. He had no inhibitions about letting an opposition member look good, either by helping out with a problem or taking a question seriously in the House. At committee hearings, he'd arrive early, shake every member's hand and make everyone feel important. If a difficult bill was going before a committee, he'd have all the members involved over to his office a few days before his anticipated appearance, pour a few drinks, give us a little jock talk and try to sound out our views. Everyone was made to feel like a confidant. He was a consummate politician who clearly thrived on the exercise of power in the theatre of Parliament.

I saw him off guard only once. My seatmate, Peter Reilly, sent Turner a note once when he was speaking in the House. It read: "Your fly is open." Turner paused in mid-sentence to read the note and the blood drained from his face. He glanced down quickly, then realizing that he'd been had, flushed red in embarrassment.

Turner was eternally the gentleman. Once when he was staying at the Connaught Hotel in Hamilton, he sought out my father just to tell him how proud he should be to have me as a son. Contrast that behaviour with the time my father welcomed Trudeau to the hotel. Trudeau was introduced to my father and said, "Oh, yeah, I know your son. He's a nice young guy. But we're still going to beat him." Such gratuitous rudeness hurt my father and offended me. Trudeau just could not resist the personal putdown.

In the fractious minority Parliament my views on youth and other issues put me on the right wing of the Conservative Party. I was not a bleeding heart; certainly no Red Tory. If my ideology became obvious, so did my capacity for painting myself into a corner by castigating party members who were not of my opinion. For example, in an early interview with the *Ottawa Journal*, reporter Richard Jackson quoted me as saying: "I don't like political labels, but you can put me down as definitely not being a David MacDonald-type Tory." David, an MP from Prince Edward Island, was on the left of the party, a Red Tory, and one of those who had not been loyal to Dief in 1966. If anyone hoped that I wasn't going to help Dief perpetuate those old wars, they soon learned otherwise.

I did attempt to be a team player, however, in parliamentary committee work. One of my more harrowing experiences was a tour of federal prisons that began in July 1973 and continued through to the fall. I was among eight MPs on a committee to investigate prison security in penitentiaries across Canada. The old Kingston Penitentiary and the Prison for Women, also in Kingston, were frightening. One, of course, had been the scene of a 1971 prison riot that left two inmates dead, many injured and parts of the structure in ruins.

The women's prison, the only federal penitentiary for women in Canada, is known as the "zoo"; I found it particularly spooky. Inside, a constant high-pitched noise bombards the ears. It is the combined cry of many inmates who have been found mentally normal by the courts but are, by less technical standards, unbalanced. The surroundings themselves are far from soothing. The place is old and outdated. While men may make macho boasts about their prison terms, confinement seems to have a devastating effect on most women.

In the women's prison, we found every inmate just jammed in with everyone else, regardless of what she had done. There were no distinctions made among offenders according to the need for minimum, medium or maximum security. Young girls who had made a single mistake or committed a crime of passion were thrust in with some of Canada's most hardened criminals. Many of the young ones just looked totally bewildered and lost. Although a few inmates might be reformed, the system rendered it all but impossible, as the alarmingly high recidivism rate clearly showed.

While the women's prison was particularly bad, all of them depressed me. We met with administration officials, but we also met with groups of prisoners in private, away from the guards, and heard their views. In Alberta, we talked with a group of twenty lifers, all of whom had been convicted of murder and appeared to be capable of just about anything. While there was never any suggestion of violence against us, just their response to our group – people they saw as authority figures – was unsettling.

At St. Vincent de Paul Penitentiary, a young French-Canadian prisoner insisted upon meeting me. The prisoner's opening line was: "So you're the youngest MP?" I replied that I was. He said, "You think that's pretty good, I suppose?" I didn't say anything. Then he added, boastfully: "I want to tell you something. I'm the youngest, too. I'm the youngest person in Canada ever to get the 'bitch.' " The prison director later explained that the courts had declared him to be an habitual criminal, a sentence known as the 'bitch' in street jargon. He might never be released from prison. I was twenty-one at the time; he was younger than I was, perhaps nineteen or twenty, and clearly proud of his status.

As a hard-working committee of Parliament, we were anxious, even eager, to find solutions. We heard many submissions and suggestions, but, in the end, the penitentiary system proved to be a situation about which one could only despair. There were too many problems of overcrowding, recidivism, lack of education, inadequate training facilities and, perhaps worst of all, little resolve to improve conditions. We recommended spending more money on trade and training programs and on improvements to facilities. We also recommended conjugal visits. Although such visits have become more common over time, few of our other recommendations were accepted by the government. If I were to take the same tour today, I expect I would find the problems even worse.

The tour and the results were typical of the frustrations a parliamentarian suffers. We were up against entrenched ways of doing things. Governments move slowly in any event, but for change to occur there has to be both political will and support from the bureaucrats. The Department of the Solicitor General was in charge of penitentiaries and was known to be hard-line and disciplinarian. In the department's view, reformers were coddlers. But this is surely short-sighted. Punishment is the reason prisoners are in jail, but they also have to be prepared for the return to society. Little will be accomplished if they are treated like animals in cages, then suddenly released.

There were other specific studies. I was given a special assignment by Stanfield, a study of the Great Lakes and the St. Lawrence Seaway. As the Quebecers might say, "*C'est pas un cadeau*" ("It's not a gift."). I knew full well that it was a makework project, one of the many dreamed up by Stanfield's staff and dished out by the leader in an attempt to make it look as if every MP was part of the "in" crowd with great responsibilities in caucus. I took my assignment seriously and submitted a sixty-one-page report calling for the weak 1972 Canada-U.S. Great Lakes Water Quality Agreement to be upgraded to full treaty status with binding requirements on the United States to improve water quality. It was clear to me, however, that Stanfield's attempts to bring me into the fold were half-hearted.

That team, however, had to get re-elected, me along with it. John Turner's May 1974 budget marked the end of my first term and of the twenty-ninth Parliament. I went home with some small notoriety after the government fell. In a final, fighting speech, Trudeau heaped scorn on all the Tory weaknesses, including our disunity. I was among the scoundrels he cited. After quoting MP Roch LaSalle's comment that there was no room for a Quebecer in the party and Jack Horner's that there was no place for a westerner, either, he quoted me, too. "The honourable member for Hamilton-Wentworth did not go so far," said Trudeau. "He just said that he thought the party should resist control by the experts in Ottawa and in Toronto." Well, he got that right, anyway. We were a ragtag bunch when it came to public togetherness.

None of this hurt me in the riding, however. I was renominated in May and spent my time lashing out at both the Liberals and the NDP for their coalition government during the minority Parliament. My favourite line was: "We've had them both and we've been had. They had their chance and they failed." Inflation was running at 10 per cent, the highest in Canada since 1951. Clearly, the Liberals were vulnerable for the way they had mishandled the economy. The Tories had a policy we said could beat inflation: price and income controls. The trouble was, the policy was unsaleable. Nobody could explain it, and though all the polls said a majority of Canadians favoured controls, individual voters must have had somebody else's wages in mind for the freeze, not their own. Trudeau stumped the country calling controls "a disaster waiting to happen." I tried to avoid the policy altogether. While voters expressed concern about controls, their real worry was leadership. For most Canadians, Stanfield could simply not match Trudeau – even with all his warts.

I did my best, unwittingly of course, to infuriate the brass and maintain my reputation as a rabble-rouser. In mid-campaign I attended a party meeting in Niagara Falls and dropped by at a birthday celebration for John Tory, then youth president. In the small hours of the morning, a radio reporter asked me if Davis would be campaigning for me. The premier wasn't scheduled to visit my riding, so just to indicate how well I felt the campaign was going I said, "No, I'm not having him come into my riding, and the truth is I don't need him." I wrongly assumed that the reporter was off duty, so I failed to indicate that my comments were off the record. Next morning my views led the eight-o'clock newscasts right across the country. I sounded like a snotty kid (which I was) dumping all over my premier (which I wasn't). Well, not that time, anyway.

Within two days, my chief fund raiser, Jack MacDonald, received a missile fired by Toronto headquarters. For my sins against Bill Davis, party election funds designated for my riding were cut off. The "ins" knew how to hurt a guy. The total Hamilton-Wentworth budget was about $30,000. Party headquarters usually paid about half the cost, and local fund raising covered the rest. At that point in the campaign, we were counting on another $8,000 from headquarters. I had just kissed that goodbye.

In desperation, I called Finlay MacDonald. In 1972, he had been national campaign chairman; this time he was a fund raiser for the national campaign. Finlay and I had always been on good terms. When I told him I needed his help, he agreed to find funds, but only if his efforts were kept secret. He didn't want his friends in the Big Blue Machine to know that he was bailing me out. I didn't hear the outcome until after the election but, as usual, Finlay's thinking was nothing short of inspired. While he couldn't raise the full $8,000, he did find $5,000 with one phone call. The source: John Angus (Bud) McDougald, chairman of Argus Corp. and self-proclaimed dean of the Canadian business establishment. McDougald was Catholic and, even more helpful in my case, regarded himself as a true-blue right-winger and therefore had little regard for Bill Davis. Finlay, of course, knew that and painted a picture of me to McDougald as a struggling young Catholic candidate battling Davis as well as the Liberals. McDougald was delighted to contribute, as much to thumb his nose at Davis as anything else.

The election results were catastrophic for the Conservative Party. In 1972, the Liberals had elected 109 MPs, the Conservatives 107, the NDP 31, the Socreds and others 17. In 1974, the Liberals elected 141; the Conservatives fell to 95 and the NDP were reduced to 16. In the Hamilton area, only four of the ten Conservative incumbents managed to hang on. Canadians may not have liked the Liberal-NDP coalition government, but they wanted Conservatives even less. I was re-elected with a reduced 1,005-vote majority, although my actual vote total went up. Although my margin was substantially reduced from 1972, I was still one of the lucky ones. I had come in with the 1972 tide and I was nearly swept out when it ebbed. Among the television commentators that night as election results were reported was Robert Nixon, Liberal MLA for Brant-Oxford-Norfolk and now Treasurer of Ontario in the government of David Peterson. At one point he turned to Jack MacDonald, who was also on hand as an analyst, and said, "If your boy can hang onto that seat tonight, it'll be his forever."

Bob Nixon was right. If I could survive that debacle, I could probably withstand anything in Hamilton-Wentworth. Yet misgivings about a lifetime in politics were beginning to set in. Deep within myself, I faced new questions about my life's direction, although I didn't yet know where to turn. So, I followed standard procedures for all good Tories when they don't know what else to do: I joined the firing squad, and we formed a circle and began shooting inward.

CHAPTER FIVE

WAR STORIES
AND BEAVER TALES

I was a parliamentary guerrilla. It's in my makeup to be a fighter, and after the 1974 election I became even more anti-establishment. In fact, during my final three years in Ottawa, I burnished the role to an unseemly sheen. There are those who claim that the constant fighting within the Progressive Conservative Party was somehow over its ideological soul, but that's not why the right-wingers and the Red Tories usually did battle. The rivalry was simply fighting between the "ins," who controlled the machinery, and the "outs," who feared they would forever stay far from the levers of power. In the end, however, both sides were responsible for the disgraceful and public party blood-letting. We were all to blame.

During the minority government of 1972-74, there was an uneasy truce. The "outs" saw Robert Stanfield as a benign leader who, with a modicum of luck, had happened to take us within two seats of forming a government. We were prepared to hold our fire and see if he led us all the way into power. The flawed 1974 campaign ended any hope of that. Stanfield's unpopular policy of wage and price controls had hurt all of our local campaigns and halted the parliamentary futures of friends who were not re-elected.

The party went into the 1974 election running badly behind the Liberals. Inflation was an issue; the Tories had an answer – wage and price controls. Controls had been urged by several MPs and some of Stanfield's policy advisors, and the party adopted the policy after the 1972 election. The policy included a ninety-day freeze on all prices and incomes during which time the rest of the program would be devised. In the heat of the election campaign, however, Stanfield was pressed for details daily and was forced to become more and more specific. With each mention of another area of the economy to be affected, new howls of protest would arise. Many Tory candidates began distancing themselves from the policy. Dief was one of several who denounced controls publicly. In the end, however, while controls were unpopular with voters, Canadians simply preferred Trudeau to Stanfield, particularly in Ontario. After the débâcle there was quiet for a few weeks while the party healed its hurts. Then Stanfield called a caucus meeting in Ottawa for August 14. This was one caucus gathering I would not miss. The *entente cordiale* was over.

The rebels were ready. Throughout his tenure, Stanfield had never really had the full support of all the Conservative MPs. While he did have a few loyalists in caucus, his main backing came from a non-elected Maritime Mafia that included backroom brokers like Dalton Camp and Finlay MacDonald. In addition, he had technocrats like Norman Atkins and his band of volunteer hotshots, who often rode roughshod over party locals during election planning.

Dalton Camp has set the style for Tory politics in Canada during the last thirty years. Since the 1950s he has been a publicist and speechwriter who guided several leaders and their parties in federal politics as well as in New Brunswick, Nova Scotia, Manitoba and Ontario. He became the federal party's director of publicity in 1955 and worked on the 1957 and 1958 campaigns under Dief. His political successes led to rewards in the form of advertising contracts (mainly tourism accounts) for his own ad agency, and in 1964 he was elected federal party president. The Liberals had won a minority government in 1963 and when they won again in 1965, Camp became the focus for those in the party who wanted Diefenbaker removed in favour of a new leader. A 1966 speech Camp gave at Toronto's Tory hangout, the Albany Club, calling for a leadership review began a bitter process that divided the party until very recently.

Norman Atkins, Dalton's brother-in-law, has become increasingly more prominent as Dalton has withdrawn from the day-to-day running of his ad agency, Camp Associates. In recent years Norman took over the firm as its president, until he resigned when appointed to the Senate in 1986. All the while Dalton was devising the words a Bill Davis or a Robert Stanfield might deliver, Norman was developing the loyal, volunteer organization (known as the Big Blue Machine) that would do everything from market the individual candidates in the ridings to fill the hall for the leader's speech. Norman's political career took off in 1971 when he ran Allan Lawrence's campaign for Ontario leader and was embraced by winner Bill Davis. In all, Norman and his team have been involved in some three dozen political campaigns across Canada. Together, Norman and Dalton form the best one-two punch in Canadian politics.

I had come into the party scarred at a young age by the events of 1966. Given our different backgrounds, then, perhaps Stanfield and I were never destined to be close. He probably thought I was too young to be an effective MP. To him I was an unabashed Diefenbaker loyalist who didn't have the maturity to control my emotions or my impulses.

My participation in meetings with him could hardly have changed his mind. I remember one discussion among a number of MPs that revolved around a letter to Stanfield from the Canadian Manufacturer's Association. The CMA castigated him on a number of topics and then showed poor form by making the letter public before Stanfield even received it. In my youthful enthusiasm and a desire to show that I was "on side" with him and against such high-handed behaviour, I said: "I think you should tell them to stick it up their ass." His withering look suggested that not only did he think it was the wrong thing to say, he expected no better from unbridled youth.

Stanfield and I simply had chemistry problems. He was a very private man who could neither get close to people nor allow others past his guard. He was also too cerebral. In my view, a party leader should operate more on raw emotion than careful compromise. I wanted to debate the issues; Stanfield wanted to defuse them. I was an Irish fighter; he was an Isaiah figure. He said, "Come let us reason together." I followed the path described in the old Irish folk song:

We tried to smooth things over
But they soon began to fight,
And me bein' strictly neutral,
I bashed everyone in sight.

Stanfield's steady perseverance and calming methods, however, did help him withstand tremendous abuse, both from the party and the press. That earned him my respect and admiration, although not my complete loyalty or affection. Even so, there were few harsh words between us. Our relations were always cordial, if a bit strained. We just felt awkward around each other; we practised different political styles.

After the dismal election results of 1974, it was time for him to go. Stanfield was scheduled to speak to that August caucus meeting. As Dief would say, he would be defending the indefensible. Ontario's Big Blue Machine had worked full out for Stanfield and fallen flat. I made my views public even before the meeting. In an article that ran in the *Globe and Mail* the morning of the caucus meeting, I was quoted as saying: "The Big Blue Machine blew it. It's one of the rules in politics that if you're given a free hand to run a campaign and you don't win it, then you have to walk the plank. So it's their turn." I said that Stanfield could stay on as an interim leader – but only for a specific period. I wanted to know the exact date of his departure. I also demanded that "the Big Blue Machine be disbanded for the federal party and that headquarters be cleaned out."

My demands were only partly met. Stanfield did announce that he would step down – but he did not say precisely when, only that a leadership convention would be called within two years. Peter Reilly was alone in making a case for Stanfield to stay. The rest of the caucus accepted his decision to resign with little or no protest. There was, however, no indication at all that the Big Blue Machine was finished, too. In fact, in the days ahead, this group – which had lost three successive federal elections – began to battle back in an apparent bid to retain control.

One of the shots was fired by W.S. Thomson, a businessman from Oakville, Ontario, and vice-president of the Ontario PCs. Thomson wrote to rap my knuckles for outspokenness: "I am sorry to read once again that you have been sounding off about the Big Blue Machine. We are not prepared to be criticized in the press by either young people or old people who still have a lot to learn. Anytime, therefore, that you publicly criticize the Big Blue Machine, you are criticizing me, and other people have found out the hard way that I am a damn tough adversary."

This was all just so much self-serving guff. I held the letter up to the light and could see that Thomson had eliminated certain lines with erasing fluid. He had hidden the part showing that copies of his letter had been sent to Bill Davis and top party officials. I wrote him a blistering reply that said, in part: "With arrogance, disdain for elected members, and disdain for the party rank and file, the members of the Big Blue Machine also take it upon themselves to discourage any expression of opinion contrary to their own. This high-handed approach is an affront to democracy, particularly within a party as diverse as the Progressive Conservative Party. Accordingly, I do reject the threat in your correspondence."

Once I made his threat and my letter public, and said I was seeking legal advice, Thomson backed down. He maintained that no copies of his letter had been sent to anyone; he had intended the letter to be a private matter. Nor had he meant his views to be interpreted as threatening. I was not mollified by his explanation and remained outraged at his attempts to intimidate me.

There were other direct exchanges with the BBM. That same month, I attended the wedding of a friend, Michael Weedon, who was marrying a niece of Bill Davis. Davis also attended the ceremony. It was the first time we'd met since my Niagara Falls remarks about how little I needed his campaigning help. The afternoon turned into a series of snide jabs between the two of us. In my defence, I can only say that he fired the first salvo. I was helping myself to a glass of punch when he noticed that his daughter, Meg, was pouring punch for herself from another bowl. He stopped her, saying in a loud voice, "No, Meg, that's not the one for you. Go take some from the one Sean's using. That's the punch for the kiddies."

The bickering continued. One of the wedding guests challenged Davis on the legislated use of seat belts, a controversial topic then very much in the news in Ontario. Davis launched into a practised and long-winded defence of seat belts. He set an imaginary scene in which he and his questioner were in two cars that collided. He painted the possible outcomes with and without seat belts. The conclusion to his spiel went something like this: "If neither of us were wearing seat belts, chances are that both of us would be dead." "Well," I said dryly, "I suppose *that* would make the news." Davis just stared straight ahead and said nothing. There was an awkward silence all round.

On another occasion, at a Parliamentary Press Gallery dinner in Ottawa, I dragged the official photographer over to Davis and put my arm around the premier. He could do nothing but paste on a smile and put up with me while the photo memento was snapped. Davis's long-time assistant, Clare Westcott, spotted my manoeuvre and was irate. "That's it," he was heard to say, "I'm going to kill that little bastard." He had to be restrained from lunging toward me. That's how far the relationship had deteriorated between Davis and me.

My rudeness toward fellow Tories wasn't reserved only for leaders. Flora MacDonald was a favourite target for Diefenbaker loyalists. She had been fired years earlier by Dief from her job at party headquarters, and she remained a symbol of the pro-Camp element and the Red Tory wing of the Party. One night when she was in Stoney Creek to speak at a Robbie Burns dinner, I couldn't resist taking a shot at her. I took note of the fact that Flora had recently been voted Citizen of the Year in Kingston, Ontario; then, reworking an old vaudeville line, I remarked: "I guess that means we can say Flora MacDonald is one of the finest women ever to walk the streets of Kingston."

As at most Burns dinners, the audience was sufficiently well-lubricated for the line to go over well. When I returned to Ottawa, I repeated it to Dief. He hooted and insisted that I write it out for him. He quickly adopted it as his own by phoning everyone on his list, beginning with Olive, to tell them. In time, after Dief had repeated the description often enough, the line found its way into print and was attributed to him.

Flora was the butt of another of my jokes. This one, however, was quickly and all too accurately attributed to me. Television producer and well-known commentator Larry Zolf, a weekly contributor to CBC Radio's "As It Happens," featured political gossip in his report, Ottawa goings-on in particular. I was one of his many regular sources. During the 1976 leadership convention, he wrote a piece for the *Toronto Sun* in which he listed me as a "very good and close friend."

As a tongue-in-cheek response, I dictated to Bunny Pound, by then my secretary, a parody of one of Richard Nixon's Watergate-era

94

statements. The one I was mimicking was issued when he was forced to release the tapes that proved he had misled the American people, while holding to his claim that the revelations did not justify his impeachment. I gave Bunny this statement to be read to Larry: "I have today instructed Ron Ziegler to issue the following statement on my behalf: 'While the *Sun* article places at considerable variance my previous statements, today's revelation in the *Sun* of being "a very good and close friend of Larry Zolf" does not in my opinion justify the drastic measures of impeachment. Accordingly, and despite the cover having been blown by Mr. Zolf, I shall refuse to turn over the tapes of our conversation to the special prosecutor. Moreover, I have no intention of walking away from the high office to which I have been twice elected. Rather I shall continue to serve the national purpose and am continuing today in St. John's, Nfld., and throughout various centres of Canada, my search for the one lonely motel which bears the plaque, "Flora MacDonald has not slept here." '

Larry enjoyed the statement so much that he quoted it in full on radio that same day. It also ran verbatim in Joey Slinger's column in the *Toronto Sun*. I had to phone Flora, make feeble excuses and apologize. To her credit, she was forgiving. (I have to say that even though we were on opposite sides of most issues, I have a great respect for her as a real trouper.) The attempted humour, however, demonstrated the them-*versus*-us attitude that dominated caucus.

After the 1974 election, I began to preach an "outs" message in various constituencies saying that it was time to return political power to the caucus and the rank-and-file party members. I argued that a conspiracy of power brokers had shunted the rest of us aside. I told audiences that some Conservatives seem "to be enamoured with the politics of complacency [and] subscribe to the cop-out belief that 'he who goes along, gets along.' " I warned that forces were at work to run the next leadership convention for their own ends. "We must actively resist any attempts by a powerful, well-organized group to gain control of the convention arrangements." I gave the speech in ten ridings and in many of them the words struck a responsive chord. The fiery rhetoric was not welcomed everywhere, of course. When I spoke in Prince Edward Island in April 1975, I got my first and only half-standing-ovation. Half the audience loved my message and stood to applaud. The other half of the gathering sat silent and glowered at me.

Not all the anti-establishment activity in the party was so public. The most common form of backroom bickering occurred in the regular bitch sessions in Jack Horner's parliamentary office. The MPs who gathered included a number of irregulars, but there was a core crowd who came together late most nights to drink and dwell upon the sorry state of the Conservative Party. Jack provided the main entertainment, pacing back and forth and complaining that his years in the party and his loyalty to the cause had brought him no recognition. The party, Horner proclaimed, was being destroyed from within by Stanfield and his staff, sellouts to Quebec and bilingualism.

For all his rough-and-tumble ways, however, Jack had an insecure side. He felt more misunderstood than menacing. One night, he stopped in the middle of his fiery rhetoric and thrust his face close against mine. "A lot of people think of Jack Horner as a son of a bitch. I'm not," he insisted. "I'm just Happy Jack." Dief loved that line when I told him and would often ask me to repeat it. For all the rabble rousing, however, there was no organized plotting against Stanfield carried out in Jack's office. It was just a blowhole on the beached whale that was the Conservative Party.

In retrospect, I am far prouder of my role as father of the Beaver Bill than of any part I played in guerrilla warfare. My Beaver Bill had its beginnings when Bernard Smith, a New York state senator, introduced a bill in January 1975 to make the beaver a state symbol. *Toronto Sun* reporter Mark Bonokowski heard about his plan, saw it as an infringement on Canada's heritage and called the protector of all things Canadian: John Diefenbaker. Keith Martin took the call. Dief was away, so Keith, sensing a good issue, told Bonokowski to call me. When I heard the details I told Bonokowski that New York's action was inappropriate. "What are we going to do about it?" he asked. Although I wasn't sure how far I could go, I sounded a clarion call anyway. "I will introduce legislation to protect the beaver as our symbol." He went to press with the story; I was committed to act.

The beaver, long associated with Canada had, surprisingly, no official status. This furry rodent, which can grow to three feet in length and weigh up to sixty pounds, was a major reason Canada had been of any interest at all to Europeans three hundred years ago and should have been a national symbol. It had graced our first postage stamp, was pictured on the five-cent piece, and was everyone's symbol of industry. "Beavering away" was part of the language. Now the beaver was about to be kidnapped by Americans. It was a great issue, a non-partisan issue and one that was already receiving media attention. It was a politician's dream. I claimed it for my own.

With the help of the experts in the party's research office, I came up with one of the simplest bills ever drafted. It consisted of one sentence: "Her Majesty and Parliament here assembled proclaim an Act to Provide for the Recognition of the Beaver (*Castor Canadensis*) as a Symbol of the Sovereignty of the Dominion of Canada." It was introduced as Bill C-373 on January 24. That might have been the end of it, since private members' bills rarely go anywhere in Parliament, except that "As It Happens" took up the cause. When host Barbara Frum asked me what Canadians could do to get action, I urged them to write to their MPs and send a copy of the letter to then secretary of state, Hugh Faulkner.

Barbara Frum and I quickly became the crusaders, with Faulkner cast as the uncaring bureaucrat. Not too many days passed before Faulkner sent me an example of the kind of letter he was receiving, just to show me how outrageous some of them were. In so doing, however, he forgot to remove a note attached by his staff saying: "Minister, for your information, at last count we had received more than 10,000 letters." That's an extraordinary amount of mail for any minister to receive on a single issue. With those kind of numbers, I knew the bill was a hit. In addition to the letters to Faulkner, the CBC gathered 13,000 signatures on a petition.

Behind the scenes, Keith Martin spoke to the Liberals to see if the bill could be passed. Ordinarily, it is not in the interest of the government of the day to let such a bill pass because it means publicity for a member of the opposition. As a result, private members' bills are traditionally "talked out," that is, allowed to be debated in the House then sent down to the bottom of the Commons agenda, the order paper, and never allowed to come to a vote. In the preceding twenty-two years, for example, only forty-eight private members' bills had passed. Most of those covered minor housekeeping matters, such as an MP changing the name of his riding to include another local geographical reference.

This issue, however, had a high media profile and there was growing public pressure, so the government agreed to proceed with the bill. The deal struck was that, yes, as long as there was no partisanship involved, the bill would be brought forward, there would be minimal debate, and it would come to a vote and pass. I approached Senator Muriel McQueen Ferguson, former Speaker of the Senate, who agreed to introduce the bill in the other place. As a Liberal senator, her involvement made it a bipartisan issue. The Liberal caucus agreed that it would neither promote nor oppose the bill.

When the bill came forward on February 21 for second reading I told the House: "There must be more to life than just financial facts and figures. There must be things to touch one's soul, heart, and emotions if we are to be complete persons and a whole nation. That is the importance of symbols." John Turner, the senior minister in the House that day, promised government co-operation in referring the bill to the Justice and Legal Affairs Committee, where it was discussed on March 12. There, one of the Liberal MPs, Robert Stanbury, noted that I had used the traditional Tory wording, "Her Majesty and Parliament here assembled." The Liberals had done away with the monarchist preamble, so those words were deleted. With that lone change, safe passage followed. The bill became law and the beaver became an official national symbol.

The Beaver Bill may not have improved the Canadian standard of living, but an oversight had been corrected. Now, along with the coat of arms and the maple leaf, the beaver is a safeguarded and official symbol of the country. Once the bill received Royal Assent in the Senate on March 24, there was a high-powered celebration that included two future prime ministers, Joe Clark (who had seconded the bill) and John Turner, representing the government. Also on hand was a future chief justice of the Supreme Court, Brian Dickson, acting on behalf of ailing Governor General Jules Léger. We gathered on the Hill for a Beaver Bill party, complete with champagne. Canadian, of course.

The response in the country was positive. A Toronto billboard company erected a congratulatory sign and Canadians sent me beavers of every description. There were stainless-steel and ceramic beavers, beaver paperweights and bookmarks, paintings and photographs of beavers. Within days, I had the largest collection of beavers seen in Canada since the days of the fur trade. I even added a beaver design to the official frank on my parliamentary mailings.

Among the gifts was a particularly unusual presentation from Bryce Mackasey, then postmaster general. On the afternoon the bill passed, Mackasey called me to his office. He explained that he had wanted to give me a giant framed print of the first postage stamp Canada issued, the threepenny beaver. The picture was on display at Post Office departmental headquarters. When he told his officials of his plan they advised him that it was not possible to give away government property. Mackasey was undeterred. He and his assistant, Pat Norris, hatched a plan. As Mackasey explained it to me: "Pat and I did what any self-respecting Irishman would do. We waited until three o'clock last night and went in and took it off the wall." Then Mackasey presented it to me.

While I was taking the high road with the Beaver Bill and looking to leave at least a small legacy of my time on the Hill, I was also working feverishly behind the scenes with one of the most publicized – and least understood – ginger groups in the Conservative Party. The "Chateau Cabinet," as it later came to be known, had its beginnings almost immediately after the July 1974 election when former party president Don Matthews began phoning party members across the country to sound out their views on the future.

Although Matthews had every reason to be bitter, his purpose was to rebuild. After becoming president in 1971, he had been defeated for the position in 1974 by Michael Meighen. Meighen, the grandson of Prime Minister Arthur Meighen, was seen by many of us "outs" as a front for the Camp forces. We felt that it was just another way *they* could retain control of all elements of the party. Unlike the power brokers, Matthews, a developer from London, Ontario, was a self-made man. He was a hard worker and had support right across the party for his no-nonsense ways. He didn't kowtow to the Toronto crowd and he didn't dodge problems. His favourite saying was,

"Let's get the codfish on the table and see how it smells."

I had supported Matthews for president and nominated him at the 1974 general meeting. We "outs" felt that Meighen's victory was unfairly gained, with the assistance of people at party headquarters who should have stayed neutral. The "outs" felt cheated. I well remember the national director, John Laschinger – who was among those who should have been neutral – saying to me: "How can you support that stupid son of a bitch [Matthews]?" The Camp forces wouldn't even let us have one elected position among all the party jobs. They wanted it all.

I complained vigorously about their actions to Stanfield during a ninety-minute meeting in his office. Stanfield wouldn't believe that his appointed officials had taken sides, and he particularly refused to believe what Laschinger had said to me. "I'm not a liar, sir," I told him. "He said it to me; I'm saying it to you." Stanfield tried to take the conversation into the future and talk about the next election and the need for unity. "There are more important things to do than to carry on old fights. We've got to get ready to fight the Liberals." I wouldn't back down. "It would certainly help if one felt that it was worthwhile fighting the Liberals and that our efforts were not going to be done in by our own, as this party constantly seems to." This was a not-so-subtle reference to what had been done to Dief and, by implication, Stanfield's role in that.

The conversation deteriorated into sullen glares on both sides. Finally, after several minutes of silence on both sides, I said, "Well, I guess that's life in the big city." Then I rose and walked out. About the same time, Newfoundland MP John Lundrigan wrote to Stanfield resigning from the party because of the support Meighen had received from headquarters staff. Stanfield was able to talk him out of that step. Jack Horner also threatened to bolt, but was convinced by friends to stay. Stanfield finally apologized at a caucus meeting, saying that whatever help headquarters staff had been to Meighen had been without his, Stanfield's, knowledge.

By December, 1974, Don Matthews had organized a lunch meeting in Toronto. Attendees included: former Ontario premier John Robarts; Arthur Harnett, provincial director of the party under Robarts; MP Tom Cossitt; Tom Warrington, a Toronto party organizer; and myself. The most enthusiastic attendee was not a party member at all. He was Kim Abbott, a former official in the Department of Manpower and Immigration. Abbott had quit his job over disagreements with Trudeau's policies and was a most mysterious character. He had no visible means of support, yet he seemed to have the time and resources to travel and promote his views. He moved freely within many circles in both the Conservative and Liberal parties, and from time to time we wondered where his loyalties lay. In the beginning, however, he was seen by all of us as someone who had spotted the excesses of the Trudeau regime early on. He argued that if Trudeau wasn't a communist, he was certainly taking Canada in that direction. He also felt that the Conservative Party was not offering an effective opposition. The party had to be galvanized. Other Canadians should be brought under its umbrella, and Trudeau had to be thrown out of office. Most of us who attended those early meetings had no such firm ideological bent. We simply disliked the direction our party had taken in the past.

For Matthews, the meeting was all about a new leader, and he had already made his choice: Robarts. A strategy paper was circulated. Its first point stated that "it is vital that before we select a new leader we must have some idea of where we would like him to lead us." Robarts left the meeting early in order to allow debate; in fact, he did not appear to be anxious for the job. The meeting ended with two people designated to convince Robarts he should run.

They were unsuccessful. Robarts remained adamant that he would not be a candidate. At the next meeting, on January 18, 1975, at a Toronto airport hotel, Matthews produced a list of every possible leadership candidate, thirty-two in all. We struck the names of those who would never gain the support of the right wing (Flora and Dalton, for example), and after several more hours of consideration, we again seemed to have settled on Robarts as the most acceptable to the group. Matthews was authorized to make another, more desperate appeal to Robarts in the hope of changing his mind.

The process appeared to be all but halted. It was only by chance that the Chateau Cabinet came about. After the meeting, I stood talking to Tom Cossitt in the hotel lobby. Kim Abbott suddenly appeared and announced that his car battery was dead and that his car would not start. While he awaited the arrival of a tow truck, the three of us went to the coffee shop to continue our conversation. It was this impromptu session that eventually led to the formation of the Chateau Cabinet. Cossitt and Abbott were violently anti-Trudeau. Cossitt had once been a Liberal and had led a walkout of the Leeds Liberal constituency executive just prior to the 1972 election. He had subsequently become a Tory. In Parliament, Cossitt tormented Trudeau about his office expenditures, the identity of those who paid for his swimming pool and the size of his liquor bill. Over coffee, we agreed that there was a need to alter both the philosophy and hierarchy of the party. We also agreed that Robarts was unlikely to get much caucus support, even if Matthews were successful in convincing him to stand. We decided that the three of us should get together weekly in Ottawa and search for kindred souls who might attend our meetings.

We drew up a list of thirty-six MPs we thought would be receptive to our views. The most responsive prospects were MPs who were not major parliamentary players in the party structure. They were the "outs," the "small c" conservatives whom Stanfield had not chosen to be official spokesmen on issues. In the days ahead, we made our careful approaches and, on the evening of March 12, 1975, met in the Quebec Suite of the Château Laurier Hotel. Because the group included no members of Stanfield's hand-picked "shadow cabinet," in a play on words, I named the group the Chateau Cabinet.

Thirty people attended, including twenty-seven Conservative MPs, a party organizer from British Columbia, Kim Abbott, and Leonard Jones, the only independent MP. All who were there came out of a sense of disgruntlement, a feeling of frustration that if we remained isolated backbenchers nothing would change, but if we gathered together, we might have some strength as a group within the party or at the next leadership convention. Everyone agreed that the session should be kept secret.

Abbott chaired the meeting and began proceedings by telling the group that we could discuss the coming leadership convention – but not the merits of any individual candidates. There was a feeling that unity among this diverse group behind any single candidate was unlikely. Instead, Abbott argued that we should formulate what he called "touchstones" or guidelines that were representative of our approach to government. To gain support of such a large bloc of MPs as this, candidates would have to respond to the call for a return to conservative values. The candidate who most fully reflected the touchstone issues would gain the support of the Chateau Cabinet's members.

Abbott had drawn up a draft manifesto for consideration. It was his document; he had not shown it to anyone prior to the meeting. Of the twenty points, for example, four related to public service reforms dear to his heart. While there was some sympathy for his views, the MPs present found his points woefully inadequate and lacking both the rhetorical impact and the subtlety of a politician's touch.

Debate about the manifesto continued for the next three hours, with MP Ron Huntington acting as secretary to record the views put forward and the changes suggested. As the hour approached midnight, we agreed to adjourn and meet again in a week once Huntington had organized his notes and compiled a revised manifesto for the group's consideration. Several weeks later, Huntington had not yet put all the points into political jargon, although he had written more than seventy-five pages and was still hard at work. That night, however, we felt invigorated and hopeful that the party could be put back on what we liked to call the "right track." We saw ourselves – and expected we would be seen by others – as crusaders, not insurgents.

How wrong we were. The heady exhilaration of that evening was short-lived. By the time the Commons met the following day, word of the meeting had already leaked to other MPs. The Chateau Cabinet quickly came to be characterized as a group of right-wingers whose sole purpose was to speed the exit of Stanfield and reverse any progress the party had made in Quebec. At the next caucus meeting, a week after the first Chateau Cabinet meeting, there were several emotional attacks on the group. Stanfield spoke, saying that the only place for such discussions was in caucus itself. He urged MPs to choose the next leader based on their own personal assessments rather than as part of any factional bloc. He also said that he "expected members to refrain from holding any more secret meetings."

Cossitt, Abbott and I were undaunted. We concluded that the

party brass wanted the meetings to end chiefly out of fear that we might actually succeed in changing the direction of the party. We decided to continue our efforts, but with a lower profile. The media soon caught wind of the group, however, and Cossitt was interviewed. He kept to a predetermined strategy of refusing to reveal the names of members (except his own and mine as founders) and described the group as a collection of MPs who were concerned about the country's future and who had met and would continue to meet in order to discuss policies and principles. With the bright sunlight of publicity, however, some members of the Chateau Cabinet ran for cover. In April and May four more meetings were held, but attendance never matched the original thirty. At one meeting, for example, although twenty promised to attend, only eight showed up. Policy matters were no longer on the agenda. Most of the discussion centred on the bad publicity we had received and whether we should continue meeting.

One of the Chateau Cabinet members, Douglas Alkenbrack, MP for the eastern-Ontario riding of Frontenac-Lennox-Addington, was scheduled to address a service club meeting in March. Because he agreed fully with Abbott's draft manifesto, he decided that he would simply read it to his audience rather than spend time writing a speech for the occasion. In addition, he made a copy of the manifesto available to a local paper, the Napanee *Beaver*. If the manifesto had gained no wider circulation than that, there might have been no problem. The editor of the Napanee weekly, however, was also a correspondent for the *Globe and Mail*. It took some time for the manifesto to wend its way into national print, but on June 28, the more controversial points of the document were presented in the *Globe* as firm policies of the Chateau Cabinet under the headline "Chateau Group Eyes Plan to Drop Fully Bilingual Civil Service."

We couldn't disown the manifesto, since Abbott had done so much to bring the group together; on the other hand, we hadn't endorsed it either, because much of it was so reactionary. The press, *Globe and Mail* columnist Geoffrey Stevens among them, used the draft manifesto to beat us black and blue. "A peculiar political manifesto," Stevens called it, going on to label its authors "a funny band of mavericks and disgruntled right-wingers." It was no such thing; we hadn't even approved it. All the group was trying to say was that there was a place and a time for a "small c" conservative party. We felt that we had to be responsive to a large constituency of Canadians who felt abandoned.

The political world, however, saw us differently. We were perceived and portrayed as a militant right-wing group because most members favoured retaining the death penalty for murder, were against abortion, for the monarchy, and against big government, welfare, and handouts. We wanted the state to stop interfering in business, and we favoured cutbacks on immigration because of the high unemployment levels. To be sure, many were against bilingualism, although I, for one, disagreed with them on that issue. I saw the Chateau Cabinet not as a right-wing group but as a body that wanted to move the party toward the right and in so doing put the party in the centre of the political spectrum. For too long we had been out in left field.

The unfortunate result of Alkenbrack's speech was to fix this working document firmly in the public mind as our policy statement. It wasn't. If we stood for anything, it was a return to traditional small-town Canadian values. After all, that's where most of us came from; those were the people who had elected us. We didn't want to please the Ottawa bureaucracy or the Toronto intelligentsia or the party establishment. Instead, we wanted to speak for Canadians who had no voice. In the ridings, our constituents were telling us that they were fearful; they didn't like the direction the country was headed. Many Canadians felt that no one had the courage to stand up and talk about the worthwhile values and the solid strengths that had built the country. The Chateau Cabinet was simply a group of elected MPs who wanted to take the Conservative Party closer to those views. It was all very much along the lines of what populist U.S. President Harry Truman had said about his time in Washington: "I tried never to forget who I was and where I'd come from and where I was going back to."

With all the national publicity about the manifesto, Stanfield wrote to me on July 18, requesting a copy of, as he put it, "a document containing the views of the group." I wrote a snippy reply: "The media reports have dealt with a draft document presented by one participant for discussion purposes only. As such, the document has no official status, nor does it represent the views of all in attendance. Should an official statement be compiled for release," I continued, "you will, of course, be the first to receive a copy."

Not satisfied with this, Stanfield wrote to me again to say that the document "has taken on a life of its own. . . [and] contains proposals which will do incalculable damage to the party if these proposals are regarded as having Conservative support." Because the House was about to rise for the summer and I knew Stanfield was taking some holidays, I did not reply. For the first time in their seven years as parliamentary colleagues, Stanfield and Doug Alkenbrack had a private conversation. It lasted long enough for Stanfield to request a copy of the manifesto. Alkenbrack, delighted by the sudden attention paid him by the press and his leader, sent Stanfield two copies.

In July, Tom Cossitt suffered a heart attack. That, combined with a long summer recess, meant that interest in the Chateau Cabinet and its manifesto waned. Until, that is, the House was set to reopen in October and Dalton Camp attacked us in his newspaper column. He called the group "an element in the Party determined to destroy it, who made Stanfield's leadership untenable, who hurried the party prematurely to convention, and who are, at this writing, determining to manage the proceedings." In fact, the Chateau Cabinet had become a shadow of its former self. There were no more meetings; Huntington never did present the final manifesto for study. It was rather reminiscent of the scene in Arthur Miller's *Death of a Salesman* when Willy Loman insists that "attention must be paid." The plea was equally successful in both cases.

During this period of party introspection, there was even a brief flurry of press speculation that I might be a leadership candidate. There was never anything to the story. It was just a rumour promoted by Keith Martin, who told someone in the Parliamentary Press Gallery that up to $500,000 might be available for my run at the top. While I didn't embrace the story when approached for confirmation, I played along with the game and didn't exactly deny it very strongly, either. I rolled the same line Stanfield had used a decade earlier when, as premier of Nova Scotia, he was asked whether he would run for party leader. Said Stanfield then, and said I in 1975: "I have considered it [a leadership bid] in much the same way I have considered ski jumping." After all, even the toughest guerrilla warriors can't take everything seriously. Especially themselves.

In addition to such harmless and not-so-harmless banter around Ottawa, I also enjoyed being a minor player on the international stage. A decade ago, when I was an MP, foreign junkets were a commonplace perq on the Ottawa scene for Senators, Members of the House of Commons and the Press Gallery as well. Salary and expense allowances were considerably less than today. As a result, these junkets were an inexpensive way to travel and a widely accepted form of lobbying by governments friendly with Canada or who wished to be on better terms with us.

There were three countries any MP could visit on a whim: Taiwan, South Africa and Israel. All you had to do was allow your interest to become known to the appropriate people in Ottawa and trip arrangements were quickly made at the host country's expense. During my time as an MP, I visited all three of those countries and many other destinations as well.

Today, these trips are depicted in the media as suspicious at best, blatant buyouts at worst. Most journalists are under instructions from their employers to turn down such "freebies" and have, therefore, become more critical of politicians who do accept them. Certainly no trip I took ever resulted in any host government or agency gaining any unfair favour from or through me. The notion that an MP is somehow compromised by accepting the hospitality of a foreign government is demeaning to elected men and women. You don't have to leave Ottawa or deal with foreign nationals to sacrifice personal integrity for personal gain, if that's what an MP chooses to do.

The issue comes down to a basic question of trust. Either an MP is going to merit the title "Honourable Member" or he is not. An MP's constituents will soon know the answer and render their judgement. Canadians must either trust their MPs or distrust them. Having known and worked with so many, I am for trusting them. Author Bruce Hutchison put it succinctly in his book, *The Far Side of the Street*. He said: "Unlike most reporters who regard cynicism as necessary

107

equipment, I speak of Canadian politicians with respect, knowing them as a species to be more honest on average, and usually more intelligent, than the men of the professions and business."

Despite the suspicion such foreign trips have raised, I saw them – and see them today – as a legitimate exercise in promoting international understanding, gaining further insight into the brotherhood of humankind and promoting peace through dialogue and mutual understanding. Part of my education in life, then, included trips to England, Germany, Belgium, Israel and half a dozen other countries in the Middle East, along with South Africa, Chile, Bolivia, Japan, Taiwan, the United States and many points in between.

Among the highlights of a lengthy tour in 1975 that included South Africa and South America was a visit with former U.S. President Richard Nixon. Nixon had resigned in disgrace the previous year and was still very much the recluse, living in San Clemente, California. Much has been written and said about Nixon over the past decade, and most of it has been critical. Nevertheless, for me he remains one of the most intriguing public figures of the second half of this century. Although I have long been an admirer of John Kennedy, Nixon also has been and remains a fascinating study. I do not agree with nor will I attempt to justify Watergate, but I know enough about the inner workings of politics to realize that the chief difference between Nixon and so many others is the difference noted in a speech Archbishop Fulton Sheen once gave to prison inmates. "Gentlemen," he began, "the only difference between you and me is that you got caught."

So, too, with Richard Nixon. Unlike many other people who stray over the line, Nixon was found out. He paid a terrible political price and an even greater personal penalty. He was universally vilified and his private life and that of his family was cruelly invaded. At the same time, I know of no other public person who, having suffered so much abuse, has ridden out the ensuing storm so well.

This was the man I was to see that November morning. I had ordered a car and a driver through the hotel to take me to Nixon's home, La Casa Pacifica. The vehicle that arrived was an ancient stretch Cadillac, two-toned turquoise and white, with the name of the limousine service announced on both sides in the kind of individual black-and-gold letters available at the five-and-dime. The

108

interior smelled like a musty motel room. It looked – as it may well have served in a previous incarnation – like a pimpmobile.

The day was hot, and although the driver claimed the air conditioning was working, the interior was nauseatingly close. At any moment, I expected that the warmth would awaken the creepy denizens I imagined must be living in the once plush seats and carpet. In an attempt to open a window for some fresh air, I pushed and prodded at various bumps and protrusions, panicked when nothing happened and struck the door harder. All I succeeded in doing was hitting the end of a screw that had once held a doorknob. The blow punctured my palm, causing it to bleed profusely.

I wrapped a handkerchief around my hand, slid over to the other window, managed to open it and sat in glum silence for the rest of the trip, looking for all the world like a secular version of Padre Pio or one of those others modest enough to cover his stigmata.

The limousine brought me to a gate in an area festooned with warning signs worthy of a nuclear test site. As the driver and I disembarked, a voice boomed from a hidden speaker: "You are in a restricted area. Please identify yourselves and state the nature of your business." We did and were waved through to a parking lot near the house. Two secret service agents led me in, while two more stayed with my driver and the pride of his limo fleet. I couldn't blame them for their caution. This bizarre vehicle couldn't have been more out of place if it had just arrived from another dimension.

As I waited to meet Nixon, I chatted with members of his staff. It quickly became clear that they were in a time warp. Nixon was "the President." All conversation was carried on as if he were still in the White House. When I was ushered into his office and the introductions were made, he was addressed as "Mr. President." Having entered this particular twilight zone, I played along.

He greeted me warmly as only a practised politician can and gave my hand a sturdy pump with his right hand while his left hand cupped my elbow. He noticed the maple-leaf-flag pin on my lapel and commented on it. As he returned to the chair behind his desk, I attempted to explain it by saying: "Yes, Mr. President, it's the Canadian version of the one you wear."

"Yes," he answered, "I recognized the tree." The tree? I thought to myself. All the reports I'd heard *were* true. The guy was off his rocker. "So you must be one of the young turks," he began, then went on to explain how, as a young Congressman, he had been called a young turk, too, and therefore intended no offence. As we exchanged opening niceties, I realized what an odd-looking man he is. His head and his hands are disproportionately large for his body. As he spoke, he gestured constantly. At times, the motions would gracefully emphasize his point. Often, however, the movement seemed out of sync with the tone and tenor of his remarks. He had all the presence and projection of a poorly trained ham actor.

After about five minutes of banalities about the need for peace and international understanding, I sensed that he was wrapping up our meeting. He talked about the importance of good relations between our two countries and what a great future there was for someone of my tender years. Clearly, he had regarded my visit as no more than a brief courtesy call and was ready to bid me good day.

I was not about to let the meeting end that quickly. I tried a ploy I often used successfully with John Diefenbaker when I wanted to change the subject, get him out of a bad mood or simply set him talking. With Nixon leaning forward in his chair preparing to see me off, I said: "That was great publicity you got all across Canada a few weeks ago, Mr. President."

"Ah, what publicity was that?" he replied, his interest obviously piqued.

"Well, Mr. President, you may remember sending a cheque for a ticket to Mr. Diefenbaker's eightieth birthday party. That may not have made the press here in the United States, but it was such a wonderful gesture that it was big news, front page in every newspaper across Canada."

"Is that so," said Nixon, obviously intrigued and pleased after all the pain of Watergate, the resignation and a tough, lonely year out of office. He relaxed, leaned back in his swivel chair and linked his fingers together behind his head. He offered coffee, then caught himself and said, "Or being from Canada, maybe you'd prefer tea?" I accepted coffee, and the five-minute drop-in became a lengthy briefing.

For the next hour, Nixon gave me a one-man seminar on the state of the world as he saw it. The session included everything from an overview of international affairs to a detailed explanation of why he had covertly provided arms to Kurdish rebels. The monologue began with what he called "the big picture." For that, he created a world map in the air in front of him, gesticulating wildly as he pointed to the U.S., the U.S.S.R., China and Canada. At one point, he actually got his arms twisted around each other as he described various political entities in the Eastern bloc then suddenly recalled Australia and made an abrupt diving motion with his hands to include that nation in what had become very crowded air space above his desk. He was like an air-traffic controller with planes stacked up everywhere awaiting his individual care and attention.

It was clear that he had lost little of his touch during his year out of office. He thrived on the international stage, he knew he was good at it, and he was anxious to talk. As I listened attentively and sipped my coffee, I noticed that the cup came complete with the Seal of the President. "My God," I thought to myself, "he even stole the china!" (As I learned later, every departing president takes the china and the lifelong use of his title with him.)

When he had verbally whirled me around the world, he made to close off the meeting again. I repeated my admiration of the contribution he had made toward détente. I assured him that many others shared my sentiments and were hopeful that he would one day play an active role again. He misinterpreted this to mean that I thought he should be president once more and advised me that not only did the Constitution not allow a third term, but that he supported that restriction.

Nixon then asked how things were, politically, in Canada. I told him that Trudeau and his government remained unpopular, chiefly because of Trudeau's manner. Nixon, who had once called Trudeau "that asshole," had not warmed to him yet. "Yeah, Trudeau's just like [Nelson] Rockefeller," said Nixon, with an obvious distaste for both men. "He got it all from his old man." As he made the comment, he rubbed his thumb back and forth across his fingers in the international sign for money.

As our meeting drew to a close, Nixon offered me an autographed photo of himself. As John Diefenbaker had done in one of my meetings with him years earlier, he produced two pictures – one formal and one more relaxed – and asked which one I would like. I chose the informal one. He then inscribed the photo in a way that both elevated me to cabinet status and made an inflated prediction for my future: "To the honorable Sean O'Sullivan, with best wishes for what I know will be a great career in the service of all peoples and the cause of peace for all mankind." And signed it, Richard Nixon.

As we said goodbye, I thought about the harm he had done to the political system and about the personal hurt he had suffered. While he remains a man reviled by many, I consider my visit with him one of the highlights of my political travels. He had honoured me, a young politician from a foreign country, with more than an hour of his time and his insights. As the car ferried me away from La Casa Pacifica, I reflected upon this lonely and sad man who had been driven into solitude by his own actions and his own staff. Tragically, he had brought it all on himself. As he said in his famous "Checkers speech" of 1952, "It isn't a question of whether it was legal or illegal. That isn't enough. The question is, what is morally wrong."

Nixon had forgotten his own directive. Yet I could only think how ironic it was that a man who had striven so gamely for peace in the world had never been able to achieve it for himself. As I turned for a final look at his hermitage, I wished for him the inner peace that he deserves.

My trip had kept me away from Canada for six weeks. Political reality soon returned, however, with a telephone call to me in Hamilton from Keith Martin. "Well, get ready," he said. "You won't believe this, but Paul Hellyer wants to see you. He thinks he wants to run for the leadership." After the culture shock of touring three continents, nothing could surprise me. Not even the thought that I might support a former Liberal cabinet minister for leader of my own party.

CHAPTER SIX

CURSE YOU, RED TORIES

By the fall of 1975, I had spent almost half my life in Tory politics and never attended a convention as an uncommitted delegate. I'd always had someone to fight for or, more often than not, something to fight against. As the February 1976 leadership convention approached, I decided this time things would be different. I'd be uncommitted, wait to be wooed and won, quietly vote for the candidate of my choice, then disappear. The first candidate to phone was Brian Mulroney, saying he'd appreciate my support. I declined. "It's not so much to do with you, Brian, as with some of the people around you." Who? he asked. "Well, let's just say that they're people the Right Honourable Member from Prince Albert and myself would find it hard to work with." As part of the Camp ouster he knew what I meant, but we ended on a friendly note: "Let's keep the lines of communication open." Of course, in politics, that's roughly equivalent to two businessmen meeting on the street and saying: "We must have lunch some time."

In mid-November, Paul Hellyer took me out to dinner and put forth a very convincing case why I should support him. He said that Trudeau would go on being re-elected unless the Progressive Conservative Party chose a leader who knew Trudeau and could attract disaffected Liberals to a party with a broader appeal than it had offered in the past. "Trudeau is leading Canada down the garden path," argued Hellyer. "His chief ally is not the Liberal Party but the Conservative Party."

Hellyer's plan was to test the waters in speeches he had scheduled across Canada, recruit others to take political soundings on his behalf and make a decision at New Year's. This approach allowed time to

113

see if any one of Peter Lougheed, Bill Davis or John Turner would be entering the race, in which case he wouldn't run. Hellyer wanted me to be his Ottawa point-man and take the pulse of caucus. I was torn. On the one hand, I was battle weary and readying myself for a departure from politics. On the other, I didn't want to let the Campites win another leadership – and certainly not by default. He argued that both of us had a duty to help the country get rid of Trudeau. "You have a chance to make a difference," he said. "It's your duty to make a difference."

Given the list of potential candidates, I realized that it was very probable the party would choose a new leader I disliked. Brian Mulroney, Flora MacDonald, John Fraser, Joe Clark and Jim Gillies were on the left. On the right, Sinclair Stevens and Jack Horner didn't look as if they would win. I could have supported Claude Wagner, but I had concluded that most Tories could not embrace a French-Canadian leader. All I could think of was the old saying: "For evil to flourish all that is necessary is for good men to do nothing." To do nothing would have meant certain victory for someone I didn't like and would guarantee continuing Tory squabbles, control by Camp and Liberal victories. I agreed to help Hellyer for his six-week sounding period.

I knew he did not come without flaws. At age fifty-two, Paul Hellyer was a controversial political figure. First elected to the House of Commons as a Liberal in 1949, he had played senior roles in defence, transport and housing under three prime ministers: Louis St. Laurent, Lester Pearson and Pierre Trudeau. He had resigned from the Trudeau cabinet in 1969 over policy differences and had sat for a while as an independent Liberal. He had also tried, unsuccessfully, to launch a new political movement, Action Canada. When that failed, he joined the Progressive Conservative Party and ran in the Toronto riding of Trinity, which had elected him as a Liberal since 1958. In 1972, he squeaked in as a Conservative, lost in the election of 1974, then became a columnist for the *Toronto Sun*.

Hellyer had made a lot of enemies among Conservatives when, as minister of National Defence, he had rammed through unification of the army, navy, and air force. (Many Tories wanted to get rid of the one-hued outfit that British Columbia Conservative MP Ron Huntington called "that green garbage bag" and to return to the distinctive uniforms for each of the three elements in the Armed Forces.) On a personal basis, Hellyer could also appear stiff to those who didn't know him. Derek Key, who would later act as a Hellyer provincial director for Prince Edward Island at the convention, was blunt: "If you rate the candidates on a scale of zero to ten, Hellyer starts below zero."

Despite the flaws and vagaries of his past, however, I saw that Hellyer had foresight and a vision for the future. I was drawn, too, by his warmth and willingness to work for others and for his country. Most important, there simply is no more decent man in Canadian politics than Paul Hellyer. As an urban developer he had won many design awards, had offered the first money-back housing guarantees and had been the first to set up a pension plan for workers in housing. His views on the economy and inflation were prescient. For all of those apparent strengths, however, his wealthy business background was tough to sell; he appeared aloof and above the ordinary man. His economic views were difficult to understand and impossible for anyone but him to explain. As soon as he began that part of his pitch, you could hear the sound of eyes glazing over in the room. He sent a copy of his book, *Agenda: A Plan for Action,* to every delegate. Most of us who became involved in his campaign hadn't even bothered to read it. On the plus side, however, he brought no party baggage; he had not been involved in any past party feuds. Yet, with that uniquely spotless record and all the experience of his service in three governments, in the end there was no more flawed leadership campaign in 1976 than his. And I share the blame for that.

In the early going, however, there were some strong indicators in his favour. In October, A.C. Nielsen Co. of Canada Ltd. was hired to survey five Toronto area ridings to see which of fifteen potential candidates people did *not* want in order to judge who might be acceptable to the most number of voters. Even though he wasn't listed, Robert Stanfield received the highest "don't want" ranking in two of the five ridings. Another highly undesirable was Dalton Camp. The most popular candidate for Tory leader was retired Liberal finance minister John Turner. Next most popular were Peter Lougheed and David Crombie, then Hellyer. This put him at the top, because the other three would not be running.

I knew that whatever effort I expended for Hellyer would be my last hurrah in politics. I was preparing to leave Parliament and enter the priesthood, although only a few confidants in the church knew. As a result, I called in every IOU I had received over the years in order to bring Hellyer what he sadly lacked – a network of friends in the Tory Party. We put together a national campaign with a high level of enthusiasm but no great expertise. Rob Lawrie, a businessman and lawyer from Mississauga, Ontario, became campaign manager. London-based Don Matthews, a former national party president, joined us and pulled in more workers from his area. Without that London mafia, as well as Keith Martin, Paul's assistant, Warren Ralph, and a few others, Hellyer wouldn't have had a campaign team at all. We may not have been all that he needed, but until then he had no one in the Tory Party to call his own.

Hellyer wisely argued that the support of MPs was critical. In addition to their own vote, it was Hellyer's view that each MP influences five other delegates. Early soundings showed that most MPs were waiting to see what candidates would emerge. If Lougheed said no, it was clear that many MPs would start to choose sides. On November 21, I met Lougheed in Edmonton to precipitate his answer. I told him if he ran I would support him and said that up to twenty-five MPs would also vote for him. He listened politely, then said: "Well, I want you to make it very clear that I'm grateful but there are still some obligations I have to fulfil here in Alberta, commitments that I feel honour-bound to carry out. I'm not going to be a candidate." He agreed that I could issue a news release to that effect. Hellyer's wooing of MPs could now begin in earnest.

Hellyer's team began by giving him honest advice, hurtful though some of it was. Peter Hunter who was then with McConnell Advertising and in charge of Hellyer's advertising, put Hellyer's dilemma succinctly. "First, Napoleon was a corporal, Hitler was a corporal and Hellyer was a corporal. We military men are a bit suspicious of him. Second, he's the only minister of National Defence I've ever known who took the salute wearing brown shoes and blue socks." Nothing could be done about the suspicion, but we thought Hunter was joking about the socks until Jack MacDonald checked and found that it was all too true.

The remaking of Paul Hellyer hardly meant a major change in his image, but it was not well received either by Hellyer or his wife. MacDonald insisted that Hellyer replace his brown suits with dark blue. Further, white shirts would supplant blue, said MacDonald. Only after sustained pressure did Paul finally consent to have some suits made, but he said he preferred his favourite blue dress shirts, arguing that he could get two days' wear out of a blue shirt. He was switched to white. He was also outfitted with a new tie that became standard campaign apparel: dark blue with a bright orange stripe, the campaign colors. His wife, Ellen, just could not understand everyone's overweening interest in Paul's clothing. "What sort of friends," she asked, "take it upon themselves to tell my husband that he doesn't know how to dress?"

Even when we were in high gear I have to say that it was amateur hour. We had little overall savvy and even less organizational skill. From the outside we might have looked good because there were handsome brochures and functionally efficient offices, but it was a piecemeal political operation. The mentality of the young turks running the campaign, and I count myself among them, was that if you looked first class and travelled first class then the campaign would achieve first place. We made the mistake of thinking that dollars and delegates were somehow connected.

Worse still, no one was really in control of expenses and sometimes we didn't even seem to know where all the money was going. We did stupid things, like ordering a union printing shop to run its presses with full crews for a weekend – at triple or quadruple time – immediately prior to the convention. People were flying everywhere on the slightest pretext; there were hotel rooms at all ends of the country, youth delegates being ferried in, and volunteer workers needing to be fed. There were full headquarters operations in three cities. Fundraising to cover that huge sum was dismal; perhaps $50,000 was gathered. Except for a $30,000 party contribution after the convention, Paul was on the hook for the rest. By the time the campaign was paid for, it probably cost Paul Hellyer, personally, close to half a million dollars.

For all our loyalty, Hellyer was almost dumped by his own team.

Don Matthews called me on December 7 to say that he had found another candidate: John Turner. Although Don didn't have Turner's consent, he had arranged for Steve Roman's plane (Roman was chairman of Denison Mines) to start in Toronto with Matthews and Turner on board. John Robarts would pronounce his blessing over Turner, and the plane would then fly to as many provincial capitals as could be reached in a single day to collect endorsements from premiers, party leaders and any other potentates who could be convinced to wave their wands. By the end of the day, said Matthews, the country and the Tory Party would embrace Turner as leader. Other candidates would drop out in astonished support.

I was bewildered by this turn of events. When I phoned again later in the day to see how the regal procession was coming, he was less enthusiastic. There were problems getting everybody where they should be, he said, but it was all being worked out. After twenty-four hours had passed, it was clear that Turner's trooping of the colours was not on. I don't think that Turner ever gave him any real encouragement. Matthews then pushed Steve Roman as a candidate for a while until that, too, fell flat, and he returned to the Hellyer fold.

Such dalliances aside, as December passed I became convinced that Hellyer could not win. He remained, however, the only candidate I would support. Paul Hellyer can't help but do the right thing, that is his nature. That was the core belief that made him likeable and a loser both. He saw that he had to run, even though he confided to me that he was not comfortable in the public eye. In an ideal world, Hellyer would have preferred to be a close policy advisor to a prime minister who would run the government and let Paul formulate the ideas. That being impossible, Paul felt he had to use his gifts to run for office, an office that he really didn't want. He was stuck with his duty; we were stuck with each other.

By December 29, however, the internal momentum was building. There were perhaps a dozen MPs, including such senior MPs as Manitoba's Jake Epp and Ontario's Walter Baker, who were supporting Hellyer. At a meeting of the dozen key supporters that day we tested his resolve – and our own – by questioning him closely on all the negatives we'd been hearing. Finally, he said, "Are you telling me that we give up, that it's not worth taking a stand, we just capitulate?

Who, then, do we go to?" None of us had an answer to that question. It really boiled down to this: If there was an opportunity to do something, there was also a duty to do it. With a sense that we were all going over a cliff together, Hellyer was in the race.

Once in, paranoia took hold. Our favourite conspiracy theory was that Camp was fielding not just one candidate but four. The like-minded candidates would, at some point, all be given a signal to come together behind one candidate. The four-finger theory we called it – with Camp as the controlling thumb. Camp was everywhere. On February 6, for example, on CBC Radio with Judy LaMarsh, Camp said that his great objective at the convention was to prevent the party from falling into the hands of the reactionary element exemplified by the Chateau Cabinet. He knew, he said, that their support was going to Paul Hellyer. "You only have to look at his nomination papers," said Camp. We were outraged. Nomination papers were supposed to be confidential and not released by party headquarters. The whole thing smelled, as usual, of collusion and control of the party apparatus by Camp. We complained to the Candidate Liaison Committee. National Director John Laschinger and MP Bill Jarvis, who was acting as convention co-chairman, said the papers were under lock and key and had not been seen by anyone other than Convention Committee officials. We were not convinced.

We simply could not allow the Campites to win control of the party for two leaders in a row. The line I was dying to use was Everett Dirksen's about repeated presidential loser Thomas Dewey, "We followed you before and you took us down the path of defeat." Camp and his crowd had held total control of the party since they began dumping Diefenbaker in 1966. They put their own leader in place in 1967, over time replaced nearly everyone on the national party executive and took over most of the party election machinery. Only in caucus was there any differing view and although that view was in the majority, "their" members, the Camp operatives, were in the sunshine. At the same time, the party had lost in 1968, flubbed the election of 1972 and got clobbered in 1974. Now it was 1976 and despite their dismal electoral track record the Campites still wanted to be in total control. The Hellyer message was to be pitched to the rank-and-file delegates, all of those people who felt "out" of this elite headed by Camp, his agents in the Big Blue Machine and the "conspirator" candidates. In retrospect, however, I guess setting ourselves up as the anti-establishment candidate just fed the fratricide image of the Conservatives.

As the convention drew closer, deals, near deals and dilemmas came three before tea. At Wagner's request, Hellyer and Wagner met on February 2. Wagner said he was being beaten so badly by Mulroney in the tussle for Quebec delegates that his campaign funds had dried up. He was thinking of dropping out. He had lost the Quebec Liberal leadership race to Robert Bourassa in 1970 and he was worried that he was going to lose again and be badly in debt. There were two possibilities. Wagner would withdraw and support Hellyer; or Hellyer would help Wagner with his funds. Wagner never withdrew. I can only assume that, knowing Paul, he did the "right" thing in human terms and helped Wagner stay in the race.

In the run-up to the convention, it was important to have Dief's support – or at least his perceived support. We certainly spread the story that Dief was on side. This upset Jack Horner. He had loyally stood by Diefenbaker, and suddenly word everywhere was that Dief supported Hellyer. Hellyer had an edge because his brochure contained a colour photograph, taken just before the convention, of Hellyer and Dief walking on Parliament Hill; it was inscribed: "To Paul Hellyer, with best regards, J.G. Diefenbaker. January 10, 1976." The members of the Hellyer campaign referred to it as "the Rose Garden photo" as if it were of a U.S. president with a visitor during a photo opportunity on the White House grounds. Dief also let it be known that he liked Wagner, but as the convention came closer, Dief began to describe Paul as "our only hope." Horner was furious and visited Diefenbaker in his office several times, blaming Keith and me for the stories of Dief's support for Hellyer. Finally, we convinced Dief to soften slightly and support Horner on the first ballot. As a result, Dief would say, in the days prior to the convention: "Jack has been very loyal to me and I can never forget all that he has done. But, he's not going to be leader, and that's all. I will give him my vote on the first ballot out of gratitude – but he's a damn fool if he thinks he's going to be elected."

As any candidate for leader moves about the country speaking to delegates, he gives the same speech everywhere. While each delegate may only hear the speech once, those travelling with the candidate hear the words until they have them memorized and the whole thing becomes laughable. Every speech Hellyer gave began the same way. Hellyer would be presented, then he would move to the microphone and say: "Introductions like that remind me of the small boy who fell head first into a barrel of molasses. When they pulled him out he licked some of the molasses from his face and said 'Lord, make my tongue adequate to this occasion.' " The barrel of molasses was only surpassed in usage by "the salami approach." It went like this, complete with exquisite Paul Hellyer body language: "The socialists' technique for the transformation of Canada is what I call the salami approach. You take a salami, remove one thin slice, hold it up and throw it away. Nobody notices that one thin slice is gone. Another slice, hold it up, throw it away. And another. Eventually all you have left is the string." From time to time, when he felt the occasion warranted it, Paul would break into song. He had a wonderful voice, and would do requests and often lead people in a singalong. The net effect of his speeches and question-and-answer sessions across the country was positive. Although our organization eventually came apart at the seams, John Manley, who had interrupted his articling duties with the Chief Justice to head Hellyer's youth workers, summarized the situation accurately: "We have three things going for us – the candidate, the candidate and the candidate."

So that campaign workers could talk freely about Paul in elevators and restaurants without fear of eavesdroppers, we gave him a code name. I chose the nickname "Harvey" after my favourite movie, *Harvey,* and the invisible six-foot rabbit of that name to whom Jimmy Stewart talked. Our Harvey had some odd turns of phrase that would regularly crop up in Hellyer's conversations. If we were talking about ending the long run of the powerbrokers who had been in charge of the party, he would agree and say, "We've got to think of the little old ladies in dancing shoes from Wagonwheel, Saskatchewan; those are our delegates." We used to joke that if there were a Prairie retirement home for aged Rockettes, we were at least going to win their votes. But failing that, who the hell had ever seen a little old lady wearing dancing shoes?

We tried to portray Hellyer as a compromise choice who could broaden the party's base. Although there was little discussion of policy, Hellyer insisted upon talking about inflation and wage and price controls, which were anathema to most of his free-enterprise supporters. He wanted to go out and sell his economic theories; we fought with him across the country to can that stuff. The race wasn't over policy, it was about personality, in many ways a glamour contest. We wanted faith, hope and charity; he wanted to talk specifics on issues.

We spent many hours and more dollars trying to track delegates' first choice, second choice and third choice among candidates – only to discover that all the information was useless. What you *need* to know is the delegate's *last* choice. At conventions, Conservatives vote against candidates, so you should try to find out who it is they hate and most want to stop – that will tell you where they will move to. That explains how Joe Clark became leader. He was the first choice of only 11 per cent of the delegates on the first ballot; he had only two MPs other than himself supporting his candidacy. Clark seemed to be a most unlikely winner.

On the final ballot, there were more people who did not want Claude Wagner than there were people who wanted Joe Clark. In Quebec, there had been too many bitter fights between Wagner and Mulroney; in English Canada, Tories just could not bring themselves to elect a French Canadian. The bad rap traditionally given to the Tory Party – that it was anglophone, anti-Quebec and narrow – seemed to be true. While we couldn't know the outcome prior to the convention, we knew we had to make Hellyer *acceptable* to the greatest number of people. Even if they didn't love him, even if he wasn't their first choice, we wanted delegates to be able to bring themselves to vote for Hellyer – if they wanted to stop a Camp candidate, for example, or just stop the feuding.

The relevations that Claude Wagner had a $300,000 trust fund to lure him into the party in 1972 hurt Wagner badly. What hurt the convention more was that the news had been leaked by Mulroney operatives. Wagner wasn't the first politician who'd had a trust fund, but it seemed to be used as a reminder to delegates that Wagner was a French-Canadian candidate. They hit Hellyer with the fact that he'd formerly been a Liberal, but they didn't castigate Wagner about that. The trust fund became a code word for "French Canadian," and the fact that he hadn't delivered for the party there.

Quebec politics are a world apart from the rest of Canada. When we were setting up the Quebec campaign organization for Hellyer, Paul gave me a free hand, but he offered one piece of advice. He said that Quebec operated under an entirely different set of rules. Their rules, he said, can involve payment of money everywhere. "Don't try to change it," he said. "That's the way Quebec operates. In Quebec, you're going to pay almost anybody who does anything for us, you're going to pay big and it's going to go on and on. So at least make sure you're getting some value for your dollar."

Mulroney was seen as the front runner. The Hellyer-Diefenbaker rump group was concerned that Mulroney would emerge as Camp's leading candidate. That would mean a race between Mulroney and either Wagner or Hellyer, depending on who was ahead. Keith Martin had tried to convince Dief that Mulroney was the main Camp candidate, but he hadn't succeeded. Dief thought both Hellyer and Wagner were doing well, but he was being cautious. He didn't want to lay hands fully on Hellyer because of his residual loyalty to Horner.

Keith had put various people up to convincing Dief to stop Mulroney but hadn't succeeded. Keith came to me and said: "You've got to convince the Chief to stop Mulroney and he's got one chance to do it – his speech at the convention." I was reluctant, but I concluded that the end justified the means. Mulroney had momentum and had to be stopped. Only Dief could do that; only I could convince Dief he had to do it.

Dief and Mulroney had had strained relations in the past. Although Mulroney had been national vice-chairman of Youth for Dief at the 1956 leadership convention, things had cooled after 1966, when Mulroney was against Dief. When the House opened in January 1973, the Press Gallery held a reception for MPs. Brian Mulroney attended and approached me. Would I get a message to Dief that he wanted to apologize for his involvement in the anti-Diefenbaker events of 1966 and 1967? As Mulroney put it to me: "When all of us thought we were so smart and so right – we weren't. He," he said, referring to Diefenbaker, "was right." Mulroney went on to say that he had been meaning to express his regrets for some time. In fact, he said, on the night his father died he had written a long and apologetic letter to Dief. Later, when he reread what he had written, he decided not to send it because he felt it was too maudlin. He said he would come to see Dief whenever it suited the Old Man. I dutifully reported all this to the Chief who remained unimpressed and unforgiving. He never sent for Mulroney.

As a result, I knew that Dief would be open to negative views on Mulroney. I had lunch with Dief and wrote him a five-page letter on February 12 that was designed to promote Hellyer and denounce Mulroney. I told him that although the race did not have a front runner, it had produced a "favourite son" – and not the traditional, regional favourite son, either. "Rather," I wrote, "the Party power brokers, and in particular Camp, have settled upon their choice in the person of Brian Mulroney." I noted that Wagner had been the front runner until the "calculated and coldly executed 'job' (*re* the trust fund) done by Mulroney's forces on Wagner" had the intended effect.

Dief's attention by now well seized, I began the pitch. "Only Paul Hellyer has the capability of stopping this complete Camp-designed takeover." Then I began to pluck every string I knew would appeal to Dief by explaining that I supported Hellyer because he had the best chance of returning the party to the "Diefenbaker tradition" of placing more faith in people than in power brokers.

> Against all those vested interests – the St. James and Bay Street friends of Mr. Drew – you succeeded and opened the Conservative Party to Canadians from all walks of life.
>
> Privately, [Mulroney] tells delegates and media people of your longstanding and close friendship, leaving the clear impression that you are supporting him. Publicly, he quotes you in every speech. Last week in Toronto he called for Party unity invoking your name and [the] admonition that "no leader can go forward when he must always be turning around to see who is trying to trip him from behind." One might ask where Brian Mulroney was and whose side he was on when you spoke those words to

us in 1966.

I feel obliged to convey to you my clear impression that the delegates are looking to you, as one who has devoted a lifetime to Canada and seeks nothing from the Party, for guidance in this crucial and complex time of decision. No one else can exercise as significant an influence over the outcome of the Convention. And perhaps, therefore – if I might be so bold as to suggest – no one carries as grave a responsibility. The future of the Party you have served so long depends on that Convention. And the future of the Nation you love hangs in the balance.

My plea worked. That Thursday speech by Dief was clearly aimed at skewering Mulroney, in the guise of an attack on Trudeau. Railing at Trudeau, Dief charged: "He shows a continuing contempt for the institution he doesn't understand." Dief noted that Trudeau had been elected as an MP only three years prior to becoming PM. "In the British parliamentary tradition, those who have achieved prime ministership have had years of experience." There was only one leading candidate Dief could possibly be against: Brian Mulroney. Only Mulroney had no seat and no elected experience. Everyone, including Brian, got the message. At the end of Dief's speech, Brian turned to his wife Mila and said: "Honey, we're dead in the water." Brian hasn't known, until now, that I put the bullet in Dief's gun. In my defence, I say this: What was done to Wagner in revealing the trust fund wasn't right. I admit that I was wrong, too. The two strategies were telling blows against both campaigns.

Going into the convention we were proud that Hellyer had become a major player. There was even an outside chance that Wagner would come to Hellyer against Mulroney. At the same time, we were also having some fun. I issued a mock press release to Hellyer campaign workers saying that Hellyer was headed for certain first-ballot victory because of his speech. "The speech brought delegates to their feet no less than sixteen times in prolonged applause. With the unanimous consent of the assembly, Mr. Hellyer went beyond the agreed limit of twenty minutes and spoke for three hours on his new macro-economic strategy for Canada. Following Mr. Hellyer's speech, all other leading contenders withdrew from the race and pledged their full support for his economic theories. The only remaining opponent was Heward Grafftey who said he really didn't understand Mr. Hellyer's plan, especially the "salami approach." Copies of his book, *Agenda*, were said to be selling for upwards of $50 in downtown Ottawa last night. The first half of the speech was given in English, then Mr. Hellyer repeated his ideas in French, breaking into song every few minutes."

Richard Nixon, in one of his more off-the-wall comments said, "You know, there never would have been Watergate except for Martha Mitchell." He explained that his attorney-general, John Mitchell, was so preoccupied with his wife and her demands and late-night phone calls around the country that he wasn't able to keep an eye on the Committee to Re-Elect the President. In that same sense, Paul Hellyer's Red Tory speech never would have occurred – if it hadn't been for Bob Stanfield.

Diefenbaker spoke on Thursday and gave precisely the anti-Mulroney speech that we wanted. Hellyer's star was in the ascendant. There was an exuberant lunch on Friday where Paul spoke well, and without notes, for half an hour to supporters. It was the zenith of his campaign, and doubly ironic because his theme was the need for party unity. Once we backroom boys got into the act on his major convention address, however, all hell would break loose causing the loss of much of the delegate support that Hellyer had cultivated so well in his campaign.

Stanfield's speech on Friday night was not gracious. Instead, I thought it was the bitter speech of a man leaving the leadership on bad terms. If MPs didn't get into line, he said, they should warm the bench rather than play. He also made a coy, but clear, putdown of Diefenbaker. "I want to thank John for his very kind remarks . . ." he paused deliberately and finally added " . . . last night."

Stanfield likely saw his speech as a warning to the party. We saw it as a denunciation of those caucus members he had not found co-operative. That was us, the MPs on the right wing, those who had been left out. "Some Progressive Conservatives would sooner fight than win," Stanfield told the delegates. "Some of us wish to elevate a legitimate concern for individual self-reliance and individual enterprise into the central and dominating dogma and theme of our party.

Why do we spoil a good case by exaggeration? Why do we try to polarize a society that is already taut with tension and confrontation?"

The conventional wisdom quickly became that, just as Diefenbaker had attacked Mulroney the previous night, Stanfield had taken a shot at Diefenbaker for causing him trouble and only being gracious at the last minute. Stanfield's message also seemed to be that caucus members should not be in the forefront as a new leader was picked. That was squarely aimed at Hellyer, who had more MPs backing him – twenty-two of them – than any other candidate.

We were all frazzled. To us in our overworked state, Stanfield's speech seemed a clear signal that the power brokers were out to stop us again. Angry and frustrated, Hellyer's senior people met at the Château Laurier. They included Jimmy Johnston, Jack MacDonald, Jerry Davies, Don Matthews, Rob Lawrie and myself. We all fed off each other. Matthews was irate and urged all manner of indignities, although he stopped short of hiring a plane to strafe Stanfield's home. The conclusion was that Hellyer's speech the next day had to be a barnburner and must respond strongly to Stanfield's warning that the party should be wary of becoming too conservative. Attendees felt that Hellyer should be summoned to join the deliberations. He refused. I urged him by telephone to join us. "There are some pretty serious concerns in the room. You'd better come here if only to calm your people." He finally agreed.

My advice was wrong; he should have stayed away. Until then he had been moving safely inside the cocoon in which you wrap a candidate. We'd tried to keep him rested, meeting delegates and away from reality. At the eleventh hour he was confronted with raw anger and a plan to answer all charges in the twenty minutes he had available the next day. Hellyer had already prepared his speech. He had taken the previous weekend off from campaigning and retired to Montebello, a resort halfway between Ottawa and Montreal, to write it himself and rehearse it. Rob Lawrie had read the speech, however, and informed Hellyer that it wasn't bombastic enough. "We have a big investment in you, you know," said Lawrie. Hellyer, I'm sure, was not overjoyed at being described as though he were a heifer on the hoof.

The last thing Hellyer wanted was to go back to square one with a new speech, but he reluctantly agreed to let me draft some notes and said that Jerry Davies and Jack MacDonald could write something as well. As it turned out, Hellyer was mistaken to listen to us. An unstoppable chain reaction had begun. I went to my office on Parliament Hill, wrote a speech and put it between the doors at Hellyer's house at about 4:00 a.m. "Mr. Trudeau is a dangerous man," I wrote. "I know Trudeau. I know Trudeau must go." The notes also touched a unity theme: "It is time to learn from the past instead of trying to relive it." Then, the message of hope and individual potential: "Mediocrity is not good enough. Laziness is unacceptable. Lost initiative and foregone opportunities are a national scourge. To my mind, there is no greater sin than to possess a talent which remains unused. There is no greater tragedy than a potential which is never pursued."

When he arose in the morning and read my draft, he decided he couldn't deliver it because there wasn't time to transfer it onto speech cards and learn it properly. He did not want to stand before the delegates and read a speech with which he was not familiar. He had made that mistake at the 1968 Liberal leadership convention and was not about to repeat it. Jack and Jerry then showed up at his house with some index cards on which they'd written all the points made by the rabble in the hotel room the night before. Hellyer's wife, Ellen, recounts how she saw the two of them coming up the walk Saturday morning and thought they were members of what was known as the Fellowship, the weekly parliamentary group that Hellyer met with for breakfast and prayers. Said Ellen: "If I'd known what they *were* there for, I wouldn't have let them in." They urged Hellyer to make their points, with some emotion, rather than use an extended text. For Hellyer, their draft efforts had the twin merits of being on handy cards and written in short, snappy sentences. As he skimmed over their work, one area did trouble him, however. "Are you sure," he asked them, "that you want me to include that stuff about the Red Tories?" They did not reply.

He agreed to use their speech, stuffed the cards into his pocket and hurried away to the convention hall to speak to provincial caucus meetings and be on hand for the other candidates' speeches to all the delegates. He did not want to enter the room "cold" for his speech, as he had in 1968. As a result, he heard some of the other candidates take direct shots at him for not being a Conservative since birth and at his failure with Action Canada. He had become, next to Pierre Trudeau, everyone's favourite whipping boy. He sensed the tension mounting around him and inside himself.

None of us had been thinking clearly for twelve hours. The last-minute change in speech strategy was a formula for disaster. Hellyer was well down the list of speakers. Even though he wasn't as familiar with the cards as he might have wanted to be, the opening minutes of the speech went well. His attack on Trudeau was strong and stirring. "Trudeau is taking us on a strange journey," Hellyer said, "and we don't want to go. I know all about Pierre Elliott Trudeau and he knows I know. I switched parties not to avoid the battle but to join it. There's much more at stake in this convention than banners and headlines. The issue is Canada itself."

Then he began to dig a hole for himself. He said that he had hesitated to join the Conservative Party for a time because he saw that it contained some "Red Tories" who were heading "where Trudeau is going and where the NDP has been." Added Hellyer: "I was more Conservative than the Red Tories but not less compassionate." The full political hara-kiri came when he launched the frontal attack on the Red Tories by saying they were like "the tail trying to swing the true-blue Conservative dog." The line brought the loudest round of boos of the day. Rather than appear to be a candidate who could unite Conservatives *and* pull votes from disenchanted Liberals, he managed to alienate many in the crowd.

After the speech, the analysis was quick and merciless. At the 1968 Liberal convention, his speech had been too wooden. This time, he had gone the other way and destroyed his chances by going off the emotional deep end. Instead of taking the high road he had hurled himself into an abyss. As he rejoined his supporters he turned to Jack MacDonald and said: "I've blown it." MacDonald could only agree. "We're finished," he said. Later, Hellyer explained that he was halfway through the first phrase about the Red Tories before he realized what he was saying. Suddenly, he recalled, he felt exactly like someone speeding along a highway only to have a big truck pull out from a sideroad. Even slamming on the brakes could not prevent the inevitable collision.

We put on a brave front. There were cheers and happy times at Hellyer headquarters, but it was as if Paul had thrown up in the punch bowl at a party. We drafted an open letter to delegates, he signed it and then decided not to distribute it. Because so many in the campaign wanted him to do *something,* and he wanted to go home to bed, he overrode his own political instincts and let us release the letter to the delegates. Wrote Hellyer: "I want you, the delegates to this Progressive Conservative convention, to know before you mark your ballots that my remarks on Saturday afternoon were not a slip of the tongue nor were they an ill-considered accident." The words only kept the wounds open.

On reflection, he said later, the times when things worked out badly for him in his political life occurred when he chose the advice of others over his own political instincts. When you've been in politics for a while, you become like the veteran athlete and develop an instinct for when to react, where the ball's going to be and what you should do to be there. When you have too many analysts second-guessing you, it undermines your self-confidence. You become convinced that all these people must be right, your own gut instinct must be wrong.

Because of my high-profile role in the campaign and because I had given many speeches attacking the Big Blue Machine, I became widely regarded both at the convention and in the party as the author of that deadly nightshade speech. I didn't write the damn speech. I do resent people thinking I did. I wrote a different speech; even if he had read it haltingly, Hellyer would have been a more credible candidate. He certainly wouldn't have had the "Red Tory" problem to deal with. Having said that, every one of us on the campaign was responsible. First, I insisted he come to the midnight "summit." Second, we agreed I would write a speech, the others would put ideas on cards and at the last minute we would give it all to Paul with no time to meld a message. Harvey was supposed to pull a rabbit out of the hat.

At the final meeting Sunday morning at the Civic Centre, floor workers were assigned to specific polling stations to be ready to work on delegates about to vote on the first ballot. In addition, there was an elaborate overlay of spotters at three different positions in the

Hellyer area as well as an additional spotter at the top of the stands. They were to keep an eye on workers and help find those delegates who were known to be leaning to Hellyer. After each ballot, cards were to be available for each provincial director detailing which delegates to chase, depending on the results. The arrangements were unnecessary. The first ballot vote showed that Saturday's speech had hurt us more than we imagined.

Wagner led with 531 votes; then came Mulroney, 357; Clark, 277; Horner, 235; and Hellyer, in fifth place, four votes behind Horner. Those Horner supporters who had intended to come to Paul on the second ballot obviously would not be coming. We decided to stay on for the second ballot to see if there would be any movement. Brief contact was made with the Stevens people, but they were in turmoil and a clean read on what they would do was impossible. Jim Gillies went to Clark, and Stevens also made his surprising move to Clark.

For Stevens, a right-winger and an "out," to go to a left-winger and an "in" like Clark was the wild-card move of the convention. When Stevens had been nominated to run for the Conservatives in the 1972 election, Finlay MacDonald had been dispatched to convince Stevens to step down as a candidate because he was seen by others in the party as too far to the right. He continued to run, and at the convention he was probably the most right-wing candidate in the field. No one had foreseen Stevens's eventual decision. Our campaign manager, Rob Lawrie, had assured us that if Stevens moved anywhere, he would go to either Hellyer or Wagner, whoever was ahead. He could have moved to either and been consistent. His support for Clark looked like a double-cross of the worst order.

Hellyer, seeing the momentum toward Clark, decided he couldn't wait for the results of the second ballot. It was essential to start a countervailing force, so he released his delegates to vote as they wished and announced that he was going to Wagner. It was too late to get Paul off the next ballot, so he had to go through the humiliation of receiving 118 votes.

As voting commenced on the final ballot, I couldn't believe we were even considering Clark for leader. To me, Joe Clark was a man of ordinary ability and extraordinary ambition. That drive was the only reason he was running. I had always found our relations in

Parliament awkward. The only time we were close came when I brought the Beaver Bill into the House and Joe had the good sense to leap up, catch the Speaker's eye and second my motion. It was my first piece of legislation. It hadn't dawned on me that I even needed a seconder. Certainly, Dief had never made any secret of his feelings toward Clark, who had been involved in his ouster. As for his wife Maureen, she and I had fallen out in YPC days and never patched things up.

If Hellyer hadn't been running, I would have supported Wagner. Although I was not convinced that Wagner would have led us to victory in the country, I felt that by electing a French-Canadian leader we would once and for all have buried the notion that the Tory Party was a party of the WASP establishment. When I joined the Conservatives, there were not many prominent Catholic members. In Hamilton, as elsewhere, if you were Catholic, you were Liberal. I felt that Wagner's election might build a base toward a truly national party. Even his second-place finish showed progress from an anglophone Diefenbaker to a strugglingly bilingual Stanfield, to 1976 when a leader had to be bilingual, to today's leader from Quebec. In 1976, I found it upsetting that the Tories just couldn't take that leap of faith to Wagner. Clark could only be a negative choice, or so I thought, because if the Tories picked him it would only prove that we were as bigoted as everyone said we were about Quebecers. I didn't want to believe that.

Before the balloting began, Hellyer and the other candidates had agreed that the runner-up would go to the platform and move that the selection of the new leader be made unanimous. After the third ballot, however, it was clear Hellyer would not be the runner-up and someone suggested that Paul vote, then head downtown for dinner. After seven hours in the convention hothouse, it was a welcome suggestion. On the way, he heard on the car radio that all candidates were headed for the stage as Clark's victory was announced. Hellyer was crushed. Despite the specific invitation earlier that only the runner-up was expected, he felt he should have known that a ritualistic appearance by all candidates was expected. He began to turn around, but it was snowing and he realized that he would arrive too late to participate. Paul, who was always the gentleman, now looked like a sore loser. He later wrote to Clark and apologized and received a most friendly and understanding reply.

On the final ballot, I was predicting a Wagner victory. *Toronto Sun* columnist Doug Fisher asked me what would happen if Clark were elected. "Why then," I said, "we'll have three socialist party leaders in Canada." It was one of those unfortunate remarks you make in the crucible of defeat. It cost me dearly. Not only had I backed two losers, I had gone out of my way to insult the majority of those Tories who had elected Clark. Reporters asked Clark later what he was going to do with the "Sean O'Sullivans" of the party.

I tried hard to be a gracious loser. I remembered Hellyer telling me that the day after he lost the Liberal leadership his first telephone call came from fellow defeated candidate John Turner. "Well," Turner had said, "I guess that separated the men from the boys." Turner had spoken to Ellen as well and congratulated them both on their campaign. The rest of the day, the phone was silent. As John F. Kennedy has said: "Every victory has a thousand fathers, and every defeat is an orphan." With that in mind, and knowing how it felt to lose, I called Claude Wagner the day after the convention. He said, "Sean, there are a lot of people today who seem to want to cry over spilt milk but I'm telling them that it's too late and I'm not crying."

I also phoned Mulroney and told him he had run a good race and should be proud to have established himself as a national figure. I reminded him that Diefenbaker hadn't won the leadership on his first try either and said I was sorry that circumstances hadn't allowed me to support him. He said: "The one thing for which I am grateful to you, Sean, is that you told me the truth from the beginning. There are an awful lot of sons-of-bitches in this party that lied through their teeth to me." As another of the losers, his phone wasn't ringing much that day, either. I was only his second caller. The first was Pierre Trudeau.

I was less generous toward my new leader. Three days after the convention, he asked to see me in his office. We were both ill at ease. I knew I wasn't running again. I regretted the "socialist leaders" comment that I had made in the heat of the moment, but I was unhappy with his victory. I thought he'd connived his way in and was unworthy of the office. He made a brief pitch that we all should work together; my reply was prickly, "I feel exactly the same way, *sir.*" "Please call me Joe," he said. "No," I said. "As long as you sit in this office, you are entitled to my respect." I was ungracious in defeat and offensive in the extreme. It was not a recipe for success. He asked what I would like to do as he assembled our parliamentary colleagues and doled out tasks for each. I was not in a mood to be wooed. I replied, suiting up in my best sulk: "I'd like to be left alone."

While I told him I would be loyal, I also said that I was rethinking my own future and couldn't even say whether I wanted to remain in public life. He misinterpreted that, thinking that I was depressed and bitter following his victory. His response indicated that he saw me as an ambitious adversary whom he had to tolerate. "Just let me assure you that I don't see myself being here for much longer than ten years," said Clark. "You're still quite young and there's still a great future for you. I would hope that you would rethink that very carefully and decide to stay." Well, he didn't get his ten years, and I didn't stay.

Through it all, I came to see Paul Hellyer as one of the most tragic political figures I have ever known. He would not like that description because it suggests some degree of pity and that's the last thing he'd want. I do, however, feel extremely sorry for his family who have suffered so many humiliations along with him. I feel badly for the country because we could have used a dram of his decency. He is gifted, has a fertile mind, and is open to new ideas; he prays and he reflects. He is not motivated by some of the baser qualities one finds in other people who claw their way to the top.

Paul Hellyer would like to have been a practitioner of politics even after he was defeated for the leadership of both main parties. He wanted to make a contribution. While I have forgiven the Tory Party much, I do remain angry for the way it treated Paul Hellyer after the convention. After 1976, he said that he wanted to stay involved as a loyal party member. There were four ridings that were of some interest. One was Norfolk-Haldimand in Ontario, where the incumbent, Bill Knowles, was retiring. It would have been a good seat for Paul; his family's roots were there. Polling showed that he could win the nomination and be elected as a member.

Some of Joe Clark's people, however, told Hellyer to stay out. There was a recurring scenario in each of the four situations. Finally, a riding president, who must have received a call from the leader's office, called a press conference and issued a statement making it abundantly clear that Clark did not want Paul as a candidate and that there was no place for him in the Conservative Party. Some people couldn't understand why he later returned to the Liberals. It was simply that he was frozen out of the Tory Party but still had a commitment to public life.

Sometimes, in politics, you have to do the less than honourable thing, the ambitious thing and spike your opponent or leak the bad news. It is refreshing to see politicians like Paul Hellyer, who operate with fresh charm and youthful naiveté. Paul Hellyer knew how to play that game; he'd been beaten up often enough by it. But he simply refused to play the game with some of the roughness and toughness required to get to the top. It's the same in private enterprise. You can get to a certain level based on your intelligence, your talents and your gifts, but there are others competing with you. They may match your skills, so you've got to be able to seize the right moment and sometimes be willing to put the skids under some others if you're interested in getting to the top.

Having said all that, as early as six weeks into the campaign, I knew we wouldn't win. A CTV poll had Mulroney ahead and Hellyer well back. In my paranoia, however, I even found a way to explain that. Camp was a CTV commentator, you see, so he must have rigged it so his man was leading. In the end I concluded that the Tory Party could not bring itself to elect Paul Hellyer. There were just too many negatives. Even so, he was the best-qualified man in the race. He would have been a great prime minister.

On May 19, I gathered some of Hellyer's key people in a private dining room at the parliamentary restaurant just to say that despite all that had happened we were glad to have stood by him. He and Ellen both came; there were a dozen people. He went around the table and said something thoughtful about everyone. When he came to me, he said: "Sean, I have one consolation in this whole endeavour. I guess we've all known from the beginning that it was going to be a dry run for you, anyway. The next time, we'll do it right." For me, however, there would be no next time. My political life was coming to an end. Just as I had finally matured politically, I was about to choose a priestly mantle. It was time to move on.

Chapter Seven

Coming Down
the Mountain

A fter the leadership convention in 1976, I could muster little interest and less zeal for either Parliament or the party. I even tried to drop all committee work, but an MP has to participate in at least one House committee, so I became a member of the Library of Parliament Committee. It met once a year, for dinner, and that was more than enough for me. My attendance in the House became spotty; I was just going through the motions. My only real political activity was to support some friends in by-elections and help Jack MacDonald's successful run for mayor of Hamilton in December 1976.

The malaise had begun to set in following the 1974 election. By then, I had spent almost half of my life in politics. My career was going well, my constituents obviously liked me and Ottawa was an exciting place to be. And yet, with all of that, I had to deal with compelling signs coming from within me. I wasn't happy. There was a void, and not enough fulfilment to sustain my interest.

Perhaps I should not have been so surprised. Others have found a similar lack in their own lives. At the end of the *Labyrinth* film at Expo 67, for example, was the thoughtful line: "Just when you think you have it all, it all starts to fade away." It was Oscar Wilde who once observed that while it is disagreeable to be frustrated, the real disasters in life begin when you get what you want. I had achieved personal recognition and professional rewards in Ottawa, but it was ego-feed in a city where the banquet table could never quite be full enough. There, a politician usually ends up more than a little hungry.

As an alternative, the priesthood was not something to which I had given much thought during my adult life. That was surprising, because there should be nothing more predictable in an Irish Catholic family with six sons than that one or more will become a priest. Yet, as adults, none of us had, even though priesthood was presented at school, in the church and at home as the greatest calling a Catholic could have. As a boy, I had considered it, but I had become side-tracked into politics by the age of twelve. In 1974-75, however, about the same time as I was searching for the "right track" for the party through the Chateau Cabinet, I began a halting, hesitant and some-times rambling parallel hunt for my own "right place." As I set out on this personal odyssey, the words of Henry Miller seemed to be appropriate: "Our destination is never a place but rather a new way of looking at things."

The search began, as these things often do, with a surprising discovery and a self-revelation. I had heard that an old grade school friend from Hamilton, Sam Restivo, had entered a seminary and was preparing to become a priest. If I had been asked to name a most unlikely candidate for the priesthood, it would have been Sam. As a youth, he had never seemed particularly pious or overly devotional. I just expected that he would lead the charmed life that seemed to be laid out for him, go into the family grocery business and be happy ever after with a lovely wife and a lively family.

I first saw Sam as a seminarian when he visited me in Ottawa just when the 1974 election was called, but I didn't feel the full impact of his new life until that fall. I had a speaking engagement in London and phoned him for dinner. I saw myself as the successful and wealthy contemporary who had made it in the political world taking a poor, starving seminarian out for a good meal. After dinner, we returned to St. Thomas Scholasticate, the seminary of Sam's order, the Congregation of the Resurrection, and chatted with some of the other students. When I arrived back in Ottawa, it was one of those times of year when the grey skies seem to collaborate with the cement and stone of the buildings to render everything three shades of dreary. The city and I both seemed equally hollow and devoid of purpose.

There was a striking contrast between the up-front men I had just seen and the backroom pols to whom I was returning. From a modern layman's perspective the seminarians had nothing. They had little money and no celebrity status. They lived in shared quarters and spent their time praying, studying and doing apostolic work among the poor and needy. What they lacked in material goods, however, they made up for elsewhere. The seminarians I saw had something that politicians only feel fleetingly – personal happiness and inner peace.

Over the next few weeks, I found myself staying in touch with Sam and seeking excuses to go to London so that I could spend more time with him and his fellow seminarians. I wanted to discover why men would give up everything that society offers, what made them different – and whether I was missing something. Through these conversations, I soon learned that my personal faith was stunted. As with so many Catholics, my beliefs had been planted at school and church at a very young age and hadn't grown very much since. My faith was underdeveloped and undernourished. When Sam spoke of Christ and the church, he was using the same words I used but we had totally different understandings of what they meant. During that fall we talked in London and Hamilton several times. Then, one December night, as we sat over pizza and wine in the Capri Restaurant in Hamilton, he put the tough question: "Have you ever thought of becoming a priest?" I turned scarlet with embarrassment and said, "No, that's not for me. There are many ways of serving people and I'm serving them through politics."

The topic was quickly dropped, but Sam had touched a lingering doubt within me. In the days to come, as I thought about my life's journey to that point, I realized that I hadn't answered his question honestly. I recalled that, as a young boy, I *had* wanted to become a priest. I wondered what had happened to that call within me. As these thoughts were revolving in my head, my eye was caught by an advertisement in *Sign* magazine, a Catholic journal. The ad seemed to speak to my innermost thoughts. Announced the headline: "Let the boy become the man he was meant to be." The copy began: "That boy who wanted to be a priest is still within you. Listen to him."

Although there was a tradition of service to the church in my family, my parents never pushed any of us toward that path. We were, nevertheless, all listening to the same sermons, and I'm sure that they prayed for this gift to be bestowed on their family. With six sons, the odds were hopeful that one would become a priest. In the end, one did – stubborn Sean. The rest all married and have families. I happen to think that choosing the priesthood is one of the few ways that a son can demonstrate to his parents and the others who have affected his life how well they have done. Faith, after all, is not something that comes suddenly or grows in isolation; it is passed on in large measure by the simple, devout faith of parents and others.

Throughout my growing years, I was often touched as I passed my parents' room at night and saw them kneeling in prayer. For me, that quiet, private act typifies their faith. There are some in the church whom I would call "professional" Catholics. For them, the church is like a big Rotary Club, simply another place to make social and business contacts. The "professional" Catholic is in every church organization, is always letting people know that he is Catholic and is forever inviting the priest over for dinner. To be sure, I had not been one of those – but what was I? It was time to reconsider my first love in life, the church.

I answered the magazine ad. It seemed like a preliminary arm's-length step that guaranteed anonymity for me because the reading material would be sent from Garrison, Maryland. I used my apartment in Deschênes, Quebec, as my mailing address and gave no indication that I was a Member of Parliament. Within a very few days, I received a packet of material and a letter from a man who would form my future much as John Diefenbaker had shaped my past. My new mentor would be Father Joseph F. Lupo. I now know him just by his initials, T.A.L. – The Amazing Lupo – and as the most successful man in the modern era at the task of vocations, convincing men to become priests. In 1961, when he became vocations director for his order, the Trinitarians, he set out to reach single males under the age of thirty-five. He consulted an advertising agency and was told that *Playboy* delivered that market. Father Lupo took out a full-page *Playboy* ad and created a raging controversy in the church, but he also became the pre-eminent professional salesman for priestly vocations.

My packet arrived between Christmas and the New Year. On the accompanying letter from Father Lupo was a personal postscript wishing me a happy birthday. I thought, my God, he knows who I am. He's checked me out; my cover has been blown. Then I remembered that the coupon I had mailed had requested my birth date. Father Lupo simply took note that in a few days I would turn twenty-three. He turned out to be an inveterate letter writer. During the next several months, I received a letter from Father Lupo at least once a week. He must have been among the first direct-mail users to employ a computer-generated personalized letter-writing system. As a result, my name appeared in each missive, and all the evocative phrases seemed to be aimed right at me. "Just yesterday, Sean, someone was asking when you were coming," he'd write. "Come home, Sean, come home." Another letter would include this compelling message: "Your place is waiting for you here. The brothers are all excited." Or this: "There are candles that only you can light."

After a few weeks of such explicit directives, I decided to find out more. One February weekend I flew down to the monastery, which is located on rolling farmland just outside Baltimore. The mother house, called Grey Rock, was a former plantation. The other structures include an office, a dormitory and various farm buildings. About forty men, including students, lived there. I very quickly realized that I was only one of many that Father Lupo treated so personally by mail. I had just arrived when one of the older priests took a look at me, shook his head and walked away, saying, "My God, he sure does drag 'em through here."

And successfully drag 'em he did. When Father Lupo joined the order thirty years ago, there were less than twenty Trinitarians in the United States. Five years after he became vocations director, there were one hundred. Father Lupo looks the part of the classic mad monk. Five feet, nine inches tall, he has a Friar Tuck girth and frizzy grey hair that stands straight out from his head. He comes on like some zany snake-oil salesman with a Brooklyn accent who is convinced that everyone has a vocation to the priesthood until proven otherwise.

The Trinitarian order to which he belongs was founded in 1198 by St. John of Matha and is the oldest order of friars in the church. Begun in the wake of the Crusades, the Trinitarians' mission was to travel to foreign lands and ransom imprisoned Christians. The money used was raised by the Trinitarians, but sometimes they gave themselves over as prisoners in exchange for a captive's freedom. Today, Trinitarians are teachers, researchers, prison chaplains and parish priests. They focus their attention on the problems of drugs, alcoholism, mental retardation, loneliness and poverty – the left-outs that the world has forgotten, the prisoners of modern society.

Father Lupo's recruitment methods are unique. Our first session did not occur in the quiet of the monastery at all. Instead, he took me to a nearby shopping plaza. He was wearing his priest's attire, and as we strolled the mall he proceeded to ask me intimate questions about my life. Often the queries were posed in such a loud voice that I was sure every shopper for yards around could hear. At one point, as we stood in a drugstore, Father Lupo held up a bristle brush used for cleaning toilet bowls and asked: "I wonder what this thing is? What do you do with that, do you suppose?" Then, as if it were all part of the same thought, he continued, waving the brush all the while: "How many brothers did you say you had? Do you suppose there'd be another one interested? You know, there were two sets of apostles who were brothers."

My plaza experience with him was not unusual. It was as if he found the juxtaposition of worldly things and religious thought stimulating. Other interested recruits told me later that he would often meet a prospect at a particular Catholic bookstore in New York. If the weather was bad, they'd talk in the store. If the day was fine, he'd walk the prospect round and round the block. Father Lupo would bring his mother and leave her sitting in his car at the curb. Every time the prospect and Father Lupo passed the car, he'd check on his mother and she'd give them some cookies to share during the next swing around the block.

For all his unusual behaviour, however, I'll take Father Lupo over all of the other religious zealots who moved in – and quickly out – of my life. During one of my trips to the riding as an MP, I managed to snag a ride with John Munro, who was Minister of Labour during my time in Ottawa and the senior representative for Hamilton. It was convenient to hitchhike with him because he had access to government planes. I recall a particularly memorable trip one April when we flew to Hamilton on a Friday and Munro brought along another passenger, an American evangelist who had befriended him.

Now, I have a rule about such "men of the cloth." Anyone who pronounces the Lord's first name as if it contains three syllables – Jee-ay-sus – is not to be trusted. This man was one of those, with his Bible clutched to his breast the whole way; it was like travelling with Elmer Gantry. The week before, I had happened to see Billy Graham on television and heard him promote a lapel pin from Tiffany's that read "Try God." Munro's preacher friend was wearing one. As an opening line, I said: "It must be nice to be able to afford jewellery from Tiffany's." The evangelist's face brightened as if he'd just seen an overflowing collection plate. He was delighted that the pin had been recognized and launched into a pitch about how he was going to save, as he pronounced the name "Mr. True-dough." Pointing to Munro, the evangelist said, "And our brother in Christ is going to help me do that." I fled to another part of the plane and hid behind a magazine for the rest of the flight.

The next day, when I returned to Ottawa with Munro, escape wasn't so easy. It was to be a luncheon flight, so in a show of appreciation and hospitality, I brought along a bottle of wine. To my chagrin, "Try God" was there, too. Once airborne, Munro, the evangelist, his assistant and I sat at a small table in the dining area of the plane. As the steward prepared to pour the wine I had brought, the evangelist intoned, "Shall we pray?" and indicated that we should all join hands. There I was, at 23,000 feet, linked to John Munro and these other two, listening to a prayer about Jee-ay-sus that lasted most of the way across Lake Ontario. Munro looked very uncomfortable, as if he'd rather be anywhere else, his eyes pleading with me to forget everything about this service in the sky.

By contrast, that February weekend with Father Lupo was a most positive experience. He made me feel wanted and told me in his inimitable fashion that the priesthood and I needed each other. After I returned to my duties as an MP, his entreating letters continued to flow my way. "I hope we made as good an impression on you as you did on us. Our prayers will be with you. Surely you won't blame us if we ask the Lord to nudge you our way."

I increased my attendance at Mass at St. Patrick's Church in Ottawa from weekly to daily. I prayed for guidance; in the beginning, none was forthcoming. At one point, I took a yellow legal pad, drew a line down the middle and listed the positive aspects of the priesthood on one side, the reasons for staying in politics on the other. It was an interesting exercise, but when it was completed I was no further ahead.

More helpful was a visit two weeks later with Bishop John Sherlock, formerly my parish priest in Hamilton and by then auxiliary bishop in London. I had met with him many times during my years as an MP to discuss the difficult decisions that a Christian politician must make on various topics. Although I had been able to discuss anything and everything freely with him in the past, my opening sentences this time were stilted. I spent several minutes spraying phrases around the room, muttering about an unidentified decision, one that I didn't have to make just yet, but I wanted his views and I wasn't sure what to do and did he mind talking to me and on and on. He listened patiently until finally I blurted out that I was considering entering the priesthood. "Sean," he said quietly, "I knew what you were coming to talk to me about."

Immediately, my conditioned Tory paranoia caused me to assume that there had been a leak from Father Lupo or Sam Restivo. "Who's been talking?" I demanded. No one, however, had needed to tell Bishop Sherlock what was in my heart. "From those years that I was your parish priest in Hamilton," he explained. "I knew that you had a higher calling than politics. I could see it in you." He went on to say that he'd observed me attending Mass with an obvious devotion that was more than just a *pro forma* approach to religion. He said that I had gifts the church needed and that my becoming a priest would be a good thing for me and for the church. From that day on, he became my silent ally.

It was a great relief to share my thinking with someone else and not be told that I was crazy. I had received affirmation from Father Lupo, but he was, after all, a vocations salesman. Here was Bishop Sherlock, who had long been in my corner, telling me that my thoughts made sense, too. He also cautioned me that it was not a sure thing. "I don't know if you will become a priest," he said. "No one knows that – it's up to the Lord. But I do know that if there is a possibility, you've got to check it out for your own peace of mind and also because you owe it to the Lord if He is calling you."

He agreed that the experience with Father Lupo was helpful and urged me to go on other retreats and pray for guidance. He suggested that as well as considering joining an order such as the Trinitarians, I should also think about becoming a diocesan priest. A diocesan priest is a "general practitioner," one who traces his roots to the first disciples, doing whatever the local bishop asks in a specific geographical area. By contrast, religious orders tend to be specialists; they have sprung up at different times in history to meet particular needs. The Jesuits, for example, are typically academics, the Dominicans are preachers and the Trappists pray for those of us who don't pray enough.

There are other important differences between a priest in a religious order and a diocesan priest. The members of a religious order live together in communities and take three vows. The vow of poverty means that they share everything in common. They swear obedience to the superior of their order and they practise the vow of chastity. The diocesan priest also promises obedience, but to the bishop of the diocese. He makes a commitment to celibacy but takes no vow of poverty, however, and can therefore receive a salary from the diocese.

I would eventually choose the diocesan route, but that was some time away yet. In order to begin the process of looking at both possibilities, I quietly visited Bishop Paul Reding in Hamilton. If I were to become a diocesan priest, the diocese where I grew up would be the obvious place to serve. He welcomed my interest, told me to continue my discussions with both Father Lupo and Bishop Sherlock and agreed to help in whatever ways he could. My long journey had truly begun.

That year, 1975, was a "Holy Year" so called because Pope Paul VI had declared it a Jubilee Year and encouraged Catholics to visit Rome. There, we were to pray at all four major basilicas and generally celebrate their Catholicism. In May, I flew to Rome on a Father Lupo charter package, and during those two weeks I fell in love with the city and its people, who live *con brio*. I was bedazzled by the splendour of the ceremonies I attended at St. Peter's, including one for the canonization of a Trinitarian, St. Michael of the Saints, a patron saint of cancer victims. I would later come to detest Rome and the

145

artificiality of some of its inhabitants, but at the time the trip was a positive step in my thinking.

In September, I attended a performance of *St. Joan* at Stratford with Bishop Sherlock. As we stood talking in the parking lot near the Festival Theatre, I told him how frustrating I was finding political life and wondered aloud how long it would be until the next election so that I could get on with what I really wanted to do – become a priest. "Yes, Sean," he said to me. "It's not much fun trying to lead a double life, is it?" The double life continued for a few more months, however, while I helped Paul Hellyer in his run for Conservative leader. Following the February leadership convention, I decided to follow Bishop Sherlock's advice about going on a retreat.

Retreats have their roots in Christ's withdrawal from the crowds to pray privately before making a major decision. Among today's most underused gifts offered by the church are centres for people to carry out retreats. The best places are run by the Religious of the Cenacle. I went on retreat with them in Connecticut in April 1976. One of the best retreat directors, Sister Elenore Woronick, was my guide. The retreat director's role is to help you shed the worries of the daily world and tune into God. In a very brief time, this specialist can discern, through grace and intuition, exactly what you need in terms of time for prayer and Bible passages to study.

On the first day of a retreat you usually rest and rid yourself of the worldly pressures of telephones and timetables. You walk in the woods and see the beauty of nature, then begin to focus on the basic questions: Is there a God and did He create all this? The secret to a retreat is the almost total silence in which you think and pray. I had my own room, a copy of the Bible and spent my time either reading designated passages there or in the chapel. I kept a journal to write down points I thought about, and once a day I met with Sister Elenore to review the assigned Bible passages and discuss their application to my life. She'd give me another assignment and I'd speak to no one until my next session with her, twenty-four hours later.

The Bible forms the core of such retreats and she led me gently through what can be a very confusing and daunting book. I quickly discovered that there is a vast difference between listening to passages being read to you in church, and reading them and rereading

Previous page: I first met John Diefenbaker in 1963, but it wasn't until he visited Hamilton during the 1965 election campaign that we had a photo taken together. I was then thirteen, already a regular correspondent with the Chief, and with lots of stars in my eyes whenever I looked up at him.

Left: This photograph by Gerry Laarakker was a particular favourite of both myself and Mr. Diefenbaker, who had only twenty minutes to pose during a whirlwind tour through Hamilton. This was 1977; we were colleagues in the House of Commons. Within a few months I would resign from Parliament to enter the seminary.

Above: The O'Sullivan family shortly after we moved back to Hamilton from Montreal in 1961. In the back row from left to right are my brother Terry; my mother, Helen; my sister, Kathleen; my father, Paul; and my brother Paul (known to us all as "Duke"). I'm in the front row at the left, beside my brothers Joe, Jacques, and Tim.

Above left: The young rebel takes on the party establishment. As president of the Ontario Young Progressive Conservatives I brought the 1971 Ontario leadership convention to a temporary halt in a well-publicized dispute over recognition of our youth delegates. The seven-minute speech remains, in my mind, the best political speech I ever gave. I won, but made some powerful enemies.

Above right: June 1972 – John and Olive campaigning in Hamilton, wearing O'Sullivan stickers. Dief called Olive "Sweets" and they remained as close and happy together as newlyweds just leaving the church. In private, Olive carried enduring hurts from political wars.

Below: Election night, October 30, 1972 – my first electoral victory and my brothers Joe (*left*) and Duke carried me on their shoulders for a victory march around the Connaught Hotel's Crystal Ballroom. At the age of twenty, I was the youngest Member of Parliament elected at that time.

Above: Every backbencher dreams of beating the odds and having legislation passed in his name. In 1975 the "Beaver Bill" caught the imagination of Canadians and more than ten thousand letters helped force the Liberals to support passage of my private member's bill that made the beaver a national symbol.

Right: Party leader Robert Stanfield and I gaze out from his Opposition Leader's office in the Centre Block. Every MP arranges a photo such as this for use in election pamphlets to be distributed in the constituency. Still, this is a rare photograph, for seldom were R.L.S. and his new young backbencher destined to be so quiet or at ease in each other's company.

Above left: One of my proudest moments as an MP came when I met Her Majesty, Queen Elizabeth. Awaiting their turn are John and Ann Wise (John is Minister of Agriculture in the Brian Mulroney government). John and I came into Parliament in the class of '72.

Below left: The most decent man I met in public life, Paul Hellyer, was destined to be the "almost leader" of our two major parties. His 1976 run for the Tory leadership was supposed to be his victorious return to politics and allow me to prepare for a graceful exit. Were we surprised! Here, Paul and Ellen Hellyer congratulate me upon my ordination as a priest.

Above: Eleven of the original first-year students preparing for priesthood at the Pontifical Irish College in Rome. The first of the major steps towards priesthood took place when we received the Ministry of Lector in 1978. This happy occasion held additional joy for me because Bishop John Sherlock (*far left*) was on hand to officiate. Bishop Dominic Conway from Ireland (*centre*) administered the rite to my Irish classmates and the Rector, Monsignor Eamonn Marron (*far right*), presented us as candidates for the journey towards priesthood.

Above left: The day of my ordination as a priest with Gerald Emmett Cardinal Carter at St. Michael's Cathedral, in Toronto, Ontario, on October 3, 1981.

Above right: My parents have bequeathed to me the solid and simple faith of Irish Catholics. They also nurtured and supported my desire and vocation for the priesthood. This privileged moment of giving them my first blessing following the ordination was the best way I could find to express my gratitude and my love for them.

Right: The "famous" billboard. The Toronto appeal for priestly vocations garnered national and international attention as Torontonians awoke early in 1983 to this stark, dramatic, and very controversial advertising campaign.

PRIEST LIKE ME

Left: John Diefenbaker is about to leave Ottawa for the last time and begin the long train journey back to Saskatchewan. I was among this group of pallbearers gathered at the Ottawa railway station on August 19, 1979. Many of us wept freely as the nineteen-gun salute sounded and the military band struck up "Auld Lang Syne."

Above: The road back from illness and chemotherapy was long, often lonely, and filled with many desolate days. But the gift of Loon on my birthday in 1985 provided a friend and companion who has worked wonders for my spirits and equilibrium. Cardinal Carter was so right when he once ruefully mused: "Every priest should have a dog, so that when he comes home, at least someone will be glad to see him!"

PRIME MINISTER · PREMIER MINISTRE

Ottawa, K1A 0A2
April 27, 1983

Dear Sean,

        Along with countless others here in Ottawa
who have great admiration for you and your work,
I was distressed to hear the news of your illness.

        I recall a story told of St. Teresa of Avila,
who once asked God why he made her suffer constant
infirmities. He replied that he afflicted most those
whom he loved the most. "If this is the way you treat
your friends," said Teresa, "no wonder you have so few."
In your case, I'm sure he took into account the fact
that, as a Tory, you're well used to coping with adversity.

        Please be assured of my prayers for your
good health and good spirits. There are not so many
like you that we can afford to have you out of action
for long.

        With warm regards,

        Yours sincerely,

The Reverend Sean O'Sullivan
  c/o St. Joseph's Hospital
    50 Charlton Street East
    Hamilton, Ontario
    L8B 1Y4

Above: More than a thousand cards and messages arrived at St. Joseph's Hospital when news of my leukemia was released. The first telegram to arrive was from Brian and Mila Mulroney, who took time from their winning leadership campaign to assure me of their prayers and to wish me *"bon courage."* This letter from then Prime Minister Pierre Trudeau was also a special favourite, representing the bipartisan nature of political friendships so rarely seen by those who only observe Parliament.

Above right: He was smooth, suave and smiling, but nobody played political hardball like the self-described "Boy from Brampton." It took until St. Patrick's Day 1986 (*above*) before the wounds Bill Davis and I inflicted upon each other started to heal.

Below right: Twenty-five years after that first portrait, I gathered the family for a dinner to honour my parents at Transfiguration Parish in Weston, Ontario. With my mother and father (*from left*), Jacques, Tim, Paul, me, Terry, Kathleen and Joe. Also on hand, Loon.

Top: Only in the Tory Party. . . . In 1976 I helped ensure Brian Mulroney's leadership defeat at Diefenbaker's hands. In 1983 I helped him to victory by urging fellow contender Michael Wilson to support Mulroney.

Bottom: Joe Clark and I had been competitors and combatants in the Tory Party even before we entered the House of Commons together in 1972. Out of an often rocky and negative relationship, however, we managed to develop a respect for each other's abilities and, in time, that bond of esteem and affection that grows between fellow survivors. That's why we could relax and laugh so heartily on St. Patrick's Day 1986, in the company of Marjorie LeBreton, a long-time mutual friend and one of the legendary figures in modern Tory Party history.

them to yourself. At first, progress was awkward and slow, but then a few words caught my attention and soon they captured my imagination. The passages actually became "the living word," and I felt as if they were written especially for me and my situation.

Among the many passages that came to be particularly meaningful to me were Chapters 43 and 44 of Isaiah, specifically these verses: "But now, thus says the Lord, who created you, oh Jacob, and formed you, oh Israel: Fear not, for I have redeemed you; I have called you by name: you are mine . . ." And this: "Because you are precious in my eyes and glorious, and because I love you." Those passages were written by God through Isaiah to the people of Israel. They helped me recognize that we are the new Israel, the new chosen people, and almost seemed as if they had been written for me personally. God said to me that even with all of my sins, "you are precious in my eyes and glorious." For me, this was very powerful stuff and set alight a fire within.

There were also passages from the New Testament, including Matthew 6:21: "Remember, where your treasure is, there your heart is also." Also, verse 27: "Which of you by worrying can add a moment to his lifespan?" And, when the whole idea of priesthood seemed preposterous, this passage (Matthew 19:26) had special meaning: "For man it is impossible; but for God all things are possible." Finally, there was a rebuke given by Christ to His disciples that hit home and remains marked in my Bible from that retreat: "Why are you so terrified? Why are you lacking in faith?" (Mark 4:40) As I pondered these and other passages over and over again, I came to regard them as love letters from God. There is a total exhilaration when you realize that you are loved, unconditionally, even with all your human faults.

In every Catholic chapel, there is a tabernacle lamp, usually a candle flickering inside a red glass. It hangs beside the tabernacle, which holds the hosts that have been consecrated at Mass. Because they have been consecrated, the hosts are no longer just bread, they are physically Jesus Christ. As a result, in every chapel and church, Catholics have the privilege of being able to talk to Him knowing that He is there, not just in word or symbol, but physically *there*. As a result of that presence, God spoke to me – not in any grand vision or great voice, but in the dialogue of prayer – telling me to trust Him and offer my love and service in return. I slowly began to learn to trust, a difficult lesson for anyone who'd been mixed up in politics for so long and who had been hurt by so many.

Sister Elenore taught me how to use memory to reflect upon my life and realize how many times God had expressed His love for me through others, pointing out that each person who had helped me was a creature of God, too, and could have treated me badly rather than with love and kindness. She also helped me realize that no one was worthy to become a priest. While a vocation is frequently mistaken as a great honour for some deserving family, anyone familiar with the scriptures or the church knows differently. Christ's disciples were very human and therefore even sinful, yet they were called and accepted. As Christ explained: "I choose the weak and the lowly in order to shame the proud." The original twelve he chose were sinners all – one even betrayed him, and ten others fled from him. In today's marketplace, they wouldn't be trusted to run a car wash, let alone a church. Nor has the Lord's taste improved noticeably over the ages. After all, there I was, being called. And called not to do great things on my own, but so that He might do magnificent things *through* me.

At the retreat I felt, for the first time in my life, that I was not just a participant in a religious ceremony. Until then, my religion had given me a strong desire to please God, a need to chalk up more credits than debits in the hope that He'd go easy on me in Purgatory. Now, Christ became personal and real; I felt loved and accepted by Him. God and I were communicating through His scriptures, through the gift of memory, by adding up my life's journey and seeing how blessed I had been. I could see that He had a message for me and a plan for my life. It was my first opportunity to experience the unconditional, intense and total love of God. Just like the love between two people, a love that does not need to be dissected or explained, the love of God is real.

It was on the third evening, after supper, that this powerful realization hit me. I had been through the awkward stage and was well into the enthusiastic stage. I felt full and complete and beloved of God. It was the most powerful experience I have ever had in my life. I wanted more of this good news. The passage for that evening was, "If you seek me with all your heart, I will let you find me." I could just sense that it was all coming together, that it was pleasing to God. I had come to find Him and He was letting me find Him just as He had promised. He was calling me, telling me to leave everything and follow Him. The next question was: "How do I return that love?" I was ready to say yes right then, sign on and follow Him into the priesthood.

Such impetuous action, however, would have been a mistake. In general, no one should ever make a major decision either at the top or the bottom of any emotional roller coaster. It is always best to wait, just as the three disciples, Peter, James and John did. They went up Mount Tabor with Jesus, witnessed his transfiguration into divine glory, and wanted to stay there, never leaving the place or the perfection that they saw. But Jesus would not let them make that choice when they were on a "high." He led them back down the mountain, back to the dust and temptations of their familiar surroundings and the frustrations of their daily lives. They would be sinners, with Peter denying Jesus and the others fleeing when he was arrested in the garden.

The priests and sisters who direct retreats today call the post-retreat period "coming down the mountain." They take you up, get you high on both life and God, then send you back to the real world again. For me, that return to real life in Ottawa was very difficult. Everything now appeared so petty. I'd vote with the troops in the House as the whip directed on clauses of bills I didn't understand, attend functions in the riding that mattered little and grow weary at constant demands for a piece of me and my time for what seemed to be trivial reasons. I began to distance myself from the grinding sadness of a process that seemed geared toward re-election and little else.

I made my decision to follow Him. While it is almost impossible to put into words what came so much on faith and from so far within, there were three key questions that I asked myself. The first was: Is there a God? If the answer is no, there is no point in considering the second two questions. In my case, the answer was a resounding yes. The second question was: Who is Jesus Christ? If He is, as I came to know him, the Son of God, then the message He brought is true and the church that He established is the true church.

Central to His teaching is to follow His example in doing the will of His heavenly Father. So, having answered the first two questions – yes, there is a God, and yes, Christ is the Son of God and gives meaning to life – then the third question was this: Based on the answers to the first two questions, am I doing what He wants me to do? If the answer is no, a person is bound to be unhappy. If the answer is yes, happiness follows.

One of the simplest yet deepest, most profound yet shortest, expressions of such a personal experience of God is the summary of John's Gospel: "God is Love." To hear, feel, sense and experience with all one's being the invitation of the Lord to "come follow Me" is to be surrounded and filled by a sense of that overwhelming love. Christ became as real for me as when He walked the shores of Galilee. The summons to me became as compelling as it was for those rough and simple fishermen to drop their nets, leave their families behind and set out on a journey with Him that would lead to the wonder of Mount Tabor, the desolation of Calvary, the exhilaration of the Resurrection and everything in between.

Every priest responds to just such a personal command. The new disciple responds to the call not knowing what lies ahead, but willing to give all that he has to honour the invitation by loving and caring for all of God's people. To be called and be so loved filled me with awe and foreboding. Christ wanted *me* to be His priest. It was an invitation that made me tremble first from fear that, like the Gospel's rich young man, I might be too manacled by materialism to say yes, and also from trepidation at what Jesus would ask of me if, like those ignorant fishermen, the first disciples, I laid down my political nets and networks and offered my life in His service.

Throughout, my self-appraisal was heightened by this awakened personal relationship with God. I was leading a healthy and active social life, so I knew it would be an ongoing struggle to remain faithful. I also came to realize that only with His help could I make it. It is difficult to talk about a "calling" because it comes in such personal language – but not because I think I'm different. Rather, it is my view that everyone has a vocation; each of us must discover what God's will is for us and how we must use the talents and opportunities He gives us. For some, that may mean raising a family, for others, learning a trade. Through prayer and the caring guidance of others, I came to realize that my vocation was to become a priest.

I also knew by then that I could not wait until the next election; I would have to resign my seat before that. I had rationalized putting off my decision for a time by convincing myself that, if Paul Hellyer were elected leader, I would have served the party by helping him and may have pleased God as well. For if Paul became leader, my plan was to resign and free up my seat in Parliament for a by-election as I left for the seminary. With the election of Joe Clark, however, I felt obliged to stay on for a time so that my decision to depart didn't feel to me, or appear to others, like sour grapes.

Although I didn't want to embarrass Clark by resigning my seat just yet, neither was I really disposed toward helping him that much either. So, I took on a Lone Ranger role, looking after my riding and setting my own schedule. Clark asked me to take on several special projects, but they were nothing more than sops to MPs he didn't want to put into the shadow cabinet. At one point, Clark called me into his office and handed me a piece of paper that outlined what he hoped would be a role I would take on for the party reviewing trade policy on steel imports. I just let the paper fall back on his desk as I told him I wasn't interested in his make-work projects.

Clark became visibly angry and blurted, "Well, what then would you *like* to do?"

"Sir," I replied, "you sound like a used-car salesman, pointing to an old wreck and asking: 'How much will you give me for this car?' "

"I don't regard it like that at all," he said. "Well, I do," I replied. The conversation was over. If I had needed final proof that my usefulness was ended, that was it. I knew for certain that I had to get out. My tenure as an MP had become no more than a waste of the taxpayers' money. I felt out of place, empty and alone.

Undaunted, Clark continued to try to bring me into the fold. In 1977, Jack Horner bolted to the Liberals and I visited Clark again in his parliamentary office. He had been on the run since the convention and he looked like a ravaged figure. Seeing me, I knew, was just about the last thing he needed. Still, I had sympathy for him because he was down. When people are up, they are often too glib for their own good. When down, they are more likely to be vulnerable and therefore more human.

With my decision firmly made (but not announced) to become a priest, I wanted to make my peace with Joe and leave on good terms. "I know these have been difficult days for you," I said, "but I want you to know that I believe you can be prime minister. I also know that I have not always been as co-operative as you might have liked, but that is over. I want to help you in any way possible, whatever you would like me to do." Clark thanked me and said that he agreed that the country was his for the winning. He said he'd think about a role for me and let me know. Soon after, he called me in to say that he felt I could become an effective one-man "hit squad" on Jack Horner in the House. I had never seen Clark so animated or enthused. He told me to dig up Horner's old speeches and questions and throw them back at him now that he was a Trudeau minister. He even mentioned how effective it would be for me, a Diefenbaker loyalist, to pose some of my questions in French. The unilingual Horner would have to answer in English. "You could just hammer him," said Clark.

I was stunned by the depth of Clark's animosity toward Horner. It also said a fair amount about Clark's view of me as a politician. Being a hit man against Horner was the last thing I wanted to do. My whole *grand geste* in going to see Clark was to leave Parliament and politics on the best possible terms with everybody – including Horner, a former colleague with whom I'd often worked. It wasn't just wrong for me, I thought it was vengeful pettiness. Fortunately, I talked him out of that idea.

Next, Clark suggested that I work under Ray Hnatyshyn, deputy House leader and co-ordinator of Question Period, on a special squad that would operate during Question Period. Clark asked me to study the possibilities and report back. This idea made more sense and, on June 17, 1977, I sent Joe a lengthy memo proposing what I called the "Blue Berets." It would be a group composed of six MPs, working with the leader, the deputy House leader and a team co-ordinator, that would pre-empt all other questions on days when a full, frontal assault on the government was required.

I proposed three types of attack. First, there would be "Scandal Days," based on government stupidity or cupidity as featured in the

152

media that day. Second, there would be "Weak Minister Days," when one flailing cabinet minister would be singled out. Third, there would be "Petulant Pierre Days," when the Blue Berets would try to provoke Trudeau into losing his temper in the House and saying something he would later regret. Although caucus approved the concept, the strategy was not enhanced by Tom Bell, the party Whip, who constantly got the group's name wrong. Rather than viewing the Blue Berets as an elite force attacking with military precision, he referred to us as the "blueberries." "Is this one of your blueberry days?" he'd ask me, somewhat defusing the squad's gung-ho nature. Still, I remained excited by the venture. We were able to try it only a few times before the House rose for the summer and the "blueberries" disbanded.

After more than a year as an MP under Clark's leadership, however, I knew that my double life had to end. One of the contributing factors in my decision to leave soon was the issue of MPs' pensions. I thought the whole scheme was far too generous for someone like myself. To be eligible for a lifetime pension, all I had to do was be in Parliament for six years. If I stayed until November 1978 before resigning, I stood to receive 21 per cent of my salary annually for life. And that $4,620 annually would be payable immediately, even though I would only be twenty-six years old. At age sixty, the payment would be raised to take account of any increase in the cost of living during the intervening years. If I lasted ten years, to an election in 1982, before resigning (or being defeated) the amount increased to 35 per cent of my salary for life, $8,400 a year, again indexed at age sixty. In my view, no former MP should receive a pension until he or she reaches a more normal retirement age of fifty-five or sixty. For my part, I didn't feel entitled to a pension from a country that had already treated me so generously. By getting out before 1978, I made sure of that.

I also had come to realize my limitations in the Tory Party. I knew that if I stayed, I might have felt compelled to run for leader at some point in order to defend policies and principles that weren't otherwise being represented. But the Conservative Party would never have elected me leader. Nor would I have been happy serving in someone's cabinet. Even cabinet, I had come to conclude, was no match for the other ministry. As Lester Pearson relates in his memoirs, his father had been a minister of the gospel, a route Pearson's mother hoped her son would follow. The day he was first appointed to the cabinet as minister for External Affairs, he telephoned his mother to tell her the news. She replied: "Well, I am glad you have at last become a minister, if only a second-class one." I do have to admit, however, that because I loved the traditions of the House of Commons and so much enjoyed the camaraderie of many bipartisan friendships, I would have thrived on serving as Speaker for a time.

I was turning away from all that, however, and on June 9, the night of the Ontario provincial election, I had dinner in Hamilton with my parents and told them of my plans, my discussions with Bishop Sherlock and my meetings with Father Lupo. They were pleased, but in a way not surprised. My father's first comment was a rueful: "What took you so long?"

I now had to decide whether I would become a diocesan priest or join an order. That summer, I spent three weeks in an orientation program at the Trinitarian monastery in Maryland. That time in July and August remains one of the happiest memories of my life. There were twenty young men in the program; I was the only Canadian. Each day was filled with work, prayer, laughter and joy. We'd rise at 6:00 a.m., pray in the chapel, eat breakfast then head out to be the modern-day equivalent of slave labour, painting, cleaning, raking and working in the fields all morning. After lunch, Father Lupo would meet with us, ruminate about his priestly experiences, tell us how to recognize the signs of a valid vocation, and generally just talk about whatever came into his mind. After a question-and-answer session, we'd head back into the fields for more physical labour. Next was supper, followed by Mass, recreation (group sports or swimming), then a reflective time together when we talked about the day and what had happened. By bedtime, we were bone weary, but in all my life I've seldom felt so alive and well-balanced as I did during those three weeks.

Because the new recruits worked, prayed, ate and played together, there was an immediate bonding – a taste of the communal life that would be experienced in a religious order. There were also long and rewarding walks that included individual conversations with Father Lupo as he counselled each attendee and tried to answer all our questions about the life of a priest. At the end of the three weeks, the committee voted to accept me if I applied for admission to the Trinitarian novitiate, the first of five or six years' preparation.

By then, there were few questions in my mind about becoming a priest. I would certainly try. But, would it be as a member of a religious order or as a diocesan priest? The three-week orientation, as I hoped it would, supplied the answer. Toward the end of the program, we were given a night off. I took another student out to dinner at a nearby restaurant. We had a fine meal and as I paid for it using my American Express card, I realized that such behaviour was not consistent with the vow of poverty I would take as a member of an order like the Trinitarians. The following day was to have been a day off, but suddenly that morning there was an announcement that everyone would pile onto a yellow school bus for a tour of Washington, D.C.

I was livid that my free day had been summarily removed, that there was no room for individual agendas. That, however, was how life worked in an order. Decisions were made by the superior and were to be followed, unquestioningly, by all members. The trip to Washington was enjoyable, even though it was hardly my first, but it helped me conclude that I was too individualistic and self-willed ever to live out my life happily in a community where all the decisions were made for me. I did not want my freedom sacrificed at the whim of superiors. I decided that I was not cut out to join a religious order. I returned to Hamilton, saw Bishop Reding and applied to become a diocesan priest.

The next few weeks were a flurry of telling family and friends of my decision. On September 6, I flew to Hamilton to inform some of my closest supporters in the riding. One of the most poignant encounters was with my mentor, Jack MacDonald, who had worked so hard and so effectively for me. His response to my news was most generous. "Well, Sean," he said, "Jessie and I have always wanted a son in the seminary."

The next morning, back in Ottawa, I issued a press release: "During the past thirteen years – over half my life – politics has been a daily companion. Those who know me also know how much Parliament and politics have meant to me. However, their importance lies in the opportunity of service to others that they provide. Throughout my political life, I have looked upon politics as a time and a way in which to serve. After much thought and careful deliberation, I have decided to leave public life. I do so for the most positive reasons, and without any negative ones. I seek the opportunity to serve others in a new and different capacity. I wish to respond to a new challenge and take a new direction in my life."

In the statement, I also took note of a letter I had written to Dief in 1965 expressing my interest in running one day for office and serving Canada. "I used to think, as I guess many people do, that politics was an evil profession and the people in politics entered only for self rewards – then I met someone who changed my mind. He was a man of great importance and power and yet he had time to see a twelve-year-old boy just because that boy wrote him a letter."

In reply, the Chief had written this on August 9, 1965: "I must tell you how pleased I am that you have decided that you are going to take part in the public life of our country. When you come to near the end of your life after such service, you will have the satisfaction that can not be exceeded outside the Christian ministry. Naturally there will be many ups and downs and you will find there are times when you will be criticized unjustly and unfairly, but that is to be expected in public service." His line about the Christian ministry had taken on new meaning twelve years later.

In my resignation letter to Joe Clark I said, "Since assuming the Leadership you have demonstrated remarkable personal and political qualities that make the loyalty owed to you by party members much more than a duty: it is a privilege to be counted among your supporters. Moreover, in our personal dealings, you have earned my lasting respect, esteem and gratitude." For his part, Clark replied with equal graciousness: "There is no question that Parliament will be poorer without you. But the talents which so suited you for that forum will also serve you well in work that is ultimately more important than the career you leave." In media interviews, I urged reporters: Don't make the same mistake that I made eighteen months ago, don't underestimate Joe Clark. He will, I told them, become

Prime Minister.

My departure was seen by some as a slap against Clark because there had been half a dozen departures since he became leader. Jack Horner and Jacques Lavoie, the MP from the Quebec riding of Hochelaga had joined the Liberals; John Reynolds, a B.C. MP, left to become host of a hotline show; Angus MacLean became PC leader in Prince Edward Island; and Gordon Fairweather resigned to head the Canadian Human Rights Commission. Most preferred to stay and fight each other. Keith Davey, a senator and long-time Liberal stalwart made one of the most pungent comments I heard about my departure. He said I had gone from the ridiculous to the sublime.

For John Diefenbaker, however, the departure wasn't distance enough from Clark. My comments had been too kindly to Joe to suit Dief. He called me to his office that afternoon and began by saying: "This morning, I could not have been more proud. As you know, I have regarded you as a son; indeed Olive and I often said that if we were ever to have a son, we'd want him to be just like you. I know how pleased she would be if she were here. Your letter touched me deeply."

Then came the pause that I had come to recognize as signalling a change in his mood. His eyes began to flash and his wattles danced as he said, "And then, this afternoon. This statement about Clark. I cannot understand it." I started to explain, but he would not let me. "No, no," he said, flapping his hand back and forth and closing his eyes, "there's nothing to be said about it. It is the most damnable business I have ever heard of after all my pride and respect for you this morning." Again, I tried to speak and again he cut me off. "As long as I live I will not understand that what you've said today about Joe Clark is what you really believe because you've been here in this office and I know what you think about Joe Clark."

Every time I tried to speak, he'd cut me off by saying the discussion was finished but then he'd proceed to start it up again. "There's nothing more to be said – however, I cannot understand . . ." The cycle continued like that for twenty minutes, as if we were caught up in a neverending minuet. In the end, I could only conclude that while he was not pleased that I had praised Joe, that was mostly a cover for his disappointment over my leaving Parliament. Becoming a priest was a noble thing, he was saying, but not for an MP – that was the epitome of service as far as he was concerned.

Later, Dief wrote to me to say: "I feel a deep sense of personal loss. It comes to a very limited few to establish the national reputation you have earned for yourself. For me who has looked on you with the pride of a father, Parliament will never be the same." I saw him only a few times after, and never again as a parliamentary colleague. Quickly and quietly, I left Ottawa. I knew if I hung around, I'd become a walking sideshow. I was off to Rome – to be in my Father's house.

CHAPTER EIGHT

GOING HOME:
THE LAST CAMPAIGN

John Diefenbaker was buried in Archie McQueen's socks. His tie, too, I think. Here's how it happened. In the summer of 1979, I was on a break from my studies in Rome and returned to Canada. I had spoken with the Chief by phone from Hamilton and promised to visit him soon in Ottawa. Shortly after, Keith Martin phoned me. "You'd better get up here," he said. "The Old Man is very anxious to see you." A few days later, I arrived in Ottawa in mid-afternoon. I told Keith I wanted to see Dief immediately and get the visit behind me. It wasn't that I was feeling callous, it was just that in the later years of his life, our dealings were not what they had once been. The visit would be no more than a predictable performance on both our parts.

Keith had already been around to see Dief at home that day and suggested I wait. I postponed my visit to the next day. I've always regretted that decision. I stayed overnight with Keith and his wife, Merle, and the next morning I was sleeping fitfully and dreaming about that scheduled encounter. In the dream, I was sitting outside Dief's parliamentary office listening to him, in full flight inside the office, raging at one of his secretaries. Suddenly, the vision disappeared as I was roused by someone opening my bedroom door. I was only partially awake when Keith announced, "Sean, Mr. Diefenbaker died at home this morning." It was the first time in the thirteen years that I had known him that John Diefenbaker and I did not keep an appointment. Instead of staying in Ottawa a few days for a visit, I stayed a week for a funeral.

Keith phoned Prime Minister Joe Clark with the news that his colleague and former leader had died. Clark's response was so matter-of-fact Keith could only conclude that he must somehow have

159

already known. Keith phoned The Canadian Press and we drafted a statement for general release to the media. Among our first undertakings was the task of creating the "official" story of the Chief's death. After all, both Keith and I as aides had protected his legend in life; we could do no less than preserve that legacy after death. Dief's body had been found by Archie McQueen, a school teacher from Hamilton, who had come to Ottawa for several summers to volunteer his services for various office duties. Archie was just another example of the kind of extraordinary loyalty Dief could command from diverse people across Canada. Archie's commitment was not ideological or political, it was purely personal, and with Olive dead, Archie was all the more welcome. In addition to helping out at the office, he was congenial and caring company for Dief at home. In that final summer, he had even moved into Dief's house in Rockcliffe to assist, along with the housekeeper, wherever he could.

It was Archie who found Dief early that Thursday morning, August 16, 1979. He was slumped on the floor of his downstairs study, clad only in tattered socks and boxer shorts. In his hand was a vial of pills that he had been fumbling with when the sudden and massive attack came. He had died quickly and without pain. Just as well. John Diefenbaker had a more intense fear of death than anyone else I knew. After Archie told me the details of his discovery, I said: "Now, here's the story. You found him in his study, all right, but slumped over his desk working on papers for the new session of Parliament. And, if anyone asks, fully clothed." Archie dutifully stuck to the story. After all, the cloak of the eternal parliamentarian had to be wrapped about Dief, even in death.

Keith and I then went to the prime minister's office in the Langevin Block across Wellington Street from the Parliament Buildings. I was still shaken by the news, but met with Under Secretary of State Pierre Juneau, his colleague from the same department, Graham Glockling, and Jean Pigott, a former MP and at the time senior advisor to Clark. Clark had given *carte blanche* for the service, which was to have the status of a state funeral. It was decided that a troika would oversee the arrangements. The three would include Pigott, to give the PM's authorization, Glockling to carry through with arrangements and either Keith or myself to ensure that Dief's wishes were carried out.

For Keith, it was like burying his own father all over again. He had devoted his life to serving Dief. For the most part, he was too emotionally drained to make decisions, so most of them fell to me. I guess I knew as well as anyone how Dief would have wanted things done.

Although the funeral plans, which had been previously settled with Dief's concurrence, were well advanced, according to protocol, there can't be a state funeral until the prime minister calls the next of kin. The same protocol dictates that, in turn, the next of kin requests a state funeral. The circle complete, the prime minister then orders events to begin. Clark was attending a meeting elsewhere, so we were shown into his office and waited there for his arrival. Clark would call Carolyn Weir, daughter of Olive Diefenbaker by her first marriage, the closest next of kin. As we entered Clark's office, an aide scurried to remove some drawings by Clark's daughter, Catherine. He stashed them in a drawer, explaining that there had been a media "photo opportunity" in the office earlier and that the fingerpaintings were kept handy to add just the right parental touch on such occasions. The rest of the time, the childish creations were kept out of sight.

The aide withdrew, leaving us alone in Clark's office. As we waited for him, as anyone else might do who had been in politics, I couldn't resist finding out what it felt like to be *behind* the prime minister's desk. I walked around the desk and stood behind his chair surveying the scene. The top of the desk was clear except for two empty file trays. As I looked more closely, I couldn't believe my eyes. I called Keith to come over and stand beside me. "Do you see what I see?" I asked. Someone had carefully used a large Dymo labeller to create the words "in" and "out," then stuck the coloured tapes with the adroit descriptives on the respective trays. Keith just shook his head and said: "We're in worse shape than I thought." It looked like amateur hour on the Rideau.

Clark swept into the room, offered a curt "Good morning," but made no comment either about Dief's death or the funeral. He didn't even have the courtesy to pass the time of day with either of us, although Keith was obviously in emotional pain and I hadn't seen Clark since resigning my seat almost two years earlier. Clark was briefed about the protocol that must be followed and was told that the Department of National Defence had located Carolyn Weir, who was on a camping trip with her family. The phone call taken care of, the Department of National Defence then flew Carolyn and her family to Ottawa to begin the difficult week.

This Canadian family, one that had stayed well out of the limelight, was about to go through the pomp and public grieving that surrounds a state funeral. We picked them up at Ottawa airport later in the day, offered our condolences, then got to some nasty business that had to be dealt with immediately. Dief's funeral plans had been given the code name "Operation Hope Not," a name that had also been assigned to the plans for the funeral of Winston Churchill. That's how Graham Glockling, whose job in Secretary of State was to organize special events for the protocol branch, had sold it to Dief. Glockling had worked on Pearson's funeral, which had had little advance planning, so he knew how helpful it was to have major decisions made in advance with the full co-operation of the person to be mourned.

As a result, the unflappable and efficient Glockling had worked out nearly every detail carefully with Dief. Dief wanted the Red Ensign draped on the coffin, a final reminder that he had fought to retain the ties it symbolized with Britain. Glockling pointed out that because this was a state funeral, the Canadian flag must be used. Finally, a compromise was reached: both flags would appear on the coffin. Dief also wanted his medals and decorations to be carried and displayed. Although he was a Baptist, he wanted the service to be held in Christ Church Anglican Cathedral because that had been the location of the funeral for his opponent, Lester Pearson, and he wanted the environs to be equally accommodating for the hordes he expected would attend. Christ Church was, after all, the largest church in Ottawa. Dief had discussed every aspect and had even scoured the details of services held for other world notables, looking for ideas and precedents.

One of his wishes, however, caused a particular problem. Dief's second wife, Olive, who had died in 1976, was buried in Beechwood Cemetery near their home in Ottawa's Rockcliffe Park area. Dief had wanted to be buried with her, but his own plans changed after she died. First, no one ever expected she would die before him. Second, at the time of her death, plans had not yet been finalized for the Diefenbaker Centre at the University of Saskatchewan in Saskatoon. Once that centre was proposed in 1978 and Dief decided he would be buried as part of the shrine there, he said he wanted Olive's remains disinterred, transported to Saskatoon and laid to rest with his at the time of his own burial. His remains were to travel there by train; as for Olive's, he left that transportation detail to the officials.

No approval had ever been received for the disinterment, so it was my difficult and unhappy task that August night to broach this topic with Carolyn and have her sign the necessary papers. I spoke to her as we sped in from the airport. After I had put the request, there was a long pause from the back of the darkened limousine. Finally she said: "You know that mother was aware something like this might happen. She spoke to me about this and she did not want it." I pressed on: "Carolyn, please, just sign." After a few more minutes of silence, she relented. I handed the papers into the back seat for her signature. In a difficult week, that was a most troublesome ordeal for us both.

The media took a morbid interest in the disinterment proceedings. They wanted lurid pictures. The last thing we wanted were photographers at the graveside in Beechwood Cemetery. To keep the media wolves off the trail, we put out a phony story, giving the wrong date and saying that the transfer would be done by DND aircraft. In fact, the disinterment was carried out earlier than announced and the remains were shipped via Air Canada. Thanks to this subterfuge, there were no photos or first-hand reports.

The numbers of people involved in the funeral arrangements grew quickly. About forty persons attended the first briefings. They represented all the various elements involved – Secretary of State for the service, External Affairs for the accreditation of the ambassadors, the RCMP for security, National Defence for transportation, and so on. It was the biggest show in town. It ran for a full week and cost the taxpayer $1 million. For me, it was like a providential perq. For that entire week, I knew what it was like to be in power or at least to have the illusion of power. With the prime minister's blessing, I did everything from dispatching Falcon Jets to overriding officials.

The zaniness started with the naming of pallbearers. Dief had specified that the RCMP were to act as the working pallbearers, but there were also to be sets of active and honorary pallbearers. We came upon several lists Dief had drawn up in the final years outlining who the chosen people should be. He had designated various categories, including active, inactive and honorary pallbearers. Names that did not appear on his lists began coming to our minds. Keith and I made a few additions, justifying them by telling ourselves that there may have been other lists that we had yet to discover. Moreover, the lists we had found were done at different times and showed that Dief, in his own inimitable and mercurial way, had added certain names one day and dropped them the next as they moved in and out of his favour.

We decided to apply our own litmus test of loyalty to the Old Man. We didn't delete anybody, but we did add a few whom we convinced ourselves Dief would want as pallbearers. As names came to mind, we'd send them over to Jean Pigott. The number of pallbearers soon grew to ridiculous proportions. Clark was monitoring everything, and Pigott said that he had expressed "surprise and concern" at this ever-expanding list of pallbearers. "Would it soon be over?" she asked. At that point, I knew from the tone of her request that it *was* over. She relayed a question from the prime minister. "He has no problems with any of the names you have suggested," she said, "but he does want to know this: was Jack Horner *really* on one of Mr. Diefenbaker's lists?" I replied by making my response into a request: "Please tell the Prime Minister yes." Although Horner had crossed the floor to sit as a Liberal two years earlier, in his day and generation, to use a Diefenbaker phrase, he had been steadfastly loyal. At the service, pallbearer Jack Horner was moved to tears; he revered the Old Man.

In those first few hours, I also put the old network together again, just as I had when we organized the leadership race of Paul Hellyer in 1976. I got Jimmy Johnston up from Cobourg, Ontario, and put him on the phone to all the Diefenbaker cronies to let them know how to pick up the tickets they would need to attend the funeral. Jimmy, in his enthusiasm – and that is a trait that has marked all his ventures – took it upon himself to mention to everyone he called that there was a train bearing Dief to Prince Albert and they were welcome to climb aboard. By the time I got wind of his generous invitations, we were well over our allotted contingent. The railway was being very strict with its available space. Travelling dignitaries would include Secretary of State officials, House of Commons personnel, government representatives and the press. The "Diefenbaker party" was to have forty-five seats; Jimmy had us up to seventy sharing a moment of history in which everyone wanted to participate. Jimmy wanted everybody on that last campaign with Dief and it led to the only argument we ever had. At the end of the day, I said to him that he had told too many people they could travel west. "If you think you can do a better job," he snapped, "then you do it."

I began uninviting some of the train guests. One of the unfortunate victims was the mayor of Prince Albert. He had flown to Ottawa on the overnight plane – known as the "red-eye special" – to represent Prince Albert at the funeral. He then planned to ride out on the train. As he presented himself at the office I had commandeered, he looked to me like a prime candidate for removal. When the secretary announced his arrival I told her to wait a minute, then usher him in. I thought for a moment, then punched up a button on the phone. As he walked in the door, I said into the mouthpiece: "Commissioner, it's all right. Tell your force that we've located him. The mayor has just walked into my office." I hung up, turned to him and said: "Mr. Mayor, you don't know how glad I am to see you. We've been searching the country for you."

"Well," he replied, "I've been flying here. John was a great MP and a wonderful friend. I wanted to come."

"Yes," I said, "it's wonderful that you're here so I can ask you this directly. How fast can you get back to Prince Albert?" He looked taken aback and said he'd just arrived and was expecting to return on the train. I needed him off.

"Mr. Mayor, in the next couple of days, the eyes of Canada will be on Prince Albert. We need you back there to make sure that everything goes right and that you give Mr. Diefenbaker a send-off that Canadians will be proud of."

He almost saluted as he said: "I'll be on the first plane." Using such altruistic appeals to duty, and every other kind of Irish blandishment, I was able to get the train list under control.

John Diefenbaker's body lay in state for two days in the Hall of Honour in the Parliament Buildings. Thousands filed past and signed the guest book. On the day of the funeral, I was standing outside the church with the pallbearers. As the hearse carrying the remains pulled up, I noticed opposite me in the back row of pallbearers the second most famous face in Canada – that of René Lévesque. I was amazed, flabbergasted and touched all at the same time that he would come to John Diefenbaker's funeral. My next thought was: What's he doing standing out here? The special section reserved for the premiers was inside. He should have been there. I could only assume that no one had communicated the arrangements to him, never dreaming he'd come.

We were all supposed to be standing at attention, waiting for the coffin to be removed from the hearse, but I called over one of the funeral home attendants and directed his attention to Lévesque. "Aren't the premiers supposed to be inside?" I asked. The attendant either didn't recognize Lévesque or didn't see who I was pointing to. "Yes," he said slowly. "Do you want me to check?" "No, no," I said, making gesticulations at Lévesque and toward the church door. "*He* should be in there." "Oh," he said, apparently understanding at last what I was fussing about. He walked over to Lévesque and asked: "Do you work for one of the premiers?" Totally exasperated, I grabbed the undertaker with one arm and Lévesque with the other and propelled them both through the doors of the church. I was irate that Lévesque had made such a grand gesture of reconciliation only to have some anglophone mistake him for an aide.

The service was ecumenical and ended with the recessional Dief had requested, "The Battle Hymn of The Republic." The roof was nearly lifted with the words: "He hath loosed the fateful lightning of His terrible, swift sword/His truth is marching on." There was a long cavalcade to the VIA Rail station. We had been through a lot of honour guards, protocol and formalities. The time had arrived for the emotion. Dief had come from the West, he'd made the train his campaign instrument because, as he said, he liked to be with the people. Now, he was headed home to the West on the train one last time. At the railway station, there was a nineteen-gun salute and a military band struck up "Auld Lang Syne." It was a most powerful moment. I, along with many others who had been in control until then, wept freely as the train slowly departed.

There were still details to be decided. We were meeting with officials from the Secretary of State's department to finalize arrangements in Saskatoon, and an Armed Forces officer arrived with a message from the minister of National Defence, Allan McKinnon. He said our request for an Armed Forces 707 to fly MPs out and back had been rejected. He argued that costs would be too high and worried about so many MPs being on the same flight. McKinnon had never been a Diefenbaker man or an O'Sullivan fan, so I was suspicious. In place of the speedier and more comfortable 707, he was offering an older, prop-driven plane that would seat about fifty.

By then, I was getting used to the levers of power and my ability to order events. I gave the officer a bald message to take back to his minister: "You tell that son-of-a-bitch to have that plane ready to go or I'll requisition two." "Yes, sir," he said, saluted and left bearing my orders. I worried no more. I also got National Defence to bend the rules and provide liquor on the return flight to Ottawa – knowing parliamentarians as I do. On my instructions, however, there was no liquor provided on the way to the funeral. As I say, I know parliamentarians.

Meanwhile, Dief's remains were moving west in a refurbished baggage car filled with flowers in the middle of the blue-and-gold Via Rail train. The members of the official party were in the front coaches, the media in the rear. As the train crawled across Canada it became a cocoon from the rest of the world. The booze began to flow and Diefenbaker's funeral procession quickly became like an Irish wake on wheels. Tongues were loosened, stories were swapped and old animosities were rekindled. Reports started to appear in the media almost immediately. Among the tales, stories about a secret trust fund for Diefenbaker surfaced. Also, battles were erupting between the estate executors and the literary executors. Reporters on the train were hearing all this and filing the stories with their offices. And the stories were appearing – unbeknownst to those travelling on the train, who continued to talk very freely.

I was not on the train. I chose instead to stay in Ottawa and keep in touch with progress along the way by phone. Now I had to move to stop the embarrassing and unfortunate stories. On the one hand there were so many scenes of respect and admiration – Canadians lining up to sign guest books and queueing at stations for a fleeting glimpse, farmers taking their hats off in the fields, people strewing flowers in the train's path. The train was running late because of the unexpectedly large crowds. On the other hand, on the train things were out of control. Reverence had been replaced by rancour. In addition to the trust-fund revelations, there was sniping between Keith and John Munro (the author who helped Dief with his memoirs) on the one side and the executors on the other.

There were three literary executors: Keith, Tom Van Dusen and Greg Guthrie. Another group of executors for the estate itself included Senator David Walker, Judge Ted Hughes, Dr. Lewis Brand and Joel Aldred. The debate among all those people revolved around who controlled the Diefenbaker papers. The estate executors argued that there was no legal meaning to the phrase "literary executor." Keith argued that it meant control and disposition of all Dief's papers. He wanted to do what Jack Pickersgill had done for Mackenzie King – release papers slowly over time to protect Dief's good name. (When it eventually went to court, Keith lost.) On the train, the bitter battle was just beginning.

Moreover, there was a rousing debate over the trust fund. Was there a trust fund at all? If there was, what had happened to it? There were charges that papers were missing. There was also some confusion about which of Dief's many wills was valid. Some claimed that the last will had been produced under duress, and others said that he had not been in complete control of his faculties when he drew it up. It was all just typical Tory fighting. Even in death, Dief remained a figure of controversy as people tried to summon his memory to their side of the fight. The feuding was most unpleasant. I knew and liked all of these people. But John Diefenbaker was dead, and there was no point to be served in anyone fighting anymore. In all, there was a lot of nastiness. Death brings out the best and the worst in people. Dief's death was no exception.

The full story on the trust fund has yet to be unravelled, but in essence it was this. John Diefenbaker went into politics without any money. On that point, everyone agrees. After that, however, there are two versions of the truth. One is that at the height of his power a group of supporters decided he should have some discretionary funds to look after those things not covered by the rather modest prime minister's salary of that era. The other version goes that it was an attempt to provide a cushion to make his departure from the leadership of the Conservative Party easier in the 1962-63 period. Perhaps, that story went, his departure could be accelerated by such a fund.

While there may be a dispute about its origins, a trust fund did exist. At his death, Dief's total estate was in excess of $1 million; the trust fund formed about $300,000 of that total. The question still remains, however, whether the trust fund was set up with his knowledge and permission, or whether, without his sanction, party bagmen went ahead with the fund anyway. His will lends some credence to the latter view since there is the curious comment that the trust fund had come to his attention only "recently." Whatever the full explanation, Dief willed the proceeds of the fund to various charities such as those for crippled children.

The debate continues. At the time, however, it was urgent that I get word to everyone on the train to hold their fire at least until after the burial. The next major stop was Winnipeg. We'd been alerted that additional reporters were gathering in Winnipeg looking for more words from loose-lipped Diefenphiles about the trust fund, the estate and the feuds. Contact became imperative. I knew exactly two people in Winnipeg who might be in a position to get such a message to the warring parties on the train. Neither could be contacted by telephone.

The prime minister's switchboard saved the day. I picked up the phone, dialled one of the PM's switchboard operators and said: "Get me the premier of Manitoba." I didn't know him, hadn't even met him, but within five minutes, Sterling Lyon was on the line. "Mr. Premier," I said, "we have a problem. We need to get someone on that train before it arrives in the station to bundle Keith Martin and John Munro off the train and get them somewhere so I can talk to them. You've got to get them off and into a safe room. Also, make sure the press doesn't get to anyone else on that train." Lyon didn't know me, and he didn't ask why I needed this odd favour, but he set it all in motion with the stationmaster in Winnipeg. People were moved off the train early; I spoke to Keith by phone and told him to keep quiet and tell others to do the same. The fires did die down, but most of the damage had already been done.

I flew out with Carolyn Weir to be on the last leg of the train trip down from Prince Albert to Saskatoon. She was so angry about what had been emanating from the train that she couldn't even speak to John Munro. He wanted to apologize, but she was too upset and hurt to meet him. I had to put her into a compartment and tell him to apologize another time, she was so angry.

It had fallen to Archie McQueen to assist the funeral directors in preparing Dief for viewing and burial. After he'd picked out a suit, Archie realized that John Diefenbaker, for all his glory, did not have a decent, matching pair of socks to his name. Nor was there a tie in any kind of clean condition. And so it was that when Canada's thirteenth prime minister was buried on August 22, 1979, he went to his grave in a pair of Archie's socks and one of his new, clean ties.

At the funeral itself, Joe Clark gave what was very likely his best speech ever. He chose eloquent words and spoke with a tone and cadence that both suited the moment and echoed the prevailing mood. He wrote the speech himself. Clark can be a gifted wordsmith when he takes the time; this was one of those occasions. He began simply, but with great feeling: "John Diefenbaker is home." His solemn closing caused some people to comment on the mild, perhaps intended, irony of his experiences with Diefenbaker in caucus and elsewhere. "God bless," said Clark and then paused just for a moment to stress the next two words, "and keep – John Diefenbaker."

After the funeral, I was standing on the Saskatoon airport tarmac worrying about my parliamentary charges and their return to Ottawa. Near the 707 for the MPs was the prime minister's Jetstar. Joe and Maureen had already boarded their aircraft, but they deplaned, came over and spoke to me. It was the first time I'd talked to Maureen since a function in my riding a few years earlier. There, the organizers had come looking for me to start the event. Maureen's comment at the time was typical of her caustic tongue. "Isn't that just like you, Sean," she said. "Always holdings things up."

I was aware that her own father had recently died. I had met him and liked him as one of the old party stalwarts, so I expressed my sympathies to her now. She accepted my condolences and added, thinking how Dief's funeral had finally brought us together: "All this brings it all back." For the first time, I could see that behind the sometimes harsh and calculating bravado of Maureen McTeer there is a softer, vulnerable human core that is only too rarely revealed.

By then, it was 5:40 p.m., and our pilot was anxious to be airborne for Ottawa. Some of the VIPs were a bit tardy. The captain wanted to take off no later than 6:00 p.m. I agreed. A few more stragglers did arrive, but some were still missing at 5:55 p.m. In the psychodrama of the moment, I recalled Lyndon Johnson's first presidential order, given on another Boeing 707 in Dallas after John Kennedy's assassination. I turned to the captain and grandly paraphrased Johnson: "Let's get this plane back to Ottawa." We bounded up the stairs and took off.

For me, it was a bittersweet week. First, it afforded me the opportunity to give John Diefenbaker the send-off he deserved. Second, I had the experience of power and that was salutary. After being in opposition and wondering all the while what it would be like to be in government and have power, I had been able to exercise it for seven days. I have to say that it made me feel good to make things happen. Because I had spent a year in the seminary I could also stand outside myself and watch my orders given and carried out. Being in Ottawa made my earlier decision seem a more enlightened one and reinforced my view that the decision had been the right one for me. Yes, the week was an enjoyable nibble at the banquet of power; and yes, it is important that some people live their lives at the centre – but not for me. If I'd had any doubts, they were gone now. It was Ralph Waldo Emerson who wrote, "You shall have joy or you shall have power, said God, you shall not have both." I had chosen joy and was happier for it.

In the end, the circumstances of Dief's death only prove the truth of the saying: "*Sic transit gloria mundi*"("So passes away the glory of the world"). They also demonstrate the tragedy of John Diefenbaker. He had rightly achieved a legendary status. People wanted to see him, to hear him, to touch him and to be with him. For many, he was a living monument in the national museum that is Ottawa. One of the

171

tragedies of John Diefenbaker's life was that while he and Olive didn't suffer financially, he really didn't have much money until his memoirs were published in three volumes, from 1975-77. By then he was too old to do much of anything with the royalties he received. If he had known about the trust fund or been reminded of it earlier, he could have drawn on the funds, either for himself or for his step-daughter, Carolyn. Keith's own belief and theory was that the people who established the fund hoped to keep it quiet and, on Dief's death, quietly dispose of the proceeds.

But after all of his achievements, what was it for? John Diefenbaker died alone. Worse, he died lonely. His parents were long gone, as was his brother, Elmer. His first wife of twenty-two years, Edna, had died in 1951. His second wife of twenty-three years, Olive, died in 1976. They were the only people with whom he'd ever been close. At the end, his only remaining love was the House of Commons and even it, he would argue, was not the place it had been. His last crusade was more a lament than a battle cry: "I want to see Parliament live!"

Those of us who worked for him wanted to be his friends, and he would have said we were. In truth, however, we were not his friends. We were his fans. That was as close as he would let anyone come. Somewhere amid the demands of the daily performance for his fans and for himself he misplaced the ability to make or maintain anything like a genuine, warm and intimate friendship with anyone. For all his populism and honest love of people, he simply couldn't make lasting friends. It just didn't fit with his battling life, the days riddled with betrayal and the memories muddled with intrigue. He never forgave any slight, real or imagined. He should have, but all those battles and all those years left him too bitter and suspicious for rich friendships.

We admired him. We even loved him. We cheered for him and we were honoured to be in his effervescent company. At the close of his life we were all more than a little sad that his final years were spent in such isolation. John Diefenbaker, our hero, had become both a prisoner and a victim of his own legend.

CHAPTER NINE

MORE IRISH THAN
THE IRISH THEMSELVES

Father Joseph Lupo was aghast when I told him where I would be studying for the priesthood. "Not with the Irish?" Yes, the Irish; specifically, the Pontifico Collegio Irlandese in Rome. "The Irish only care about two commandments," he declared, "the sixth and the ninth. And every sin is mortal." Only Father Lupo could put theology in such graphic terms. He was happy about my decision to become a priest and the fact that I was going to Rome – but the Irish! An Irishman, according to his stereotype, worries only about adultery and coveting his neighbour's wife; sex equals sin and sin equals sex.

The truth was I had little choice. In Rome, most major countries, including Canada, have national colleges where men study to become priests. The Canadian College, however, is quite small and exists only for priests doing postgraduate work. Of the other English-speaking colleges, the North American College, despite its name, did not then accept Canadians, but was open only to U.S. nationals. The other three possibilities were the English College, the Scots College and the Irish College. The first two were already full for that fall, so by a process of elimination the choice became the Pontifical Irish College. In the end, the Irish was a happy choice for my next three years.

The Irish College is an historic institution. The current building, the fourth to exist, was built in the early part of this century; it is near St. John Lateran Basilica, forty-five minutes by bus from St. Peter's and is typical lace-curtain Irish. Behind the kelly-green iron gates, the three-storey beige stone building sits amid lush lawns, gardens and fountains. Inside, the foyer is marble and there is a polished staircase with a narrow red carpet. At first sight, it appears to be the equivalent of a gentleman's finishing school for the Irish church hierarchy.

That fond view altered as I was shown around. Away from the front façade and fine foyer, the building was in severe disrepair. My high-ceilinged room was spartan and contained only an antiquated wooden slat bed, a wardrobe for clothes, a desk, a chair and a sink. The only personal items were the trunk I'd brought, some family photographs and my cassette player. The college was in such dire financial straits that during the cold, rainy months from November to March, the central heating was turned on for just two hours in the morning and two hours in the evening. To survive, everyone bought supplemental electric heaters, and on particularly raw nights all the heaters glowed and the circuits always blew. The communal bathroom was down the hall. Outside there was a swimming pool that was actually no more than a cement box into which cold water was poured after the first-year students had cleaned out the collected leaves and debris.

In all, the college housed about seventy-five residents, sixty of them studying for the priesthood, the rest doing graduate work. In my own class, there were fourteen first-year students, most of them younger than myself because they had proceeded into theology directly from university. Despite my Irish name, I was the only non-Irish seminarian. It wasn't until Christmas that my past as an MP in Canada became public knowledge among my fellow seminarians. I welcomed that anonymity because I was able to become integrated into the community, with only my accent and my age making me any different.

Living with so many Irish students I was able to discover much about my background and the country of my forebears. I had never been to Ireland, but I soon came to know Irish ways and understand my own bull-headedness better. As a people, the Irish suffer from an inferiority complex that renders them melancholy and brave and defeatist all at once. It is the co-existence of these apparent contradictions that shapes the Irish psyche.

I learned that the Irish of the North and the South are as dissimilar as Canadians and Americans. And within Ireland, there are many distinct cultures; they are not a monolithic people. Speech, views and customs differ widely from county to county. I absorbed enough that by the end of my three years, I sounded like a south Dubliner. Once, an American student trying to enrol used me as an example of a non-Irish student who had been admitted, but Monsignor Eamonn Marron, the rector, turned him down and explained my presence by saying: "He's more Irish than the Irish themselves." I also saw the deep and abiding faith of the Irish and heard all the arguments about the Northern Irish problem as well as every possible solution. I sadly concluded that the problem is intractable; there is no clear way out of the very tragic situation there.

The students at the Scots College were the best party-goers and they were also the keenest students. The Irish would party, too, but have the good sense to sleep it off the next day. Not the Scots. The morning after, Scottish students would be sitting in the front row at lectures, furiously taking notes. Predictably, the Irish regarded the residents of the Venerable English College as pompous clerical dilettantes. It was said that there were three qualifications for becoming a bishop in England. First, you had to be male; second, you had to be baptized; third, you had to be graduated from the Venerable English College. In cases of necessity, the story went, the Vatican was willing to waive the first two conditions.

Becoming a student again after the freedoms of Ottawa was a severe adjustment. One day I had a staff, car and money; the next I had regressed to an austere seminary setting. On the first Saturday night, a student from another college and I went out to dinner. When we arrived back at the college it was only 11:30 but the gates were padlocked shut. I stood outside staring up at the vice-rector's darkened window, debating whether to ring the bell and risk his wrath. I decided on stealth instead. With the help of a motorscooter that was leaning against the fence, the other student's shoulders and a coat placed over the spikes atop the gates, I climbed up, jumped down into the grounds and, fortunately, found an open door for my furtive entrance. In the days ahead, every student obtained a copy of the "underground" key to the gates (to which the powers that be turned a blind eye).

The food at the Irish College in that era was abysmal and by Christmas I had lost fifteen pounds – about 10 per cent of the 158 pounds I weighed when I began. Breakfast consisted of a hard roll called a *panino,* some butter, industrial-quality milk and pots of strong, lethal tea. Since all lectures were given in Italian, we spent the first month trying to learn the language. That effort turned out to be one of the great disappointments of my time in Rome. The teacher assigned to the first-year students was a woman who had grown up Catholic but was no longer practising her religion. In fact, she had become anti-clerical. If that had been her only problem, she would have been tolerable. This was, however, her first assignment *and* she was a terrible teacher. As a result, each day was siege warfare between us. Only two of the fourteen students achieved anything like passable Italian. I was not one of them.

The college regimen was rigorous. Up at 6:20 a.m., chapel at 6:40 for prayer and meditation followed by breakfast and hours of classes interrupted only by lunch, then a short but welcome siesta prior to more classes, then Mass, dinner, studies and lights out by 11:30 p.m. In all, there was more than an hour of scheduled prayers daily as well as a forty-five minute Mass. There were also the usual student high jinks. One night, as I sneaked into my room after being out late, I had the strangest feeling that someone was already there. The moonlight was shining through the window, and I suddenly saw that there was a body under the covers of my bed. Only the head was visible, staring up at the ceiling. I let out a muffled gasp. Then I recognized the face: it was the college's life-size plaster statue of Ireland's patron saint, St. Patrick. Once the initial shock had worn off, I was left with the practical problem of how to get the heavy statue back to its pedestal down the hallway. Several students had probably been involved in this traditional trick that was routinely played on new students. Since it was long past curfew, and no one was around to help, I had to drag St. Patrick back quietly by myself.

The Irish College, like the other national colleges, was a place to live, celebrate Mass and receive spiritual formation. During the day, however, we took our classes elsewhere. Students from all the national colleges attended one of the three papal universities in Rome: the Lateran, the Angelicum or the Gregorian University. Without a doubt, "the Greg," where we studied, was the best in Rome. It had traditionally been a place for the training of priests, but today a number of lay people as well as religious sisters study there also.

The professors at Gregorian were Jesuits from around the world – all teaching in Italian. The use of Italian was a small concession to modern times. Until fifteen years before, all classes had been held in Latin. In first year, classes contained two hundred students of many nationalities (and languages) working toward the degree of Bachelor of Sacred Theology. We took five courses each semester in such subjects as moral theology, Latin, Greek, scripture and the Sacraments. Classes began in mid-October and ended in June with two sets of exams every year. The professors took the standard Jesuitical approach and looked, in turn, at the teachings of the Old and New Testaments, the early Church fathers, the Councils of the Church, Vatican II and current theological opinions.

With so few students or teachers working in their mother tongue, it was a wonder anyone survived the workload. In my first two years, six fellow Irish College students packed their bags and went home, unable to withstand what's called "being on the rack" – the mental anguish of feeling unable to live up to God's demands on those who wish to wear the cleric's collar. For the rest of us, however, there was collaboration to get around the system. At the North American College, for example, senior students who had become fluent in Italian would protect their fellow students who were not. The seniors would sit in on first-year lectures, transcribe them, then translate them overnight and make copies available in English the next day.

The secret, then, was to befriend a student from the North American College (the Pontifico Collegio Hiltonese we called it, because it was so posh) and obtain photocopies. The exams, both oral and written, were done in the language of your choice. As a result, you could graduate after three years of attending lectures in Italian, as I did, able to understand the language somewhat but unable to speak it beyond ordering a meal. Out of my experience in Rome grew a personal sympathy for any immigrant struggling with a new language.

Rome was a pagan city when Peter went there as Pope and it remains a pagan city today. When I first visited Rome in 1975, I was swept off my feet by its grandeur and glory. Seeing it up close for three years made me realize that I had been blinded by enthusiasm and idealism to its less impressive and less edifying side. While the Jesuit teachers were brilliant and dedicated, the city was also home to clerical careerists just hanging on to sinecures in the church. These are the bureaucrats who gravitate to the Vatican and calculate their way up the ranks – ambitiously attached to a bishop, archbishop or cardinal. They handle mail, receive visitors and generally serve the curial officialdom in the most unctuous manner. We even had a saying about this sad side of Rome: "Blessed are those who have seen and yet still believe."

"Ambition," it is said, "becomes the lust of the clergy." If you take healthy young men and tell them that part of their commitment to the church is to remain celibate, the easiest way to compensate for thwarted desire is to become overly ambitious. Unfortunately, these careerists tend to feel that it is their duty to maintain the church's hierarchical structure, to be support staff to a clerical empire. Thanks to my experience in politics, this role did not tempt me. After all, I had been the victim of my own vaulting ambition before, and I knew how shallow it could become. For me, the church is at its best in the company of everyday people, nurturing their faith.

I was beginning to see myself as I yearned to be, as a servant of God, not a slave to my lesser self or another stifling system. Those who remained in Rome apparently thought they were somehow closer to Heaven; they were not. Heaven was to be found in the streets and the homes and hearts of the people of God. Outsiders think it must be edifying to study in the shadow of St. Peter's, but after attending a couple of papal audiences and sending the appropriate postcards home, I stayed far away from "the office," as we called the Vatican, except for rare and specific events. In July 1978, for example, two other students and I skipped exam cramming one Saturday to attend a concert in the audience hall of the Vatican. The concert was not the reason; we wanted to see Pope Paul VI. We felt a bond with him and knew he had been ailing for some time. That evening, we sat about ten feet from him. He died the following month.

More important than coming to terms with student disillusionment, however, was something I learned about the church and, by extension, about myself. As I studied theology for the first time, I realized that Christ was far more compassionate and less judgemental than I had previously imagined. I could see that the church needed to reflect that truth more forcefully. Jesus had come to earth not just for Catholics, but for everyone, and He came out of love for all of us. What I learned was a broadening and deepening of the love I had felt during that retreat in Connecticut, a lesson that also had applications to my previous political life. I grew to know Christ as truly loving us all, even with all our failings. Further, he only asks one thing in return – that we love one another as well, even those who have hurt us. For me it was the beginning of a new challenge for my life, one of forgiveness and understanding toward those who, in the past, I had blindly regarded as enemies.

The man who most helped me discover this insight and guided me through the difficult times was my spiritual director. Every student had such a spiritual mentor; mine was certainly a godsend. He was Father Dan Ormonde, prior of the Irish Augustinians in Rome, and he regularly listened to me let off steam about everything from petty complaints over the food to my deepest concerns about my spiritual well-being. For the most part, he was a cheerful soul who consoled and counselled, but he could also be quite tough. On one visit, as I ranted on about all the things I thought were wrong in my life and said I was considering giving up my studies for the priesthood, he grew irate. "This is exactly what Satan would want you to do," he said. "You can go back to Christ in prayer and ask for the strength to see you through the storm or you can do what Satan wants and give up." Father Ormonde quickly brought me to my senses.

Although I avoided most of official Rome, there was one cardinal who befriended me and was not like the others: Sergio Pignedoli. He had been papal nuncio in Ottawa before I was an MP and had spent one summer travelling through Canada in a Volkswagen van meeting people. In Rome, the much-loved Pignedoli was president of the Secretariat for Non-Christians and his role was to promote dialogue with those not of the Christian faith. He'd heard from friends in Canada that I was in Rome, so in my first year I had a call from him and was invited to his office.

In a city of stuffed shirts and ambitious capes, Cardinal Pignedoli was an exception. When I met him he wore the simple black cassock of a priest and was a cherubic and friendly man. Our chat was brief – about Canada and his admiration for John Diefenbaker – but it was refreshing to find such a candid and open person in the hierarchy. After that, he invited me to lunch a few times. At one lunch, the topic was the Vatican budget. He wanted to make the actual expenditures public because he felt that people would be surprised at how low the budgets were. The entire Vatican, he said, ran on $50 million a year. He himself got by on a mere $1,200 a month. His instincts were correct. Such public honesty would have confounded the sceptics and silenced the cynics – at least about the Vatican's exaggerated wealth.

Another interesting man I met was Monsignor John Magee, who had been private secretary to three popes. He would regularly come to our college and talk about times past. Typical was the story of Pope Paul VI and how he permitted the departure of men from the priesthood by a process called laicization. At the time, the requests were flowing in by the hundreds and only the Pope could approve a priest's departure. After all his other work was done each day, Pope Paul VI would sit, late at night, in terrible pain because of his arthritis, and personally review every application. According to Magee, the Pope called the exodus of priests "my crown of thorns." Before he approved each by signing his name, the Pope said two prayers, one for the man so that God might grant him peace, the other for himself so that God might forgive him. Every laicized priest was also remembered individually in the Pope's prayers the next morning.

As seminarians, we heard many stories about Pope Paul VI, details that made him human for us. Toward the end of his life, for example, he travelled to the tomb of a cardinal who had treated him cruelly years earlier. For a long while, this cardinal's name could not even be mentioned around the Pope, the feelings were so bad. At the end, however, the Pope made the pilgrimage and forgave him, saying: "I beg pardon of all those to whom I may not have done good and I grant it freely to all those who may wish it of us. May the Lord give us His peace." Toward the end of his life he reflected often that we didn't thank God enough. Another snippet of information we had was that he liked to watch cowboy movies. Details, like the cowboy movies, that revealed his human side were important for us as

180

seminarians, especially since the deification of the Pope seemed to preoccupy most of clerical Rome.

His successor, John Paul I, the smiling Pope, should have stayed with us longer than the thirty-three days before his untimely death. We needed his good cheer and refreshing simplicity. I never believed the stories alleging that he was murdered. Indeed, Monsignor Magee told us that John Paul's first words to him as Pope were a complaint about a headache, with more to follow. The symptoms of a stress-related death were there right from the beginning of his term in office. The election of his successor was a marvellous time to be in Rome. There was the vigil, the first puff of smoke (it was meant to be black, indicating that the conclave had failed to choose; but it came out grey) and then the rising excitement as the selection process went into the second day.

When the announcement came, we were all truly witnesses to history. A Polish Pope, the first non-Italian Pope in more than four hundred years, had been chosen. By the time John Paul II came onto the balcony in St. Peter's Square, the sun had set and a full moon lit the scene and rendered everything an ethereal silver. He won everyone's heart and imagination by beginning his address in Italian. "When I make mistakes in your – " then he corrected himself " – *our* language, you will correct me." It was a night for celebration. With this dynamic and dramatic departure from Italian entrenchment, we students all thought the church would free itself from the burdensome Italian bureaucracy and welcome a refreshing modern era. That did not occur. Our naive high hopes were soon dashed upon the rocks of Roman reality. Popes may come and go, but the Italian bureaucrats remain as unyielding as ever.

Of all the people I came to know in Rome, however, the one with the greatest impact on my life is the man who became my cardinal. Emmett Carter was bishop of London when I first met him in Rome in 1977. We knew each other only by reputation, and I think it's fair to say that we approached each other with similar wary prejudice. I expected to dislike him and I'm sure he expected the same about me. He had invited me out to dinner at the urging of his auxiliary bishop and my mentor, John Sherlock. I would be the lowly seminarian going through the motions of dinner with a visiting bishop from home. It would be an evening of duty for us both.

We came away from the evening, however, with newfound respect for each other. There was the give-and-take of forcefully exchanged views, which we both enjoyed, and a genuine rapport was established that grew as time passed. He had a way of crystallizing his views that combined humility with insight. The next day, for example, as we crossed the piazza on the way to a papal audience, Bishop Carter said something that has always stuck with me: "Remember, Sean, the church is a divine institution which the Lord has entrusted to a bunch of miserable sinners."

In 1979, at the end of my second year, Gerald Emmett Carter became a cardinal. During his stay in Rome for his induction, I was pressed into service to act as a tour guide on one of the three busloads of people carrying his family and friends around Rome. After pointing out some of the sights, I gave them their final instructions as they climbed off the bus for an afternoon of shopping. "Now, remember that you're Canadians," I advised. "Don't go acting like a bunch of those obnoxious American tourists." It was only then that I learned that my busload contained a significant contingent of the new cardinal's American friends. I was just not meant to be a diplomat – or a tour guide.

I flew home with Cardinal Carter to spend the summer working as a seminarian at Holy Rosary parish in Milton, Ontario. On the flight, I chatted with Gordon Walker, an Ontario cabinet minister, friend of the Cardinal's and part of the official delegation. Gordon was a straight-shooter, often a controversial one, so I listened with interest and genuine surprise as he told me that the age-old question of Ontario government funding for Catholic high schools was ripe for resolution. It was a surprising turnaround for Bill Davis, a premier who had secured his first majority in 1971 by rejecting full funding.

A lot of Catholics, myself included, recalled with little warmth the hostile emotions of that campaign. Anti-Catholic sentiment seemed to be a powerful force in many parts of the province, particularly in those areas where the Conservative Party traditionally held its safest seats. I couldn't see any leader, least of all Bill Davis, tampering with that bloc of votes in Orange Ontario. That day, however, Gordon Walker, himself a member of the United Church and an MLA from the Protestant enclave of London, argued forcefully that the Conservatives now recognized the new political realities of Ontario. They realized the need to increase their support among ethnic (and largely Catholic) voters.

Gordon said that there were only a few diehards left among his colleagues who were opposed to funding Catholic schools. Further, he saw the appointment of Emmett Carter as archbishop of Toronto and his elevation to cardinal as making him one of the most potent forces in Ontario society – including its political life. The time to settle the issue was at hand, said Gordon, and Carter was the man to bring about a resolution that would be good for the church and the party. Walker felt that the cabinet and caucus could be brought around by the right arguments from the right people. He asked me to convey a sense of urgency to the cardinal and to work on any political contacts I had.

I was excited at the prospect of helping realize this elusive goal for Catholic schools and lost little time in contacting Hugh Segal, a friend from politics and one of Bill Davis's chief aides. Over lunch, he assured me that it was not only a goal worth working toward but one that he thought was attainable. He did, however, name a few individuals whose change of position would take a good deal of work and persuasion. Among them was my old adversary from the 1971 leadership convention (and elsewhere), Eddie Goodman.

I took my accumulated political information back to Cardinal Carter. As I arrived for the meeting, I felt like a retired intelligence officer suddenly called back to active duty. I told the cardinal about the cabinet and caucus positions, the Tory concerns over the Catholic vote and my assessment that a settlement was a remote, but real, possibility. Reflecting upon my own years of experience with the Tory Party, I also offered the gratuitous advice that he should play "hardball" in any dealings he had with politicians and their advisors.

As is his custom, the inscrutable Emmett Carter offered no response to my advice, it being neither requested nor required by one of the shrewdest strategists – from church or state – I've ever encountered. What transpired in those next few years will probably continue to be as much a source of speculation and misinformation in the future as it has been in the past. What is known is that in 1984 Davis unexpectedly announced full funding for Catholic high schools, received all-party support for that move, then resigned early in 1985.

What was a thoughtful and correct decision, however, struck many people as being arbitrary and unfair. The decision was too sudden for many. Before it could be properly explained, the province was plunged into an election. School funding became a major issue and during the campaign some dark and frightening voices reminded everyone that anti-Catholicism remains a poison in our society, one that is all the more potent because it is often kept out of sight. While I can offer no inside information on the political decision made by Davis, I do know that it is preposterous to suggest, as some have, that funding was the result of any Machiavellian deal between cardinal and premier. Cardinal Carter and the other Ontario bishops had been working for years to bring about just such a change in the government's position. They had been supported by thousands of parents who had felt their children were being discriminated against by a policy that was outdated at best and bigoted at worst.

For my part, I thought that funding was appropriate for all legitimate schools of various denominations that wish to operate under established standards of educational excellence while also providing supplementary religious teaching. Faith is such a precious gift to pass on to young people. Instead of nurturing their spiritual side at every opportunity, we pretend that they will absorb enough religion at home or in church. This is no longer so. How tragic it is to encounter so many young people for whom life has no meaning, joy or purpose simply because we have kept from them the greatest and most valuable lessons of all.

By pure chance, on the night Bill Davis made his full funding announcement, I was at dinner with Cardinal Carter. In a private moment, I mentioned that the day's news must have brought him great relief and much satisfaction. He put his massive hand on my shoulder and said: "Yes, Sean, and now I truly feel I can pray: '*Nunc dimittis servum tuum, Domine . . .*' "

Those words rocked me to the very core, for I recognized them immediately as the original Latin version of the church's Night Prayer, the prayer with which each priest ends his day. Translated, they mean: "Lord, now let your servant go in peace." They are taken from the scriptures as the last words of the elderly and devout Simeon who, having been promised he would not die before he saw the Saviour, held the Christ child in his arms in the temple. Realizing the Lord's promise had been fulfilled, his words implied he could die contented.

So, that night, one of the greatest dreams and goals of Emmett Cardinal Carter, the pre-eminent leader of the Catholic Church in Canada, was finally realized. Yet, even in the joy of this achievement, there was the unspoken lament that there might not be many more victories to claim – or time even to fight any major battles. By then, he had endured a stroke, and I had contracted cancer. Those crusades, we realized, might soon pass to others either younger or healthier than us. And when he finished the prayer, that realization had brought us both to the point of silence and the brink of tears.

I came to serve under Cardinal Carter in a rather roundabout way. As I finished my third year in Rome, Bishop Reding of Hamilton told me he wanted me to stay on for further studies in canon law. He thought it might be a good idea for me to become a church lawyer, interpreting not the scriptures but the man-made laws. Perhaps he saw me as a potential candidate for bishop one day, since canon law is often the route to that position. But I did not feel called to be a bishop – my days of seeking higher office were over. And if canon law was a convenient stepping stone toward such consideration, I fell back on my justification for avoiding such temptations of the lust of the clergy. I didn't get out of elected politics to get into ecclesiastical politics. Besides, I did not want to study canon law; to me it was boring. During the summers I had done parish work in the diocese and I wanted to continue with what was interesting and fulfilling. Moreover, I did not want to be a "celebrity" priest, the kind that people come up to and say: "Didn't you used to be an MP?" Putting me on the "fast track" of anticipated ambition just guaranteed that I would have that sort of unwelcome pressure. I didn't want to become a canon lawyer, but if Bishop Reding wanted me to, I would submit.

My old friend Father Lupo ended the dilemma. He visited me on one of his whirlwind trips to Rome and we went walking in the rain. When I told him what was planned for me, he stopped in the middle of the road and roared: "Boy, they've really made a seminarian out of you, haven't they?" In total disgust, he continued: "What's happened to you? You can't do this, you'll be ruined, it's not *you*." He asked what other choices I had and I flippantly said I could leave Hamilton and go next door to Toronto, a large enough diocese in which to be absorbed anonymously as a parish priest. When Father Lupo heard that I knew Emmett Carter, and that he would likely accept me, he was ecstatic. "Take my word for it," he said. "This is a sign from God. He is calling you to Toronto, believe me."

A few months later, I had a chance to present my alternatives to Emmett Carter in person: study canon law for Hamilton or be a parish priest in Toronto. "One of the differences between Hamilton and Toronto," he said, "is that in Hamilton you will always carry your past with you. In Toronto, for the first couple of years someone in your parish might ask, 'Weren't you the guy who used to be an MP?' And after you've answered yes, they'll say, 'Now, what's on TV tonight?' " It was a brutal put-down but it was bang on the point, too. In Toronto, I would be just another priest. And a happy one.

The answer came on a retreat in France. I laid out my problem for another priest, one who knew nothing of me or of Canada. His response was insightful. "Look for the door that has 'service' marked over the top of it; that's the door to walk through, not the door marked 'ambition' or 'pride.' " If my priesthood was to be one of service, not notoriety, I needed the anonymity of Toronto. Bishop Reding was disappointed and hurt when I told him my decision. The rivalry between clergy in the two dioceses can sometimes be as keen as the competition between fans of the Hamilton Tiger-Cats and the Toronto Argonauts. As a result, some in the Hamilton diocese assumed incorrectly that Toronto had wooed me and had won me through the appeal to clerical ambition. One wag in the Hamilton diocese even came up with a nickname for Emmett Carter – Cardinal Catch-a-Tory.

When I advised the cardinal of my desire to transfer, he accepted me and said that I should come to Toronto *quam primum*. I looked at him blankly. I know now that *quam primum*, meaning "as soon as possible," is quite a common expression in the church. Although I had studied Latin in Rome, I had no idea at the time what he was talking about. That was proof positive, if additional reasons were needed, that the study of canon law – with its heavy emphasis on Latin – was not my *métier*. I had been right to choose parish work in Toronto. Especially because I honestly felt it was the will of God.

In September 1980, I took the next step toward priesthood; I was ordained a deacon and dispatched to do parish work for a year with Father Tom McCann in St. John's in Toronto's east end. Father McCann is truly a great parish priest, a hard-working man with no pretensions. We hit it off well together. I enthusiastically preached, took communion to the sick, did my share of baptisms and weddings and generally got my feet wet in the myriad duties of parish life. In addition, I served as chaplain to the 1,007 students at Notre Dame, the girls' high school next door.

Notre Dame was the kind of Catholic school that exists all too infrequently today. Much of the teaching staff and administration was made up of sisters who cared about their work and their charges. Discipline was strict, but there was plenty of spirit, too. I discovered what vast changes had occurred in high school life in the eleven years since my graduation. What had merely been rumours in my day – sex and alcohol and drugs – could become daily decisions facing these students. There was tremendous pressure on them; it was not an easy time to be a teenager. Father McCann, the sisters and the students taught me so much. All in all, it was a charmed year for me.

My ordination as a priest, originally scheduled for the summer of 1981, was postponed when Cardinal Carter suffered a stroke. He made a remarkable recovery, however, and in October my ordination was his first public function. The ceremony at St. Michael's Cathedral in Toronto was, for me, a glorious celebration of God's love and the love of so many family and friends. At one point, as all priests do, I prostrated myself on the sanctuary floor, face down with my head in my arms, signalling submission and a total abandonment of my life to God. At the same time, the cardinal led the congregation in the Litany of the Saints, a series of prayers asking all of the church already in Heaven to join in praying for the new priest.

A beautiful and sentimental gift I received at my ordination came from the "girls" of the parliamentary restaurant. One of my perqs as an assistant to Dief was a pass to the restaurant and, of course, during my time as an MP I was a frequent diner as well. The food was good and inexpensive. Besides I had never learned to cook, beyond hot dogs and Kraft Dinner. The parliamentary waitresses felt protective toward me and offered a kindness and caring that I didn't mind at all. I invited them to the ordination. They couldn't all afford to come but they took up a collection and raised enough money to send one of their number with their gift of a priestly stole.

After my ordination, I was assigned to St. Bernadette's Church in Ajax as associate pastor to Father Reilly O'Leary. My posting to this growing community east of Toronto was for three years, so I plunged in, zealously, meeting families, learning names and trying to help out in a parish that received me very warmly. I had been in Ajax less than a year when Bishop Pearse Lacey, one of the auxiliary bishops and director of personnel, phoned to ask if I would take a transfer – to director of vocations. I was flabbergasted. Given the shortage of priests in the archdiocese, this was an unexpected position for someone so recently ordained. Cardinal Carter cautioned me that it would be a difficult job and that I shouldn't expect any thanks for it. As he put it, "I learned long ago in the priesthood not to expect any thanks, this side of Heaven." When I told Father O'Leary I was being transferred I received one of the shortest and most complimentary job reviews ever, when he said, "Oh, shit."

And so, in July 1982, I was appointed director of vocations – full-time recruiter – for the archdiocese of Toronto, a jurisdiction of 195 parishes and more than one million Catholics. Certainly, there was a desperate need for more priests. In the previous twenty years, 125,000 priests had retired around the world. Within fifteen years, fully half of all priests currently serving the church will probably have retired. The archdiocese of Toronto was in worse shape than most and had one of the worst priest-to-people ratios in North America. We had one priest for every 3,000 Catholics and that was expected to grow quickly to one for every 4,000 Catholics as the priests, with an average age of fifty-four, grew closer to retirement.

My instructions were to take an aggressive approach. I knew that the old route of speaking from every pulpit was not enough. The campaign had to be high profile; it had to challenge even those who weren't attending church. I turned to three people for help: Father Lupo, the dean of recruiters, long-time friend and writer Marc

Giacomelli and Toronto advertising wunderkind Martin Keen. They contributed their time and services free of charge. As the master of the business, it was Lupo who came up with a mass-market approach. Looking over the prices for various forms of advertising, billboards gave the biggest bang for your buck. We didn't have much money, but the Knights of Columbus became interested and raised more than $60,000 for the project.

The concept and the slogan were Father Lupo's as well: the billboard would portray Christ on the cross with the slogan, "Dare to be a priest like me." Marc and Martin added the final pizzazz that made the campaign so compelling. Rather than use a drawing of Christ, photographer Nigel Dickson shot a model "nailed" to a cross with a city skyline behind. Usually crucifixion scenes show Jesus after death, his head bowed. In the photograph, however, He was looking straight at the viewer with beseeching eyes. I thought it was dramatic and just what the campaign needed. Cardinal Carter approved it, although he did caution: "You're going to get some heat for it."

The billboards were set to run for three months in thirty-eight locations in the Toronto area beginning in January 1983. Media interest was immediate and amazing in intensity. Everyone wanted to do a story on the campaign and the recruitment problems behind it. Within a matter of days, Associate Director of Communications Margaret Long and I did seventy-five interviews with most of the major Canadian and American print and broadcast outlets. Mediacom, the billboard company, attempted later to put a value on the additional free coverage we received and came up with a rough estimate of $3 million.

Not everyone was a fan, to say the least. A small group of dissident feminists in Toronto saw the campaign as an opportune time to press their case for the ordination of women as priests. Some of them possessed theological degrees from the Toronto School of Theology (TST) or were in the process of completing their studies. TST had been set up as an experiment in ecumenism, with professors and students from Catholic and various Protestant denominations studying together to promote greater dialogue. At least, that was the noble theory. However, instead of clarity and dialogue, our students often received a muddled theology that promoted polarization and seemed especially aimed at the Roman Catholic hierarchy and traditional teachings. Some of the feminists sent me applications, using initials instead of their given names, in the hope that I would somehow let one slip by. None succeeded. After all, while they may have been aiming at me, their real argument was with the Pope and two thousand years of Catholic tradition. As the recruiting officer for future priests, I was in sales, not management.

The response from serious candidates was overwhelmingly positive. In total, we had more than one thousand telephone calls and sent out five hundred information packets. Within a few weeks, we talked to about one hundred young men who were genuinely interested. Attendance at retreats increased from twelve to forty. I was pleased, but cautious. After all, on average, it takes three years of ongoing contact with a vocations candidate before he finally decides to enter the seminary. From the early response, however, we were able to launch Serra House, near the University of Toronto campus, as a new residence for undergraduates who were interested in the priesthood. When Serra House opened in 1985, twelve men who otherwise wouldn't be considering studying for the priesthood moved in. Today, there are sixteen living there. Overall, our student population for the archdiocese doubled from thirty-one to more than sixty. That April, there was another retreat weekend and the atmosphere was buoyant. I felt the pleasure of the Lord within me for what had been started.

On the Monday after the retreat, however, I awoke with what I thought was a cold. My throat was slightly sore, my nose was running and I felt run down enough to cancel a few appointments. I tried to keep others, however, and maintain the momentum of the vocations campaign. The next day, my symptoms included nausea and a fever, and on Wednesday I consulted my doctor by telephone. He said it sounded like the flu and prescribed penicillin, just as a precaution. The next day, I was to have dinner with another doctor friend, Dr. Greg De Marchi. When I phoned to cancel because of my flu, he said he'd drop by to see me.

At the time, I was living in Scarborough at the archdiocesan seminary. Greg, worried that there was no one there to look after me, suggested that he drive me to my parents in Hamilton on the way to his home in nearby Dundas. During the trip, he said: "It's probably just the flu, but do you know that you have symptoms of something more serious?" "Such as?" I asked. "Well, you might be having a reaction to some of the cold remedies you've been taking – or it could be something quite serious, such as leukemia." "Oh, forget that," I said. "I know myself. I've got the flu and I'll be fine in a few days." At his urging, however, I did agree to go to St. Joseph's Hospital in Hamilton the next day for tests.

On Friday, April 15, I was seen by Dr. Jim Gibson and Dr. Brenda Copps, sister of Sheila, at St. Joseph's. They took blood samples and kept me overnight for observation. I slept well and awakened late. At around 11:00 a.m. as I was shaving in my hospital room, Drs. Gibson and De Marchi entered. "Oh, you've come to tell me that I can go home," I said. Then I saw the pain on their faces. "No," said Dr. Gibson. "I'm afraid we have some bad news for you. The blood counts look abnormal. We want to conduct a bone-marrow aspiration to be sure, but we have to tell you that there are signs which are symptomatic of leukemia." By 6:00 p.m., they were sure. It was acute leukemia, cancer of the bone marrow.

My mind reeled as they threw more information at me than I could hope to take in at the time. One thing I did understand, though; the odds were not in favour of survival. Without immediate treatment, I wouldn't live beyond six weeks. With treatment, there were no guarantees. As I tried to comprehend what had happened to me and how I had come to be invaded in such a stealthy and deadly manner, the hospital staff went into action around me. More tests were conducted to confirm the diagnosis; treatments were debated; all visitors except family were barred from seeing me.

One old friend, however, did manage to sneak in. Marc Giacomelli showed up at the front desk, bedraggled and unshaven, wearing a black T-shirt, black pants and a white trenchcoat. Somehow, he managed to convince the hospital staff that he was my personal physician and had just flown in from Beirut. When he arrived unannounced at my bedside, I looked up at him and said, "Well, I guess He didn't like the billboard."

CHAPTER TEN

TO THE BRINK AND BACK

Leukemia was not the first diagnosis suggested by two of the doctors who examined me at St. Joseph's Hospital. One thought I simply had a viral infection. The other, noting that I was a Catholic priest with an Irish name, ventured that I might be suffering from chronic alcoholism. Blood tests soon showed them both wrong. The normal white blood cell count is 5,000-10,000; mine was high at 12,000. Platelets (the cells that promote clotting), usually at 250,000, were a low 90,000. Worse, the blood samples also turned up an abnormally high number of "blast" cells.

Confirmation could only come from a bone marrow aspiration, the first of twenty-five of these painful tests I would endure over the next three years in which the hip bone is punctured to enable marrow to be drawn out from within. The skin, fatty tissues and muscles, even the bone covering, can be anesthetized to some extent, but inside the bone itself cannot be frozen. As a result, there is sharp pain as the bone is punctured and the marrow removed.

During the initial tests, my mind was racing. This can't be happening to me, I thought, there has to be some mistake. My head would not believe, but my heart knew. The bone marrow aspiration was done on Saturday afternoon. I waited with my Aunt Joan, the hospital's director, for the results. They were some time in coming, because Dr. Peter Powers, the hematologist who would become my supervising physician and grow to be a friend as well, wanted to be absolutely sure of his diagnosis. At his request, a colleague from the Henderson Hospital came to St. Joseph's and looked at the samples under the microscope. He agreed with Dr. Powers's diagnosis. I had acute myelomonocuytic leukemia.

193

Greg De Marchi and Peter Powers told me the bad news at 6:00 p.m. I accepted the information as a death sentence. Chemotherapy was held out as the only possibility. I recoiled in horror. Chemotherapy, I knew, was a treatment that could be almost as bad as the disease. Dr. Powers acknowledged all my fears, but said, "This is one of the ways of getting this thing into remission."

Remission was a word that carried heavy freight. "There is no cure," he added, "just a remission." The cancer falls quiet, but it never disappears. A relapse is always possible. "Using chemotherapy, you have roughly a 60 per cent chance of getting a remission," Dr. Powers said.

"And if we don't get one?" I asked.

"Well, then we'll try a second time, or," he paused, "it may just not work."

"What if we didn't do anything?"

His reply was blunt: "In six weeks, you'd be dead. I think we should begin chemo as soon as possible." Without treatment, I was dead; with treatment, I still had a 40 per cent chance of dying. Even if the chemo were successful, there was only a 10-20 per cent chance of living for two years. Even the good news was bad. I couldn't comprehend it well enough to make clear-headed decisions. We settled upon a minor operation the next day to implant a Hickman catheter, a tube that runs almost directly into the heart, so that transfusions and medication could be administered more easily during my stay.

A few minutes later, I told my parents the grim tidings. We sat in my hospital room too stunned to react. There were long periods of silence that spoke volumes. I thought about the other symptoms that the doctors told me had likely existed during recent weeks. Signs of leukemia had been there: bleeding gums, body bruises that I couldn't remember causing, recurring throat infections and constant fatigue. I had mistakenly put them down to the excess work load associated with the vocations campaign. I shuddered to think what would have happened to me had Greg De Marchi not come to visit that evening, taken me home and insisted I have blood tests immediately.

What I knew about leukemia I'd learned at the hands of Hollywood. Leukemia was the disease in *Love Story* that sneaked up on Ali McGraw. At one point, she mentioned that pet cats wouldn't stay where someone was dying. Shortly thereafter, the cat left and Ali McGraw died. In the last few hours, I had learned much about leukemia. In the weeks to follow, I would learn a lot more, especially from Dr. Mahmoud Ali, who was head of the hematology department. Mahmoud Ali and Sean O'Sullivan became fighters together.

The word *leukemia* literally means "white blood," but it is not, as it is commonly called, a blood cancer. It is a cancer of the tissues in which the blood is formed, mainly the bone marrow, and sometimes involving the lymph nodes and the spleen. In Canada, various types of leukemia strike 1,900 adults annually and claim 1,400 lives. If allowed to run its course, the aberrant cells will overproduce and squeeze out the good white cells, the good red cells and the platelets, leaving only a sludge. In a person with a body weight of sixty-five to seventy kilograms, leukemia shows itself as an illness when the weight of tumour tissue in the body reaches one kilogram. That one kilogram of tumour tissue likely starts with a single aberrant cell that doubles and redoubles *ad infinitum* until it kills.

My family began telling others and, on Sunday morning, just before the anesthetic for the catheter insertion was administered, I was anointed by the hospital chaplain. Using the oil of the sick that has been blessed by the bishop, the priest anoints a layman on the forehead and the palms of the hands. Because a priest's palms have been consecrated at his own ordination, he is anointed on the back of his hands. For both, the prayer is the same: "May the Lord through this holy anointing heal you and raise you up."

Cardinal Carter phoned. Referring to the billboards that were still on display, he said: "I guess the Lord is taking you at your word." I had been scheduled to preach that day at St. Michael's Cathedral; the Cardinal took my place. Later, I heard it was one of the most moving sermons he had ever given. He spoke about the vocations campaign and my leukemia. Here was a young priest, he told the congregation, being asked to live out the message of the billboard and perhaps yield up his own life.

As the knowledge sank in that I was dying, I began to wrestle with the myriad emotions within me. In the seminary, I had studied *On Death and Dying,* the classic work by Dr. Elisabeth Kübler-Ross. I had applied her thinking to patients I had ministered to and had seen them go through the various stages she described. Now I was suffering them first hand: denial, anger, bargaining, depression and acceptance. As Dr. Kübler-Ross indicated, most patients exhibit two or three stages at once.

My emotions were kaleidoscopic. At first, I was totally obsessed with the fact that I had a terminal illness. I thought I was the only cancer patient in the world. Then, I looked for an angle, a fix, any deal I could do that would make everything right again. That was followed by disbelief, then resignation. I heard myself saying, "This is madness, it's all over, I'm doomed." Then, the kaleidoscope would turn again.

There were also moments of lucid thought about practical matters. I realized, for example, that I had not made any funeral plans. On Saturday night, after the family had left, I pulled out a yellow legal pad and listed my funeral arrangements. Again, Dr. Kübler-Ross would find all of this quite predictable. Attending to "unfinished business," she calls it. I wanted a service in St. Michael's with burial in the O'Sullivan family plot in Hamilton. I listed some Bible readings, named the pallbearers and said that one of the hymns should be "Lead, Kindly Light" by John Henry Cardinal Newman. I wanted the homily to be delivered by Cardinal Carter or, if he couldn't attend, Bishop Sherlock or Father Sam Restivo. I also made it clear that there was to be no eulogy. Rather, the occasion was to be used to celebrate life, our shared faith and the gift of priesthood that had made so much difference to me.

Writing out the arrangements was a morose project, but it was also one of the rare times during the next few weeks that I had something to do and the strength to carry it out. The rest of the time, I was neither heroic nor stoic. I had the whole panorama of petty thoughts. Why was God punishing me? Why did he want me dead at thirty-one? It all seemed so wrong and so unfair. Most of the time, the only reason I wasn't more petty was the fact that I was so sick and devoid of energy that I just wanted to escape through sleep.

On Tuesday, April 19, chemotherapy began. I was put on the leukemia protocol (treatment) developed at Roswell Park Memorial Institute, a cancer-research hospital in Buffalo, N.Y. This particular protocol employed adriamycin and cytosine arabinoside. That first phase, known as the induction stage, *looks* so benign, just orange-coloured liquid flowing from a bag into your body. At root, however, chemo is actually a poison used to kill off the cancer cells – but chemo also destroys some normal cells. The idea is that when the bone marrow starts to produce white blood cells again, they will all be healthy this time around.

Since chemo is designed to shut down the production of your own blood supply, you have to be kept alive by a series of transfusions of blood and blood products from donors. Chemotherapy also wipes out your defence systems, thus rendering you susceptible to all kinds of infections. Most leukemics die as a result of an infection – pneumonia, for example – rather than the cancer itself. I had been admitted with an infection; they feared more would strike. As a result, I was receiving megadoses of antibiotics: tobramycin, tetracycline, cloxacillin, Mycostatin, and Septra. It seemed to me that I was losing most of them through the constant diarrhea and vomiting that began three or four days after chemo started. Nothing would stop the vomiting, not even THC, one of the active ingredients in marijuana. All the THC did was make me spacey. No one could figure out why I just wanted to stare out the window. They finally took me off THC and my brain went back into gear.

The vomiting, however, continued. If I was wheeled down the hall for x-rays, I went clutching a pail in my lap. I was throwing up with such force that all the blood vessels in my eyes broke. The insides of my mouth grew so raw with ulcers that I couldn't eat; the membranes were literally falling off. Every time a nurse tried to insert an intravenous needle, the vein would collapse. A rash began on my thighs, and itchy blisters spread all over my body. Infection set in around the Hickman catheter. Even though there were few whiskers left on my face to worry about, I couldn't shave for fear I might nick myself. The chemo had killed off the platelets, too, so I could have bled to death. I didn't want to shave, anyway; I couldn't look at myself in the mirror. I had only a few strands of hair left, my face was sunken, the skin was discoloured and the whites of my eyes were now bright pools of blood. My self-esteem was long gone. I looked like a freak. I was so emaciated and weak that I could hardly lift myself up off the bed.

Anyone who suggests that a cancer patient undergoing chemo is somehow carrying on in the manner of Ernest Hemingway's "grace under pressure" has never seen the reality. There is a happy heresy abroad about what it is like to be desperately sick. Melodramatic television shows and maudlin movies are mostly to blame. Hollywood would have you believe that critical illness is a time of profound spiritual or emotional heroism. The celluloid portrayal shows nobility in the face of adversity, an inspiring, if ailing, superman. That was not my experience. Nor do I think it is the experience of most cancer victims who have been through chemo. When you are sick, you are sick. I heard no distant trumpets calling me. I just wanted to be left alone.

As I lay dying, however, there was one religious image that brought comfort to me: the Agony in the Garden. On my trips to Israel as an MP, I had felt a sense of occasion at only two of the many shrines I visited: the Mount of the Beatitudes and the Garden at Gethsemane. The other holy sites, with their crowds, commercialism and competing Christians, could just as easily have been K-Marts in Cleveland. In the Garden of Gethsemane I was deeply moved by the place where tradition holds that Jesus wept in such fear and loneliness that he sweated blood. Today, the site is a large black rock with a church built on top. When I visited, I was the only pilgrim present on a cold, damp day. I was much moved and felt His loneliness all about me. After praying there, I rose to leave, hesitated and recalled John Kennedy's lament about the original burial site for his infant son, Patrick: "It's so lonely out there."

Lying in that Hamilton hospital bed, cut off from the outside world except for visits in shifts from my family and the few friends who were allowed to see me I remembered the Agony in the Garden. This, I thought, must have been what it was like for Him. I felt so utterly doomed and abandoned. "Oh where," I lamented, "is God?" Jesus, too, had felt equally bereft. Supported only by that rock, he had cried out: "Father, if it is your will, take this cup from me; yet not my will but yours be done."

From those depths of despair flowed an inner peace from the same Lord who had endured such lonely agony. He would, I came to feel, see me through. He was asking me: As a Christian and a priest, are you for real? Do you truly believe what you preach? Do you trust Me?

Just as Jesus had trusted the Father and finally abandoned Himself to the Lord, so I faced the same option. Give in – or give myself over to Him. "Father, into your hands I commend my spirit . . . Not my will, but yours be done." I trust you.

On Saturday, April 23, eight days after I'd been admitted, I came as close to death as a body can and still live. Chemo had begun that previous Tuesday, my defence systems were non-existent and infections were setting in. The antibiotics were not sufficient and the fever rose all week. On Saturday night, my temperature hit 104 degrees and was still climbing. For an adult, that level is close to the danger zone where brain damage can occur. I was hallucinating on that dark night of the soul – and body. One side of me was angrily fighting the treatment the nurses were attempting with the cooling blanket meant to lower my body temperature. The second me, quite detached, was watching all of this and saying, "O'Sullivan, shut up. You're making a fool of yourself." As the fever burned and my strength wasted away in waves, I could feel the tension of those in the room. I sensed that this was the end; I wasn't going to make it. Later, Dr. De Marchi told me, "We left you that night fully convinced we wouldn't see you in the morning."

Indeed, I came very close that night to accepting Jesus's invitation to enter into His whole life. I knew what it was like for Him to go through the Agony of the Garden. Yet Sunday morning arrived and I awoke. In my bed. I still felt sick, but I was alive. My recollection of the crisis was dim, but even in my hallucinating state I knew that my temperature must be falling because of the delight registered by the nurses.

The cause for the change was not medical alone, although those magnificent nurses were the glue that kept me together that night. No, the turn toward recovery came from another source. For no obvious reason, on the very night that medicine had done all it could in an apparent losing battle for my life, the fever peaked and began to abate. No one knew why.

I know now. I had not been convinced that week that the chemo would work. I wasn't alone in that view; the cancer had spread so far, so fast. I was so weak that the staff's heroic efforts were really desperate measures. The slow return to health that began that night

199

came not from science alone but in answer to the sincere prayers offered by countless people. The fact that I came through that night and am around at all today is an example of the efficacy of prayer. Prayers work. Especially prayers for others.

The turn for the better certainly did not come in response to my own prayers. Sister Joan had moved into the hospital and visited me at least three times a day. She held me when I wanted to cry and listened to all my complaints. Every night after the floor had grown quiet, I would hear her familiar footsteps. We would talk for a few moments about small things, hold hands, recite the Our Father, the Hail Mary, and the Glory Be and I would respond to three invocations: "Sacred Heart of Jesus – I place my trust in Thee." "Immaculate Heart of Mary – Pray for us." "St. Joseph – Pray for us." Most days that would be all the praying I could muster.

I later expressed my guilt to Father Sam about saying so few prayers. He reminded me of the old seminary maxim. "Pray while you are well, gentlemen, for you won't pray when you are sick." How true that turned out to be. As a result, I was carried by the prayers of so many others. That was Christianity at its best and most effective. At its best, because most of the prayers were the spontaneous acts of charitable people whom I may never meet and can never thank – this side of the veil. At its most effective, because they were answered.

In true Irish Catholic tradition, I think my relationship with God had been rather formal, far-off and often based on fear. Oh, I had preached a lot about a God of mercy and compassion, but I had worked hard to be a good churchman (which is different from being a good priest) in the unspoken hope that all that activity might cause Him to overlook a lifetime of failures. One of the most difficult things in my life had been learning trust. As a priest, I had entrusted my life to God, and in my weaker moments I was bitter that this illness was my apparent thanks from Him. With the help of some sensitive and talented priests, I came to understand that God especially asks us to trust Him when we don't understand what is going on.

None of this was in the hospital's two-paragraph official statement May 2 announcing that I had leukemia and had just completed a ten-day program of chemotherapy. The statement gave the barest details in response to the queries that had been tying up the hospital switchboard for days. On one single day, there were more than four hundred telephone calls inquiring after my condition. My friends kept the hospital in flowers, and I received more than one thousand cards and letters from well-wishers.

One of the letters that touched me most deeply came not from anyone rich or famous but from a parishioner in Ajax where I had stayed such a short time that I doubted I had been helpful. "You don't know me but I was a parishioner at St. Bernadette's, the note began. "One day, I came to you very troubled to go to confession. You treated me exactly as Jesus Christ would have in granting me His forgiveness. I will never forget you. Thank you." That message spoke directly to my heart and reminded me that it was not up to me to decide when I was doing His will. I was learning part of the mystery of being a priest and of bringing God to man and man to God. What may seem like failure may actually be a moment when He is using us to express His love in the life of someone else.

There were also the letters from the loonies who said cancer was a conspiracy of the drug companies and the doctors. The notes often included information on clinics where alternate therapies were available from health food cultists who recommended everything from coffee enemas to beet roots. I heard, too, from the born-again Christians. They generally fell into two camps. One group said that my cancer was punishment for the billboards. The other blamed my Catholicism, calling Rome "the whore of Babylon." One telephone caller who managed to get through said he wanted to bring in his family immediately to receive my blessing before I died. When I said that I was hopeful of surviving, he became quite belligerent. "Look," he said, "I have a direct message from God here that you're dying and we're to get your blessing." He was irate when I refused to tell him my room number. Mediacom announced that the billboards would stay up for another six weeks, without charge, as a tribute. The gesture was thoughtful, but I was so weary of the whole thing that all I could say was: "Please get them down, just bring them down." The signs were removed.

I received a more inspirational message from Cardinal Carter during his trip to Rome that spring. He had an audience with Pope John Paul II and told him of my campaign and condition. The

Cardinal reported the Pope's comments in a telegram to me: "Tell him that his suffering will bring vocations." Certainly, Jesus offered His suffering to the world, so as His disciples we should also offer our suffering for worthy causes. For my part, I offered my suffering for three good causes: as reparation for my own sins, for the cause of vocations and for unity within the Church.

Although the ten-day chemo treatment was finished on April 29, another week passed before my life began to return to something like normal. The sores in my mouth were slow to heal. I drank apple juice to test my tolerance. It was non-existent. I spat the juice toward the closest wall and have avoided it since. I was able to swirl a little mouthwash for the sores and eventually swallowed half a glass of ginger ale. Solid food followed days later. The other highlights of that early recovery period were the daily bath in tepid water and the escape of watching reruns of *Happy Days*. No visitor, no matter how far he'd travelled, could interrupt my time with the Fonz and his friends.

Four weeks passed after my admission before I began to feel human again. I even hauled myself down to the nursing station one day, trailing intravenous tubes and scrawled a name, more as a forlorn hope than anything, on the discharge section of the blackboard: "O'Sullivan." Just as I was coming around, however, the treatment began again. All it takes is one leukemic cell for the disease to come roaring back.

One measure of progress – or lack of it – throughout that time was the white cell count. Two weeks after my admission, my white count had fallen to 200, my lowest recorded level. The chemo had done its job. There followed a period of ten days when I was extremely vulnerable to any kind of infection. By May 3, however, the white count was 400, and a week later it was 1,200 – a long way from the healthy 5,000-10,000 range, but a vast improvement, nevertheless. The next day, the count was up to 1,700; the day after, 2,900. My bone marrow was recovering. The leukemia was in remission.

In May, I went home for a few weekends and was readmitted several times for testing; but by June, my white blood cell count was up to 5,000 and the platelet count was 249,000, both within normal range. Although there would be other consolidation treatments during the summer, I celebrated by attending a gala evening when the billboard campaign was awarded a Billi, the prize for the best outdoor advertising campaign in Canada during the previous twelve months. The prize properly went to Marc Giacomelli and Martin Keen, but the celebration of winning was a tremendous boost to my spirits, too. I was beginning to feel whole and human again.

Still, the suffering continued in unexpected forms. Many times I could sense the frustration, disappointment and irritation of friends who expected me to feel better than I did or have more strength than I had. The fact that I was in remission and looking better were certain signs to them that their prayers for a full recovery had been answered. Their prayers had achieved remarkable results, to be sure, but those same friends were baffled by, even intolerant of, any suggestion that I wasn't fully better.

For some patients, the second (or consolidation) stage is often not as bad as the induction stage. Not so with me. The first consolidation treatment, using AraC and adriamycin, lasted for seven days in June. The second, in July, used M-AMSA and AraC, and took only three days, but all of the sessions were terrible. Part of the reason was that M-AMSA was still experimental and I was given very large doses. Use of that drug has since been largely discontinued; it can cause severe and sometimes permanent bone marrow damage. I was angry at the whole medical profession. I could not understand why the doctors would take a relatively well person, as I thought I had become, and make him sick again. I came down with new infections and complications and had to be pumped full of antibiotics for the umpteenth time.

The whole chemo process is experimental and chancy, like a television set that goes on the blink. You give it a few good kicks, turn the control switch briskly off and on a few times and hope that the reception is restored. Every patient who undergoes chemo is, in a way, a guinea pig, because the treatment is an inexact science, even an art. From their panoply of medicines, the doctors choose a treatment bearing in mind your age, condition and weight, then try to estimate the proper dosage and duration.

As time passed and I began to understand more about leukemia, I also realized how shaky were the gains I was making. Remission buys a little time, perhaps twelve to eighteen months at the most. No one can predict whether you will join the successful group and achieve a remission. Nor do they know why some treatments work for one patient and not for another. Or for how long. All I knew was that I didn't want a relapse. Most leukemics who suffer a relapse are resistant to any help from chemotherapy the second time around.

I also knew that the chemo could not continue. My future would unfold in four-week stages: a week of treatment, two weeks to recover and one week of feeling normal. No one could tell me how long that would go on or how successful it would be. That's why I listened attentively when Dr. Powers raised an alternative to more chemotherapy – the possibility of a bone marrow transplant. Because the secret of dealing with leukemia is to rid yourself of the aberrant cells and grow new, healthy ones, the chances of growing those healthy cells increase substantially if they are introduced from a healthy person. I was so sick of being sick, so bloody tired of leading a life of quiet desperation that I seized upon this new possibility like the dying man I was.

Marrow for such a transplant had to come from a naturally compatible brother or sister. My brother Terry turned out to be the closest match. The best-known transplant centre was in Seattle, Washington, where the Fred Hutchinson Cancer Research Center had been doing them for about twenty years. The cost, however, was staggering: up to U.S. $100,000. The Ontario Hospital Insurance Plan would reimburse 80 per cent of that, but full payment to the Seattle hospital had to be assured in advance. The Archdiocese of Toronto guaranteed payment and I was booked to begin in September.

I left Hamilton with high hopes but aware that my life could soon be over. People always called me a young man in a hurry; now we knew why. I yearned to live, but I was ready to accept death. As Pope John XXIII had said about his own cancer: "My bags are packed and I'm ready to go."

In Hamilton, I had been among friends; Seattle was a city of strangers. St. Joseph's was run by my aunt; at the Hutchinson, I would be just another patient. Still, I could understand why the staff seemed aloof. Much of the transplant work is done with children – and the operations don't always work. As a result, the hospital concentrates on efficient medical care in order to keep a professional distance and prevent burnout.

My hopes were soon much diminished. When Terry and I first talked to one of the doctors in Seattle, his opening sentence was a heart-stopper: "You know that all of this is experimental and one day we'll know whether or not it works?" Then he spewed pessimistic statistics: "You have a 50 per cent chance of being alive one hundred days from now." Just in case I still didn't understand the odds, he handed me a single-spaced typed document that ran several pages and spelled out all the possible complications of the transplant. Terry faced little risk, but he would undergo the most pain as they removed a quart of mushy, pink bone marrow. He would have to stay in Seattle for up to two months in case I needed transfusions. If the operation worked and I survived, I might be in Seattle for a year.

I had little choice but to proceed. Hamilton offered only chemo and limited time. At least Seattle held out half a chance for life. I spent the next five days going through daily tests as they monitored my condition in preparation for the transplant. Although I was not afraid to die, I had enough residual pride that I worried about *how* I would die. Dying of leukemia can be quite peaceful; you just quietly slip away. So, too, if an infection sets in; a coma results and final sleep follows.

The transplant, however, held out worrisome new prospects. The first step was a final round of chemo and total body irradiation to get rid of any remaining bone marrow cells. Then came the actual transplanting of Terry's bone marrow into me. Between the two steps, however, I feared the need for respirators and other hardware to keep me alive and breathing. I didn't want to go out thrashing and frothing at the mouth, like some lunatic struggling all the way down.

The day before the radiation was scheduled, one of my test results was not to their liking. My liver, which had been healthy until then, was suddenly not functioning properly. The liver is a key organ for the procedure because it helps the body handle the toxic chemicals used in the final chemo treatment. One of the most common causes of death after a bone marrow transplant is liver failure when that organ cannot respond to all the chemicals, medications and blood products being stuffed into the system. Transplants work well for teenagers, less well for those in their twenties, are chancy after thirty and have very limited success over forty. At thirty-one, I was already in the grey area.

A second test confirmed the findings of the first. I had contracted hepatitis from one of the more than forty transfusions of blood and blood products I had had while in hospital. Nothing had shown up until now because hepatitis requires an incubation period. There are fatal forms of hepatitis that can be detected when blood for transfusion is screened, but the type of hepatitis I had – known as non-A, non-B – could not be picked out by the screening methods. While it was not a fatal hepatitis, my liver had been damaged. My chances of survival, previously at fifty-fifty, sank precipitously to 13 per cent. They told me to come back when the hepatitis had cleared up.

The world around me went black. I felt that I was on some slippery slope to my grave. I had said my goodbyes in Hamilton and come for the cure. On arrival, I had learned that it wasn't a cure at all, it was only an experiment. I had agreed to proceed, anyway, and now they were sending me home to what appeared to be certain death or a chemo-riddled life of brief and painful duration. In my newly depressed state, I could see little difference between the two options. By then, I was a psychological zombie.

I couldn't stay another day in Seattle. The place of hope had become a charnel house. I just wanted to get the hell home. The fastest route was CP Air from Vancouver. The only way to get to Vancouver was by bus. I didn't even have my shoes. I had so few long-term expectations that I had brought only one pair of dress shoes – and they were worn right through on one side. I had dropped them off at a Seattle repair shop for a $20 mending job while I was undergoing tests at the Hutchinson. We flung all our clothes into our suitcases, checked out of the hospital lodgings where we were staying, picked up my shoes and hurtled onto the bus.

At some point in the hustle to leave town, I wrenched my back badly and spent the four hours on the milk-run to Vancouver in agony. I felt like a doomed man. The hope for a cure was gone and the acute back pain just added to my misery. Because of the liver problem, I had been cautioned not to take any medication or alcohol for either the depression or the pain. We boarded the aircraft and as the flight attendants turned down the interior lights, I thought, well, perhaps the in-flight movie will distract me for a while. As the screen flickered on, I saw to my horror that the selection for the day was, of all things, *The Terry Fox Story*.

Back at St. Joseph's, a liver biopsy confirmed hepatitis. Because there was no treatment recommended (it would clear up on its own), chemotherapy was suspended because it would just weaken my system for the eventual transplant. Greg De Marchi, the first to diagnose leukemia six months earlier, knew what I needed now. "Go to Serra House," he said. "Those students will give you a reason to live." And so, sporting my third new head of hair that year, I went to work with the students I had recruited. Although I lived in the shadow of death, their energy gave me new strength. As the weeks passed, the hepatitis did not improve. The bad news was that the transplant looked less likely. The good news, however, was that maybe I wasn't going to need it. The regular bone marrow aspirations showed the amazing news that my leukemia remained in remission.

Earlier that year, Bishop Reding had contracted lung cancer and had been undergoing periodic treatments in Detroit. One night, by coincidence (or more likely Providence) we were both at St. Joseph's taking tests and spent ninety minutes together, in our bathrobes and pyjamas, sharing cancer stories. The hurt he felt after my decision to join the Toronto Archdiocese was forgotten as we spoke of our faith and our journeys as priests. Together, we enjoyed a catharsis of forgiveness as we tried to understand what God could possibly have had in mind for us, two cancer victims. At the end of our conversation, I knelt to receive his blessing, which he gave. Then, as I stood up, he dropped to one knee and in a magnificent gesture of humility, asked for my blessing in return. As he rose, we embraced, weeping freely.

Bishop Reding was planning a trip with Bishop Sherlock to the shrine of Our Lady of Lourdes in France. When Marc Giacomelli heard this, he said that he would accompany me if I wanted to make such a pilgrimage, too. On the day Marc and I were in Boston ready to set out on the next leg to Paris, we received word that Bishop Reding had died. I was shattered. A bishop was far more important to the church than a mere priest. He must have had more people praying for him, I thought, and was certainly more holy. Even so, cancer had claimed him. What hope was there for me? I was torn between continuing to Lourdes and returning to Hamilton for the funeral, so I phoned Bishop Sherlock. "One of our problems was that Paul and I kept delaying the trip too long," he said. "We kept thinking that after the next round of treatment it would be time to go. If you feel up to it, go." We did.

For me, Lourdes was a deeply moving experience. The shrine began to have significance for Catholics in the nineteenth century when the Blessed Mother appeared and spoke to Bernadette Sourbois, a humble, peasant girl. Mary told her to dig in a particular grotto and a spring of water would bubble forth. She said that people were to wash in the spring and drink of the water. Today, that custom continues at the same grotto where Mary appeared, using the same stream that Bernadette uncovered. A church has been built, and at the top of the hill is a room with long banks of confessionals where priests extend forgiveness in many of the world's languages.

I joined all the other supplicants going to confession, renewing their faith and asking Mary to pray for them. I washed in the water, drank of it and at one point submerged myself in it. The visit was a most humbling experience, corresponding to the moment during my ordination when I was prostrate on the sanctuary floor. For me, as with the millions who have journeyed to Lourdes, the pilgrimage and the prayer are a public acknowledgement of what is in the heart. By visiting Lourdes, we pilgrims admit that human effort is not enough; we need the superior power of God. And from that humble beseeching comes new strength.

Did Lourdes help me? Well, it certainly was a spiritual force. The visit was an opportunity to escape the daily grind of hospitals and doctors and treatments. It spoke to me of the many people who were praying for me and helped me to see my recent experiences through the inner calm that accompanies simple, devotional faith. Lourdes let me find and feel an almost childlike trust in God and confidence that He listens to prayers. Because Lourdes is a Marian shrine, the pilgrimage also reminded me that God listens to the prayers of those who are already in Heaven, especially Mary. Devotion to Mary is not some Catholic abstraction or pious nicety. Mary has a particular maternal love for priests that dates from Jesus' death when she was left to look after his disciples. In honouring Mary, I feel closer to Her Son. At Lourdes, I experienced the grace of Her loving protection.

I did not leave Lourdes, however, thinking that I had beaten cancer. There was no miracle, nor had I expected one. In harsh, practical terms, I knew that the next test could show leukemia's vengeful return. Out of all the patients who had been treated at St. Joseph's Hospital with my type of leukemia, only one had lived for three years. Nevertheless, I had finally done for myself what so many others had done for me – pray. I had been so sick for so long that my prayers had been truncated and irregular. I had just been coping with cancer. At Lourdes, I prayed for continued life and renewed hope and the encouragement to carry on with what I had begun of His work. I received it.

My work at Serra House was energizing, but the dilemma and the depression continued into 1984. It had been almost a year since my initial diagnosis; I was even feeling sorry for myself that leukemia hadn't changed me spiritually more than it had. I was alive, yes, but I didn't feel any more holy. Unless it was convenient, I wasn't saying Mass every day. Unless I was actually in residence at Serra House, the breviary went unread. I did say the rosary daily, but that was often the extent of my prayer life. It was not a very impressive output for any priest and certainly not for one who was alive because of prayer.

Some aspects of myself, however, came roaring back. My Irish temper, for example, showed itself on the occasion of Cardinal Carter's birthday in March 1984. I arrived at the gathering in his honour and was uncomfortable and self-conscious. I felt that my invitation had been mostly out of sympathy for the "sick boy." At the door, I met a waiter bearing a tray of full champagne glasses. I took one and, as he began to walk away, said: "Wait right there." I drank it, hoisted a second, then polished off a third and a fourth while the waiter watched, wide-eyed. I took the fifth, parked it in my hand to sip as I met the other celebrants, and dismissed the waiter, ready at last to face the rest of the world.

After dinner, another attendee, a rather pompous church bureaucrat, said, "Tell me, Father, have your doctors got you on Librium or Valium or anything these days?"

I regarded him quizzically: "No, but why do you ask?"

209

"Well," he replied, "I've just noticed that ever since this whole illness began, you've been so laid back, so *laissez-faire*, so unusually calm about life that I figured they must have you drugged." I was stung that he'd reduced my fight for life to little more than lackadaisical lounging. I was not, however, without a riposte. "No," I said, "It's just that through it all, I've realized two things. First, I've learned to stop worrying about a lot of things I used to worry about. Second, I've realized that the things you worry about are bullshit." So much for my determination to be a peacemaker!

Our difference of opinion that night, however, was minor compared with the major schism I began to see brewing in the Catholic Church in North America. There are two churches emerging, both composed of "professional Catholics" – priests, religious, theologians and activists. Both sides are discontented and their relations are growing more strained. One side will become a remnant of the traditional church. Its adherents will place extra emphasis on fidelity to the Pope and pronouncements from Rome. Those on the other side will view themselves as reform-minded Catholics although, in fact, they are little more than neo-Protestants.

For this contemporary crowd, Christ will be viewed as a perfect role model because of His concern for others. The liturgy – as they will insist on calling Mass – will use bread and wine as just symbolic reminders of the Last Supper, no longer accepting Jesus's true presence. For them, priesthood will become a temporary status accorded by the community of believers, not a mysterious pact between God and his chosen male celibates. These contemporary Catholics will champion female priests, a married clergy and anything innovative for worship. They will be increasingly less concerned with individual salvation, and will place more emphasis on social activism.

The traditionalists will regard the contemporary Catholics with the contempt reserved for heretics, while the contemporaries will dismiss the traditionalists as psychologically repressed misfits who cling to outdated structures. One group will become shrill and intolerant; the other, smug and indifferent. Both will believe they have a corner on Christ and a growing monopoly on His true message. Both will give righteousness a bad name.

There will be no new heresies in the coming schism, just the old ones dusted off and presented in new wrappings for today's consumption. Some of the divisive issues will be very familiar to students of Catholic history: our understanding of the divinity of Christ; His true presence in the Eucharist; the authority of the Pope; the efficacy of the seven sacraments; the distinctive characteristics of the priesthood; and the conflict between the claims of other-worldly things and the here-and-now.

The majority of Catholics are puzzled by the factions and stand somewhere in between, unaware of the developing rift. As the differences become sharper, those in the middle will be forced to make a choice and the schism will be complete. If this occurs, the Catholic Church, like the Anglican, will be divided into "High Church" and "Low Church" adherents. People in the middle will drift or be carried along to that expression of Catholicism with which they feel most comfortable – or, sadder yet, with whichever side is the most convenient.

In the time I have remaining, I would like to help build bridges between the two groups, and beyond. We are all called as Christians to be people of hope. The church has survived for two thousand years and will live for another two thousand, despite, in the words of Cardinal Carter, us "miserable sinners" to whom the Lord has entrusted His church. The healing must begin with forgiveness, a quality that I have begun to learn and tried to live these last three years as a leukemic.

The best lessons about forgiveness have been taught to me by the acts of others. Since I fell ill, I have heard from many fellow cancer victims or their families, asking for my prayers or a visit from me. Such visits remain painful for me because the sight of a cancer victim brings back my own nightmare. When I can, I go, but it is agonizing. And when the victims die, as they often do, I feel guilty to be alive and desolate at my own fate that draws closer with every passing day. Sometimes, I am ashamed to admit, I find excuses not to go because I can't always cope, physically or emotionally, with the reminders of cancer and its ravages.

There was one call in particular to which I responded, however, and I will always be glad I did. A hospital social worker phoned me to describe a young woman, a leukemic about my age, who had relapsed after a remission of three years. Active treatment was now stopped and her situation was bleak. She had followed the press reports of my illness and was anxious that I talk to her.

And so I did. Despite all her suffering, her lively personality shone through and her determination convinced me that she would wage a strong and lengthy fight. As we held hands and prayed, I could sense that the residual Catholicism of her childhood was both a comfort and a complication for her. She told me she was an actress. I did not recognize the name and assumed that the big break had eluded her thus far.

Her family background was troubled. She was reluctant to speak of family and there was only one brother who ever visited. There were a few close friends who obviously cared for her but who quickly withdrew from her room when I arrived. As her strength ebbed, she would pray and speak of faith. She was open to God's love and forgiveness, but she resisted confession, saying that she would let me know when it was time. However, she lapsed into a coma before the time arrived and I was angry with myself for not being more aggressive. I had grown quite fond of her and, after administering the last rites, bade her farewell with an awkward embrace and the kiss of someone who had come to regard her with true tenderness.

After her burial the social worker phoned to thank me for my kindness. Yes, there were family problems, she said, and that had made my acceptance of her that much more important. And yes, she was an actress to the end. For she had spent most of her adult years as a prostitute on the streets of Toronto not far from the hospital where she died. At first, the revelation shook me. I quickly overcame my hang-ups, however, and saw the experience as a grace-filled encounter with another of the Lord's Mary Magdalenes.

I am no St. Paul, but I have tried to imitate him by being a loyal son of the church. He, too, did what he could in the time allotted to him and warned those who were to carry on of the tensions and divisions that would continue in the church. I pray for the grace to persevere, so that I may approach my rendezvous with the Lord with the same consolation given to St. Paul: "I have fought the good fight; I have finished the race; I have kept the faith."

It is fashionable to say that one has no regrets. But, being human, of course I have regrets. I regret all the good I could have done and did not do. I regret any harm or hurt I may have caused others. And now, as I live out my life and try to apply its lessons, I think of Woody Allen's line: "I'm not afraid of death. I just don't want to be there when it happens." After all, we all want to go to Heaven – but nobody wants to die. Death awaits, however, and it will not be on my terms nor at a time of my choosing.

CHAPTER ELEVEN

SO MANY CHANCES

ll my life I've been a fighter, the result of a combination of an
Irish disposition and the circumstances of fate. At the tender
age of twelve, I went to war, following the colours of the
controversial John Diefenbaker in the chronic skirmishes within the
Progressive Conservative Party. During my time in youth politics and
my five years as an opposition Member of Parliament, I fought for
principles, but I battled my own colleagues as well. In 1977, I resigned
my seat to enter the seminary and became a priest to fight for souls,
including my own, in the eternal struggle of good over evil. The
biggest battle of my life, however, is still under way – along with
about one-quarter of a million other Canadians with cancer. In my
case, I have enjoyed Irish luck. The leukemia has been in remission
three years – though it could return any day. And that too, teaches
humility.

Some of what I have to say about the time I spent in both my
houses – the House of Commons and the House of God – may be
seen by a few prudes as treating life too lightly or seeing faith as too
much fun. Well, as one who has felt the hand of death, all I know is
that I love life and have learned that laughter can lead to faith. As a
human being who is little more than a warm grab-bag of vul-
nerability, I take my faith seriously.

Theologian Reinhold Niebuhr has written about faith and how it
relates to humour. "It must move toward faith or sink into despair
when the ultimate issues are raised," he says. "That is why there is
laughter in the vestibule of the temple, the echo of laughter in the
temple itself, but only faith and prayer, and no laughter, in the holy
of holies." If there are still those who receive my message of hope,

forgiveness and reconciliation for politics, for the church and for the sick with raised eyebrows and pursed lips, I summon Sydney Smith to my defence. As that English man of letters once wrote to Bishop Bloomfield, the bishops "must not think me necessarily foolish because I am facetious, nor will I consider you necessarily wise because you are grave."

When I met John Diefenbaker, Canada's thirteenth prime minister, for the first time in Hamilton in 1963, there was an immediate magic between us. For some in the Conservative Party, a group much ravaged by rancour, the Chief could do no right. For me, he could do no wrong. Yet for years I was so blinded by his strength that I could not see his weaknesses. With the hindsight that comes with maturity and the second chance at life I have been given, I know now that John Diefenbaker could often be a bitter man. No wonder. He had been assassinated by his own party in 1966, an event that divided Conservatives for years.

In his final years, the Chief was abandoned by most of those around him, a lonely and misunderstood man. Yet I believe he wanted forgiveness and he wanted to forgive. Given half a chance he would have had both. When he died in his Ottawa home, on his desk nearby was a note written in his own hand. It began: "Olive. I have an abiding faith – God has been good and merciful to me. Almost eighty-four." He then paraphrased a passage from St. Paul. "All things brought in work together for good, for those who love the Lord." Through all the hurts and disappointments and betrayals, he saw his life's pattern as having worked out for the best. With God's help, I have learned earlier in my life the vital lesson with which Dief was struggling at the end of his. Though I have spent most of my adult years locking horns with people I hardly knew, I have come to know that reconciliation, not condemnation, is the right course.

During my five years in Parliament, it is safe to say that many in Ottawa and my party did not particularly like me. Often, the feeling was mutual. There were times when I did not much like myself. I was an MP at twenty, at that time the youngest ever elected to the Commons, and I was fearful of not being taken seriously. Having pushed myself that far, I was determined to succeed in the face of my own insecurity. As a result, I often came across as cocky, ambitious

216

and arrogant. It was as though I had landed the role of a backbencher in a school play and was anxious to perform according to expectations – even if I had to write my own script.

Still, just being elected that young was an achievement that would have a lasting impact on my life. As an unrepentant Diefenbaker loyalist, I embraced his tendency to be overly critical and negative about many people. Because I was scarred in 1966 by Dief's overthrow as party leader, I was a more than willing collaborator in the ongoing vendetta against so many that he held responsible for his downfall. At a time when the party needed to pull together under leader Robert Stanfield, I lost few opportunities to keep the old wounds from healing and cause new hurts as well.

While I remain proud of having sponsored the bill to recognize the beaver as one of Canada's official symbols, there was a behind-the-scenes role I played, of which I am equally proud and which I can now reveal. The Official Languages Act had been law since 1969, but in 1973, the Liberals introduced a bilingualism resolution in Parliament. The public rationale was to affirm the principles of bilingualism in the public service and make Quebec feel more a part of Confederation. The hidden agenda was to unearth the divisions in the Tory caucus. The objective was bound to succeed; Dief and many other members from western Canada were adamantly opposed to the resolution. Many MPs wrongly presumed that because I was a Diefenbaker loyalist I would also oppose the resolution. They were wrong; I was in favour of bilingualism.

The issue quickly took on a life of its own. For many of my colleagues in the Conservative Party, bilingualism represented all that was wrong with Trudeau and his regime. Others simply saw it as a chance to embarrass Stanfield. After all his efforts to woo Quebec, the party had been able to elect only two members from that province in the 1972 election. Both groups formed a rough coalition. Because some of the anti-bilingual MPs mistakenly saw me as one of their own, I heard first-hand reports about the strength of their ranks. It soon appeared that up to thirty Conservative MPs were preparing to vote against the resolution.

Such an outcome would have been disastrous. The political damage, not just in Quebec, but among all Canadians suspicious of a narrow-minded Tory Party, would be incalculable if so many of our MPs took that view. Stanfield's staff was remarkably sanguine. They expected that Diefenbaker would lead a tiny rump group of no more than seven or eight renegades against the resolution. I knew otherwise, and that inside information led me to play double agent.

My contact within the party hierarchy was Finlay MacDonald. When Finlay arrived in Ottawa early in 1972 to serve as election campaign manager, I was then an aide to Dief. Finlay called me to say that, as a joke, party headquarters had presented him with some fake telegrams welcoming him to Ottawa. One of the messages purported to be from Dief. I'd never met Finlay, but he asked if I would phone headquarters and say that my boss had heard about this unauthorized use of his name. I was to tell headquarters staff that the Chief was irate and was drafting a question of privilege to be raised in the House that afternoon. I was delighted to comply; anything to have fun and stir up trouble. Headquarters was suitably chastened and chagrined by my call until Finlay told them the truth. Nevertheless, he had arrived in Ottawa just as he wanted, trumping their own practical joke. As a result, Finlay and I became friends.

Finlay was flabbergasted at my prediction that up to one-third of the Tory MPs might vote against the resolution. He agreed that he would not tell anyone – including Stanfield – that I was his source, so we could keep the information flowing, and we set to work to reduce the number. I began to feed information through Finlay about who was wavering on the issue. Finlay, Whip Tom Bell, and a few others began cajoling, threatening and twisting arms to convince MPs to change their minds or, if they wouldn't alter their vote, to take a walk and be conveniently absent when the resolution came before the House. When the vote was held, sixteen Tories voted against. That was too many, but likely only half what it would have been if I hadn't played the mole and helped reverse the hemorrhaging.

While I talked to MPs on this issue, it became clear that while bilingualism was a problem for some, Stanfield himself was an even bigger difficulty for most. Many MPs saw him as a self-styled patrician who had little personal rapport with them and didn't even seem to know their names. We seemed to receive more attention from Liberal Finance Minister John Turner than we did from our own leader. They saw their anti-bilingualism as a way of expressing their dissatisfaction with Stanfield.

After the vote, I wrote to Finlay pointing out that there would be other similar disciplinary problems unless Stanfield changed his ways. I listed some things Stanfield could do to improve caucus relations. They included such simple steps as talking to individual members after Question Period each day, getting to know more names and using them in conversation, and holding regular breakfast or lunch sessions with MPs. My ideas were not startling, but underlined that there were a number of MPs who simply needed to know that Stanfield cared about them.

Finlay agreed with my analysis and I allowed him to give the memo to Stanfield, with my name removed. Stanfield was furious that anyone saw him as a less-than-competent leader. He called Finlay in, waved the critique covered with his own copious notes, and demanded to know who had written it. Finlay refused to tell him. Finally, Stanfield broke the impasse by declaring, "All right, don't tell me. I know who wrote this. Joe Clark wrote this." Stanfield never knew differently until now. Nor did he do much to follow my suggestions.

It wasn't until years later, at the swearing-in of Finlay MacDonald as a senator in 1985, that Stanfield and I made our peace and came to understand each other better. During a break in the ceremonies, I was sitting on a bench outside the Senate. Stanfield made a point of coming over and sitting beside me. Until then, our relationship had been, at best, cordial and correct, as they say in diplomatic circles.

That day in Ottawa, however, his conversation showed a degree of feeling he had never before shown toward me. "I'm very glad to see you here," he began, "and I know Finlay is." We reminisced about Finlay and the widespread good feeling in the party about his appointment. Stanfield then went on to explain that for all his difficulties as party leader – and he didn't need to spell them out for me – in the end there were very few people with whom he could not get along. "I found that if I allowed people to make judgements of others for me, then I would be cutting myself off from these people." Then he paused and continued: "But if I took people just as I found them, there were really very few that I could not talk to or work with."

In fairness to Robert Stanfield, through a very difficult time in the party's history, he was willing and able to take people exactly as he found them. It was sad that too many of us – and I include myself most of all – were unable or unwilling to extend the same courtesy to him.

Robert Stanfield has many reasons to be bitter and disappointed after the loss of three elections and his mistreatment at the hands of his party, but he shows no signs today of either bitterness or disappointment. I admire his persistence through some difficult years as he tried to hold the party together, fight Trudeau, learn French and mount an effective opposition. He was both criticized and ridiculed, yet he never failed to act like a gentleman. He was a gentleman at a time and in a business that demanded a street fighter, and I can't fault him for that.

Brian Mulroney is equally easy to admire, although for different reasons. On August 31, 1978, I was on vacation from my studies at the seminary in Rome and was invited to lunch with Mulroney at the Mount Royal Club in Montreal. Brian was at his charming best; there was a staff of four looking after three of us in a private upstairs room. The table was so broad that when I asked for the salt, it couldn't be passed from one diner to another across the table, but had to be carried around. Good wine flowed freely, and at the end of the meal, I pulled out some Robert Burns cigars I'd bought in the States. When Mulroney saw them, he said: "Get rid of those goddamned Presbyterian cigars," and buzzed for the house cigars, explaining that they were Fidel Castro's special selection. Amazed by all the splendour around me, I finally said: "Brian, I can't get over all this." He turned to me and said, "Sean, can you imagine if we'd won?"

Little did Brian know that day that I was a major cause of his losing the leadership convention in 1976 by convincing Dief to make his anti-Mulroney speech.

Just as I helped do Brian in then, I like to think I helped him win in 1983. I was in hospital with leukemia during that leadership campaign, but I was an avid supporter of Michael Wilson. After the first ballot, Michael decided to drop out of the race. Which candidate should he go to? He and a small group of close aides and workers had met in a private room at the Château Laurier Hotel to discuss all eventualities prior to the vote. The group was evenly divided. Half said Michael should go to Crosbie, the other half said he should back Mulroney. Long-time Wilson supporter Don McCutchan suddenly remembered that there was an absentee ballot to be cast. Mine. When Don had phoned before the convention to review all possible scenarios, I expressed my view about whom Michael should support if a choice were required. That tie-breaking vote could now be cast – for Brian Mulroney. Although Michael did not feel bound by the advice, it was to Brian Mulroney's box he walked, taking a majority of his one hundred and forty-four delegates with him.

Way down deep, Brian Mulroney is probably as insecure as the rest of us. What he pulled off in uniting the Conservative Party and winning the 1984 election, I would not have thought possible. He has brought discipline to the Tory caucus, unity to the party and delivered the biggest majority ever.

As with most politicians, there is a good Brian and a bad Brian. He's truly Irish in his tribal loyalties to old friends. When I resigned my seat in 1977, he sent me a long, hand-written and most welcome letter of encouragement. The very first telegram I received when I was in hospital with leukemia was from Brian and Mila. Just as Brian has often showed me his warmth, so has Mila, who must rank as the most helpful political spouse Canada has ever seen. Without her, Brian would not be prime minister. When the Pope visited Canada in 1984, Mila phoned me with an invitation to attend the Ottawa papal mass and sit with them as their guests. Regrettably, my condition at the time prevented my attendance.

Brian has been raised believing in traditional values and wants to do the right thing. However, he has been so scarred by the political process that sometimes he lets paranoid advisors convince him to be mean-spirited. Perhaps the problem is that it all happened too fast for him and on too big a scale. In less than two years he went from businessman to prime minister. It would have been better if he'd had more time to prepare for office.

Most Canadians, I sense, would like to like him; they would like him to succeed as prime minister. They would like to be able to trust him. To achieve all that, he must very soon let us know Brian Mulroney's vision for Canada – what he's going to do as prime

221

minister, not just that he's thoroughly in love with the office. Every man, goes the old adage, should have within himself a cause for which he would rather die than surrender. Brian Mulroney has to have such a cause and he has to articulate it. If he is to be more than one-dimensional, if he is to be a flesh-and-blood leader, we've got to have that inner self exposed. I can only hope that Canadians see past the often inaccurate portrayals of the prime minister to the Brian Mulroney I know.

Brian and I and a lot of other Tories came out of student politics, the raw spawning ground for future politicians. Politics at the student or Young Progressive Conservative levels is played with such intensity that if you can survive there, you can certainly survive in the big leagues. Student politics is tougher, more vicious and more intense than at the senior levels. Although Tories tend to do more of their savaging in public than the other parties, youth politics in all three parties is more Byzantine than it is in later life.

Still, some of what has been said about me and my nefarious youthful doings has been wrong. It is true that as a YPC member I formed a mutual support coalition with several others of similar views. We called ourselves "The Shysters." In *Contenders*, the 1983 book describing that year's Tory leadership convention, we were elevated to an exalted status. "So fervent," says the book, "was the zeal of the right wing that some of its members even formed a secret society called 'The Shysters,' which was dedicated to the pursuit of their ideology. (The society's rituals included an oath-burning cere-mony and the kissing of a sacred ring.)"

There was a group that included Keith Martin, Bill Hatton, Wayne Taylor, Georgia Allan, Paula Marsden, Warren Ralph, Ian McPhail, myself and several others. But there was no constitution; and there were no official meetings – only the occasional gathering of kindred souls on a slim pretext such as showing the Robert Redford film *The Candidate* in a rented hotel suite. There certainly was no ring-kissing or oath burning, whatever that may be. We acquired our name, "The Shysters," at the time of the 1967 Conservative leadership conven-tion. Keith and Bill, who were heading the Youth for Diefenbaker movement, asked for a list of delegates so they could make contact and promote Dief. A party functionary at convention headquarters

222

refused because, at that point, the leader they represented was not yet a declared candidate. In addition, the functionary didn't like Dief and let Hatton know that. The two engaged in a shouting match that finally ended with the functionary saying: "Look, fellow, I don't have to listen to you; get out of here, you're nothing but a two-bit political shyster." They didn't get the lists, but they got themselves a label.

For us the term "shyster" denoted a political operative, a conniver, anyone who was less than honourable. As the youngest delegate to that convention, I was a Dief supporter; to me, anyone who wasn't was less than honourable. Applying the label "The Shysters" to ourselves was thus a tongue-in-cheek gesture of defiance, ironic in its intent. In turn, we called our opponents "the bastards," as in, "What are the bastards up to today?" After Robert Stanfield, with help from Dalton Camp, won that convention and ended the reign of our beloved Chief, they became the mortal enemy.

I brought this us-them mentality with me to Ottawa as an MP. For many opposition members, fighting within the party was an outlet for the frustrations that resulted from the overall inability to effect change. You're in Ottawa chasing power, telling yourself you want power in order to make changes for the better. The other reason, of course, is because power is tempting in and of itself. Both reasons help MPs put up with the long days that begin with breakfast meetings and end with late dinners, and that can include five functions in a single day in the constituency on top of all the other demands on your time. You want to be re-elected, be in government and become a cabinet minister so you can make changes. At least that's how you feel as a young MP. I guess in the end I have to say I deluded myself about how much an individual really could achieve. There is a lot of inertia to overcome in the system, particularly the bureaucracy.

Even with those frustrations, however, most of the politicians I know come to Ottawa with genuinely sound principles and good causes they want to forward. They want to make a contribution, to give of their time and talent to serve their constituents. To be sure, some politicians do give in to the perqs of power and the allure of the levers at the top. But you can only take so many first-class flights and attend so many embassy dinners. By themselves the trappings of power are not enough to sustain most people; you have to be driven from within to make things better.

Politics can be a dirty business that treats people badly – even those with a strong inner core of decency. It wreaks particular havoc on families. An MP should serve before the children are born or after they're raised. Trying to serve country and a young family is all but impossible. If the family moves to Ottawa, the MP sees them late at night, then disappears to the riding for the weekend. If they live in the riding, the kids see their MP parent as one who changes clothes between functions in the riding and gives time as a local celebrity to everyone but them. Resentments build and relationships suffer.

There are decent people in all parties who have been badly treated by the harsh realities of politics. In 1984, I was still recovering from the ravages of cancer and its treatment, so I fled to Bermuda for a few days of rest and recuperation. John Turner was also there, taking his first break after the election in which he was so roundly trounced by Brian Mulroney. We met over dinner and talked about his recent campaign and some of its more painful memories. A political realist, John spoke candidly of the job he faced in trying to rebuild a Liberal Party shattered by that defeat. He was well aware that he might be just a transitional leader and that someone else might be the beneficiary of all his efforts.

We shared a bone-weary fatigue with life that gave us a kinship like the survivors of separate shipwrecks beached on the same island. We knew we had to get over our respective tragedies and get on with living. I felt an overwhelming sadness for this good man, a victim of the political cycle, who had gone from being a prime minister of such promise to one of the loneliest men in Canada. That night, I thanked him for the times he had come to see me in hospital in the aftermath of chemotherapy. During those four anguished months when I was in and out of hospital, he had often phoned and had taken the time to travel to Hamilton to visit me. Once he stayed forty-five minutes, another time for an hour and a half, even though there were no votes to be gained in that hospital room.

On one of those welcome visits, John gave me the kind of fiery pep talk he can do so well, telling me that life was worth the fight. I badly needed to hear that speech; it lifted my spirits and I loved him for his devotion. "You may never know how much those visits meant," I said. "I only wish I could do for you what you did for me." In the silence that followed, our eyes filling, we changed the subject.

Among the stories he asked to hear was the inside account of the Paul Hellyer campaign for Conservative leader. As I began, I mentioned that I had originally vowed not to work for any particular candidate, but had relented and agreed to support Paul, as I put it, "When Paul got to me with the only argument to which I did not have an answer. He told me it was my duty." "Tell me about duty," John replied in a voice tinged with both pain and resolve as he stared off into the dark distance of the nighttime Bermuda sky.

To me, that single sentence captures John Turner. He left his comfortable and safe haven of a Toronto law practice because enough people had convinced him that it was his duty to offer new leadership after the trauma of the Trudeau years. He will continue to do his duty, whether that be continued service to Canada or putting his party's fortunes ahead of any personal ambitions. He is a fighter, to be sure, but he is also a man who consults his conscience and will do the right thing. And he will continue to command the respect and affection of many of us who went to Ottawa fearing him as a political opponent and left with the special privilege of his warm and true friendship.

As I like to joke, the reason I became a priest was all Paul Hellyer's idea. I supported him for Conservative leader at the 1976 convention. Later, I turned to him for advice and said: "Paul, I've been here five years. What are my chances of becoming a minister?" He replied: "A minister? Sean, with your name I think you'd be better off becoming a priest."

Well, since he was so good at giving advice, I then asked: "Where should I go to seminary? There's a seminary here in Ottawa, there's one in Toronto and there's one in London."

"No, you should go to Rome to do your studies."

"Why go all the way to Rome?"

"Sean, don't tell me that you've been in politics all this time and haven't yet realized that most basic of political lessons? If you're going to seek the nomination, you should live in the constituency!"

I did become a priest, but not because politics didn't make me

225

happy; it's just that along the way I found that I had a heart with other needs and yearnings. When I was the MP for Hamilton-Wentworth, I thought I had everything I wanted. There was the prestige of a profile in the riding and the perqs that came with the office in Ottawa. During twelve years of party membership I experienced the pull of power, the exhilaration of victory and the desolation of defeat. But I learned the dangers of being seduced by victory at any cost and so easily losing those ideals and high principles that bring politicians to serve in Ottawa.

For me, the role of politician was and remains a badge of honour. But for all of that, there was something missing in my life, a peace, an equilibrium that caused me to continue my search and discover a very simple truth. The key to living is to do the will of God. I left politics to become a priest because that is what He wanted of me, and in the end, I gained more than I gave up. In politics you deal with issues in the abstract and people in the most general of terms. A lot of the time, I really wondered whether anything I did made any difference at all. The call to politics makes you open to the pursuit of power. You ask "How can I gain?" The call to the priesthood is to service. You ask "How can I give?" As a priest, you know you are making a contribution. Unlike politics, where you want to be the groom at every wedding and the corpse at every funeral, as a priest, you can be happy as a member of the supporting cast.

The life of a priest is not so much a sacrifice as it is a gift. I believe that the Lord has a plan for each of our lives. The secret to happiness is to find that plan and follow it. Although I retain an interest in national issues and have many friends in politics, I will not return there. Being in politics, especially Conservative politics, must have been like surviving the Great War. You wouldn't want to have missed it, but you wouldn't want to do it again.

Many people have also asked if I miss marriage and having a family. It is true that everyone has genuine, natural desires. It is also true, although some wrongheaded thinkers would insist otherwise, that priests are more or less human. Therefore, it is logical to assume that priests have genuine, natural desires, too. To the best of our abilities, however, we do model ourselves after Christ, thus allowing us to be free of family responsibilities so we can give ourselves to others. Deep inside, every one of us would like the support of a spouse and the continuity of heirs. However, the term "father" used to describe a priest was not carelessly chosen. It is the precise role that a priest plays with the people entrusted to his care. Celibacy is not so much a denial as it is a freedom to be a father to all.

When people ask if I have any regrets about choosing the priesthood, it is almost as if they want to rationalize their own spiritual lethargy. Well, there have been difficult moments, to be sure, but I have no regrets about saying yes to the Lord's call. American President Harry Truman once said that regret is the most enfeebling of the emotions and he was right. During those difficult times, particularly in the seminary in Rome, I drew strength from many sources. One such source was a letter from Senator David Walker who wrote: "You are going to have some rough moments. When they are really rough, let go and let God."

It is nearly a decade since I first heard His call and tried to respond with the classic words of Isaiah, repeated by all God's messengers through the centuries: "Here I am Lord. Send me." It was not easy to give up my seat in Parliament and all my political ambitions. It was not easy to revert to student status, to live as an anonymous stranger in a foreign seminary in the Eternal City that was so obviously unimpressed by yet another idealistic young seminarian. Nor has it always been easy simply to go where I've been sent, to take on tasks not of my choosing.

Most of all, it has not been easy to understand why, if I was meant to serve the Lord, I ended up in a hospital bed, desperately ill. I am coming to understand. Emmett Cardinal Carter, prince of the Catholic Church and Archbishop of Toronto, suffered a stroke in 1981. As he recovered, he wrote to his flock: "When we suffer and above all when we suffer as He suffered, helpless and held back, we may be at the highest point of our lives, not the lowest."

In getting to know any priest's story, the central symbol that will emerge is Calvary, where Christ was crucified. Each of us is called – or is it carried? – by the Lord to Calvary. He does not call any of us, then abandon us, although at times He may seem very distant or unfeeling. In living out my vocation, I feel the warmth of His presence, the guidance of His hand and the blessing of His love, which I do not deserve but cannot lose. To be a disciple of the Master is to feel loved and alive and cared for. He is real. No one could ask for anything more.

This is not to suggest that every day is filled with the rapture of blissful enjoyment. Indeed, since we never lose our human side, so do we never escape our human failings. Often, we become confused whether we are doing His bidding or ours. When I lay in St. Joseph's Hospital in Hamilton, among the messages was this from Sister St. Christopher, who was also a patient in the hospital. "How surprised you must have been to have your plans for God interrupted by God's plans for you." It was a poignant reminder about who is in charge.

I have done many things wrong in my life, but there's one thing I did right. I said yes to Christ's invitation to share His priesthood. When I wrote to Cardinal Carter to tell him my decision, he sent a most apt reply: "The movement you give yourself is from God. Simply look on it as a grace, not as if you were doing something for Him. You are the true beneficiary."

Life's experiences have taught me that love and suffering are mysterious links to God. We must take the risks of love even when that involves suffering, hurt and misunderstanding. Always love. Never be afraid to love. I don't know – can't know – what the future holds. I do know the statistics, and I know the nature of leukemia. In fact, I know more about leukemia than I care to. I also know myself, my body and my psyche, and I'm doing whatever I can to prolong my life and my usefulness. Priesthood has made my life all the more worth fighting for.

A similar fight faces many other people. In Canada, one death in four is caused by cancer. When I first came down with the disease in April 1983, doctors told me that I stood only a 10-20 per cent chance of living for two years. I have now lived more than three years. There is no medical reason at all for me to be around today. I think about that constantly and thank God for this bonus time He has given me.

I do not hold myself up as someone for other cancer victims to admire. I was just desperately ill and coping. Even months after my release from hospital, I still felt weak, vulnerable and leached of all life. The end of active treatment was not the end of the illness, it was just a pause. So, while those well-meaning friends grew exasperated,

I had to say, honestly, that I still felt sick, although I learned to couch my responses in euphemisms: "Well, I have my good days and my bad days, but don't we all?" I was impatient with myself, too. I could only sympathize with the comment of a friend reading another newspaper update. "I'm tired," he said, "of reading about the sick priest."

Me, too. In my defence, I can only say that the truly sick person does not enjoy his predicament. Nor is he wallowing in illness just for the attention and sympathy; it's not worth the price of the trade-off required. There is little heroism involved. Healing takes a long time and is accompanied by acute anxiety, frustration and bouts of depression. While putting up with someone who is sick may not be easy, believe me, there is little joy on my side, either.

Although I set out sincerely to serve people as a simple parish priest, that was not God's will. As director of vocations running a very successful and high-profile billboard campaign, and as a former public figure with leukemia, I became the very celebrity priest I didn't want to be. I know that a lot of people – including other priests – may feel jealous or resentful that their own work is over-shadowed by my notoriety. I feel their coolness toward me, not to mention the loneliness and the hurt that causes. But that situation is also a constant reminder of who is really in charge when you hand your life over to the Lord and become a priest. God, as Sister St. Christopher wrote, interrupts our plans with His.

No one would choose to have leukemia or any form of cancer, but I do not begrudge my experience. In many ways, I am thankful for it. I've learned not to look for explanations; I simply trust God. Many of the things He does are not what we want, but His ways are not our ways. Facing death has taught me three things. First, it has taught me the simple and wondrous joy of living. I no longer demand that He submit His plans for my approval. I embrace the daily experience of a healthy life and believe in the simple goodness of people. Second, it has given me the privilege of joining the cancer battle and the chance to meet hundreds of cancer patients and their families. Third, and most important, the door of death showed me that God's love for all of us is not unconditional. He said we must forgive others; that's a condition of His forgiving us. If we are going to have peace and goodwill on earth, we must forgive and seek reconciliation with others.

My term as vocations director ended in 1985. I felt that, with all that had happened, three years in the role was enough. While the number of men considering the priesthood was up, I knew I was no longer the right man for the job. I asked to go back to the simplicity and fulfilment of a parish, working with the people of God in all their needs. I was concerned, however, about having sufficient energy for the daily commitment that a congregation requires. I do need a great deal of rest. My current regimen requires eight hours of sleep a night or I get run down and risk ending my remission. Every other week, I spend most of one day in Hamilton for blood tests and sometimes a painful bone marrow aspiration, then wait in trepidation for the results to see whether I am still able to carry on. And every sixth week, I must flee my duties and rest for the entire week, recharging my batteries for the days ahead. Without that time away, I would collapse on the job. As it is, my energy reserves are more limited than I would like for my current role as an associate pastor in a suburban Toronto parish. I live there and assist the other two priests with Mass, confession and all the other duties an active parish demands. In December 1985, I was assigned the additional post of publisher of *The Catholic Register*, a weekly church newspaper.

This new role will let me build bridges and be a force for reconciliation. I hope I have already begun. In 1984, I had lunch with former colleague David MacDonald. By that time, we were both ex-MPs, and both active in our own denominations, I as a Roman Catholic priest, he as a United Church minister. One of his projects was to promote a religious television network and he wanted my advice on how Catholics might become involved in the project. We were able to dispatch that topic within twenty minutes. Then we spent the next three and half hours talking in ways that we had never been able to talk before. It was the first time in almost twenty years that we had spoken to each other with our guard down.

I felt free to be open; I was living on borrowed time. He had no further political ambitions; he had been secretary of state in the Joe Clark government and was out of politics for good. We talked about the Conservative Party and the bad things it did to people. I realized for the first time how much anger I carried toward the party. I had been able to make friends more easily with MPs in other parties than in my own. David and I had been, if not enemies, certainly adversaries. That's what the party did to us. It put each member into a category; none of us trusted anyone in another category.

I was a Diefenbaker Tory; David was a Red Tory. From my vantage point, they were the bastards who had done Dief in. As far as policy was concerned, I thought they should have been in the NDP; they were hypocrites who called themselves Conservatives but really weren't. We sat on the same committees; we had to. There was cordiality, but there was never any warmth. I related to David the time that there had been rumours that he would join the NDP or sit as an independent. When Jack Horner joined the Liberals and it became clear that David MacDonald would remain, I remember I saying to Tory colleague Pat Nowlan: "The only thing that bothers me more than Jack Horner's leaving is David MacDonald's decision to stay."

The majority of my fellow Tories had been against Dief in 1966 and the wounds stayed open for years. They were kept festering by the bilingualism debate and the 1976 convention, but I didn't realize the depth of the problem until the distance of the years, the choice of a new calling and the cancer. I was angry and disappointed with myself when I realized the part I'd played as a collaborator in the self-destruction. The constant knifing not only kept the party out of power but also fouled up personal relationships. That day with David we found each other – and liked each other – for the first time.

After being a long-standing opponent of the party hierarchy, I have also come to know and like the members of the Ontario organization who worked for Bill Davis and for federal leaders. The Big Blue Machine is not a mechanistic device made up of cogs and flywheels, it is a gathering of people who share hopes and happiness – and, to be sure, win a few elections. Although I took some time to realize this, I guess the process began for me when I went to the seminary in Rome in 1977. As I studied the scriptures and examined my own conscience and life, I was also introduced to a process called "the healing of memories." All of us have memories that are still as intense and painful as the event was itself, no matter how long ago it happened. We were taught to turn those hurtful memories over to God and pray for the person in question. If you wish God to forgive your sins, we were reminded, you must forgive others.

I realized through that process that I had accumulated a lot of baggage that could not be dumped overnight. In fact, the process took years. When I returned from Rome in 1980, for example, I would see Ontario Premier Bill Davis on television or read about him in the media and still feel the hurt of 1971 when I was president of the Ontario Young Progressive Conservatives. He had promised me an honourable way out of my executive position and then reneged, leaving me twisting in the wind like a thief at a public hanging.

On the long road back that started in Rome I reached an important turning point in Lake Forest, Illinois, in 1985. I had met David Camp, son of Dief's nemesis, Dalton Camp, years earlier when David was a member of the Parliamentary Press Gallery in Ottawa. We had corresponded over the years and in 1985 he asked me to help officiate at his wedding in Lake Forest. After the rehearsal, Dalton and I stayed up until past 3:00 a.m. What began as a perfunctory effort by the two of us to get along for the sake of David and the wedding became several hours of learning about each other and building a bridge across the chasm of the years.

The bull session started with each of us trying to outdo the other with old political stories. It was an interesting pastime, because we would recall the same incident but from quite different vantage points and each with the warm blur of faulty memory that placed us or our side in the best light. For example, I recalled a story about Dalton meeting Dief in a receiving line at some event at the height of the controversy over leadership review, when Camp, as party president, set out to change the party rules in a way Dief believed was aimed directly at him.

As Dief told the story, he had greeted Camp, saying: "Good evening, Mr. President." A flustered Dalton had replied: "Good evening, Prime Minister." Dief, by then leader of the opposition, was delighted his rival had restored him to what he regarded as his rightful place. "Now I like that," Dief said. "You just keep that up." That night in Illinois, Dalton explained his flustered response. His wife had preceded him through the receiving line and Dief had refused to shake hands with her. Taken aback at Dief's rudeness,

Dalton was fumbling for a response and had blurted the wrong title. Of course, when Diefenbaker told the story, he never revealed his own petty behaviour.

My life in politics, I realized, had been one of chasing ghosts. I hadn't known anything about Dalton Camp except from the erroneous perceptions of others. The irony was that we had spent all those years and all that energy attacking people we never really knew. We had been like soldiers in a trench firing blindly through fog at an unseen enemy in a battle over imagined indignities from another era. That night, in Lake Forest, Illinois, the bitter cycle that had begun two decades before finally came to an end.

At a dinner in my honour on March 17, 1986, a lasting peace was declared. Even the location was appropriate. The dinner was at the Albany Club, where Dalton had made his first speech calling for a review of John Diefenbaker's leadership. That 1966 address was the beginning of a bloodbath in the Conservative Party that tainted my view and divided the party for two decades. Now, on a March night twenty years later, Dalton Camp honoured me by sitting at the head table. So did Robert Stanfield, William Davis, Joe Clark and Norman Atkins, who organized the extravaganza. Brian Mulroney joined us via a videotape. The room was full of Tories who were celebrating something rare in the party: forgiveness.

Someone said to me before the dinner, "Boy, you're really working both sides of the street." That night, I hope the Tories finally stopped relegating people to one side of the street or the other. Standing in their midst, I realized that I had lived and worked on a divided street for too long a time. As Terry Fox explained during his valiant cross-country marathon attempt: "Somewhere the hurtin's got to end."

The hurtin' may not all have ended that night; there will always be differing views wherever there are strong people. But in the good humour that elevates humankind above all other creatures, in the fellowship of wanting to be kind toward each other, in the healing balm of forgiveness, there was a glimpse of how the world can be. I have found that it is better to forgive than to try to settle old scores. I'm much more calm and at peace with the world, with others and with myself. People blessed with longevity may count their years. Some of us, blessed with full lives, prefer to count our friends.

I appreciate the simple things in life more than most. The freedom to take a shower rather than a tepid hospital bath while still connected to intravenous tubes. The chance to walk in the sunshine rather than be tied to a bag of chemotherapy. The joy of sitting with people discussing everyday problems rather than listening to the doctors bring bad news. I have learned to trust God, yet I still have doubts about being good for the long haul.

Whatever time remains I will use to develop my trust in God and promote reconciliation among people. I want to be an agent for reconciliation because it has been important in my own life's journey to realize how silly and unnecessary it was to hurt others, dwell on their shots at me and focus on paying them back in the future.

But little of value is achieved without cost. I have felt the cost of the bitter fights I have had in the past. I have paid the price of serious illness. Even with that pain and suffering, however, I am not afraid to live. Nor am I afraid to die. For I have the comfort of friends and the strength of my faith. It was my privilege to count Arthur Maloney as a close friend. He was a great lawyer and ombudsman for the people of Ontario even before the office was created. In the final days of his life in 1984, he reflected on his beliefs and said to me: "I cannot conceive of a God who is anything but merciful." Then, he added, ever so gently, "He gives us so many chances, so many chances."

So many, indeed. And I have missed a few of those; with His grace, my life has been extended and I have been given a few more chances to do His work. In our daily lives, we can aspire to boast about our own human achievements. But as our life draws to an end, we find those petty gains for self are but hollow phrases. Better we should work to serve others. The reality of the funeral Mass causes everyone to ask the haunting question so often posed by the Irish: "And sure, at the end of the day, what does it all matter?"

In his mercy, the Lord has allowed me some time of service in both the secular and spiritual care of His people – in both His houses. Also, a period of grace, beyond what I expected, to put my own house in order. He has also allowed me the opportunity to suffer as all priests must, for our own sins and, with Jesus, for the sins of His people. As Cardinal Carter wrote prophetically to me on the eve of my ordination: "The Priesthood of Christ has been the joy of my life. No privilege of the highest human order can compare with it. I offer you a life of dedication, sometimes of very real hardship, but, with grace, perseverance and self-donation, a life of joy and fulfilment. It is exactly on the cross that we are our truest priestly selves."

I have been on that cross; soon, I may be summoned home. But sing no sad songs for me; for I am a Christian. Without merit of my own and trusting only in His abundant mercy, I go gently toward that glorious goal. To other cancer victims and their families, to Catholics and all people of goodwill, I say: Remain steadfast, keep stout hearts and hold unwavering hope. Fear not, our God is still at work. However dark the coming days, He will triumph and be with us always, even until the end of time.

INDEX

meetings, 79; Chateau Cabinet, 99, 101-6; fighting within, 89, 100-1; federal elections (1972), 73-4; (1974), 87, 89-90; (1984), 76; general meeting (1966), 11-14; in Hamilton-Wentworth riding, 65-6; leadership conventions (1967), 20 -4; (1976), 113, 122-3, 125ff., (1983), 220-1; Ont. leadership convention (1970), 34-9; O'Sullivan's interest in, 7; treatment of Hellyer, 134-5; wage and price controls, 89, 90. *See also* Young Progressive Conservative Association

RALPH, Warren, 116, 222
Reding, Bishop Paul, 145, 155, 185, 186, 207
Reilly, Peter, 77, 82, 92
Religious of the Cenacle, 146
Restivo, Father Sam, 138, 139, 200
Reynolds, John, 157
Ridge, Ishbel, 69
Ridge, Jim, 67
Robarts, John, 32, 33, 35, 37, 101-2
Roblin, Duff and Mary, 24
Roman Catholic Church: colleges for priests, 173-77; diocesan priests, 145; importance of Lourdes, 208; in O'Sullivan's early life, 3, 139-40; need for more priests, 188; ordination, 187; O'Sullivan's first trip to Rome, 145; O'Sullivan's decision to enter priesthood, 139ff., 150-1, 155-6; religious order priests, 145, 155; retreats, 146, 148-9; tabernacle, 147; traditionalists and

contemporary Catholics, 210-11; Trinitarian order, 141-2, 145, 154
Roman, Steve, 118
Rome, 145-6, 177-8
Royal Connaught Hotel, 1, 4, 7-8, 73
Ryan, Monsignor Gordon, 3
Rynard, Dr. P.B., 44

ST. Bernadette's Church, 188, 201
St. Christopher, Sister, 229
St. Joseph's Hospital, 191, 193, 207, 209, 228
St. Michael's Cathedral, 187, 195
St. Paul, 212, 216
Salinger, Pierre, 69
Sauvé, Jeanne, 75
Scots College, 173, 175
Seattle, 204-5, 206
Segal, Hugh, 183
Selling of the President, The, 5
separate school funding, 182-4
Serra House, 190, 207, 209
Sévigny, Pierre, 10, 21
Sheen, Archbishop Fulton, 108
Sherlock, Bishop John, 144, 145, 146, 181, 207
"The Shysters," 222-3
Sign, 139
Slinger, Joey, 95
Smith, Bernard, 96
Smith, Sydney, 216
Sourbois, Bernadette, 208
Stanbury, Robert, 98
Stanfield, Max, 30
Stanfield, Mimi, 72
Stanfield, Robert, 28, 29, 32-3, 53, 61, 70, 73, 75, 84, 85, 96, 106, 115, 233; bilingualism, 217-19; Chateau Cabinet, 102, 105-6; final speech, 126-7; leadership convention, 22, 24,

PHOTO CREDITS

Lloyd Bloom/Gage Park Studios, iii; christopher blythe, xv (top), xvi (top); CanaPress, v; Tom Delemere, xv (bottom); Nigel Dickson, x-xi (bottom); Hans Eijsenck, viii (bottom), x (top), xi (top); Herbert Fichtner, i; *The Hamilton Spectator*, iv (top left), xii, xiii; John Evans Photography Ltd., viii (top), ix; Bill McCarthy/PMO, xvi (bottom); Chris Wade, iv (top right)